THE ORDEAL OF EQUALITY

THE ORDEAL OF EQUALITY

Did Federal Regulation Fix the Schools?

DAVID K. COHEN
SUSAN L. MOFFITT

Harvard University Press
Cambridge, Massachusetts
London, England
2009

Library of Congress Cataloging-in-Publication Data

Cohen, David K., 1934–
The ordeal of equality : did federal regulation fix the schools? /
David K. Cohen, Susan L. Moffitt.
p. cm.
Includes bibliographical references and index.
ISBN 978-0-674-03546-1 (alk. paper)
1. Children with social disabilities—Education—United States.
2. Education—Standards—United States—Evaluation.
3. Educational accountability—United States—Evaluation.
4. Federal aid to education—United States—Evaluation.
5. United States. Elementary and Secondary Education Act of 1965.
I. Moffitt, Susan L. II. Title.
LC4069.C56 2009
379.1'580973—dc22
2009017609

For Magdalene, Lisa, and Sarah

—D. K. C.

For Judith, Julia, and Madeleine

—S. L. M.

Contents

Acknowledgments

Our work on this book was eased, and the book much improved, by the help of colleagues, officials, educators, friends, and organizations.

Many people who worked in and around Title I gave generously of their time and knowledge in interviews. What they told us, and the documents that they shared with us, were always valuable and sometimes invaluable. We owe a great deal to Gordon Ambach, Cynthia G. Brown, Christopher T. Cross, Charles Edwards, Paul Hill, John F. (Jack) Jennings, Michael Kirst, Mary Jean LeTendre, Jessica Levin, Mary Kennedy, Phyllis McClure, Hugh Mognihan, Tom Payzant, Danica Petroshius, Rich Rasa, Cheryl Sattler, Brett Scoll, Marshall S. (Mike) Smith, David Stevenson, Brenda Turnbull, Susan Wilhelm, and Bayla White. Readers who attend to the notes will see at least some signs of our indebtedness.

Several of these people and some others were kind enough to read various drafts of the manuscript, point out errors, and comment helpfully on the analysis. Thanks to Cynthia G. Brown, Christopher T. Cross, Richard Elmore, Susan Fuhrman, Simona Goldin, John F. (Jack) Jennings, Phyllis McClure, Lorraine McDonnell, Milbrey W. McLaughlin, Fredrick (Fritz) Mosher, Bella Rosenberg, Brenda Turnbull, William Taylor, and Maris Vinovskis. If we succeeded in taking their advice, which in some cases was terrifically helpful, readers will never know how very helpful they were. We are responsible for any remaining errors and infelicities.

The initial research for the book was supported by a grant from the Carnegie Corporation of New York; thanks to Michael Levine for his help. Continuing research was supported by a grant from the School of Education at the University of Michigan; thanks to Cecil Miskel for his help. Neither organization is responsible for views expressed in this book.

We also owe many thanks to Elizabeth Knoll of the Harvard University Press, for her interest in the book, her encouragement, and discerning advice, and to Melody Negron of Westchester Book, for her capable editorial assistance.

Carol Barnes, Susan Faja, Heather C. Hill, and Terri Ridenour also gave us advice and assistance along the way.

THE ORDEAL OF EQUALITY

The Transformation of Title I?

The Founding Fathers feared that the United States might disunite shortly after it began. The several decades that followed ratification of the U.S. Constitution saw fierce arguments about the authority of the national government and the states. George Washington, Alexander Hamilton, John Adams, and other Federalists believed that their chief task was to secure the authority of the central government and establish its superiority to the states. Republicans like Thomas Jefferson and James Madison sought to reduce central power and saw the Federalists as homegrown near monarchists. Leaders on each side thought that the nation's success hung in the balance and feared that the federal union would dissolve if the other side won.[1]

The United States did not dissolve, but the argument was not settled. The Jeffersonian view was set back by Justice John Marshall's decision in *Marbury v. Madison,* but it gained in Andrew Jackson's opposition to the national bank. The argument erupted in the Civil War, as North and South divided over the Southern states' authority to maintain slavery within the Union. Though the North won the war as a military matter, the South won the battle over its states' authority, as the former Confederacy destroyed Reconstruction and crushed the black civil rights that the Union victory had briefly created. The argument over state versus federal jurisdiction also marked the presidency of Theodore Roosevelt in his efforts to use the national government to solve social problems, and this same argument was central to the conflict over Franklin Delano Roosevelt's efforts to use the central government to regulate markets and solve social and economic problems.

The argument had evolved—no states seceded over Theodore Roosevelt's reforms, the federal income tax, or the New Deal—but fierce battles over central versus state authority again fractured U.S. politics in the 1960s, when the national government moved to break Jim Crow by securing black civil rights in Southern states. Secession was not a serious option, but Southern politicians threw nearly everything else into their resistance to federal support for black civil rights; the political battle realigned the major political parties and fundamentally changed national politics.

The same sort of divisions framed efforts to send federal aid to public schools.[2] Liberal legislators in Washington tried to pass federal aid in the late 1950s and early 1960s, but they failed. Southern legislators, all of whom were white, wanted no federal presence in their states' segregated schools, and civil rights advocates wanted no federal support for Jim Crow schools. Catholics would support a bill only if it aided parochial schools, and many Protestants and civil liberties advocates opposed such aid on First Amendment grounds. The conflicts among these various groups were so intractable that leading experts declared federal school aid a dead issue.[3]

John F. Kennedy's murder and pressure from the civil rights movement gave it new hope, and Lyndon Johnson's political influence and skill gave it new life. The Elementary and Secondary Education Act (ESEA) became law in 1965, and Title I was its centerpiece. Title I established a federal priority in education, to improve education for children from poor families; it brought federal aid—nearly one billion dollars—to public schools; and it set major changes in the politics of education under way.[4]

ESEA was a breakthrough. Not only did it bring Washington to local schools, but it also set the first of many federal priorities for those schools. Title I's priority tied up a rich mixture of motives and ideas: it was a convenient fig leaf for federal aid, a politically feasible way to respond to the civil rights movement, and an expression of the old American idea, set down in Horace Mann's twelfth report, that public schools could be the "balance wheel of the social machinery," righting wrongs that the economy and society imposed on children.[5]

Yet if Title I broke through some barriers, others remained intact. There would be federal school aid and some federal influence on schools' priorities, but the aid was distributed in a way that greatly constrained federal influence. The governance arrangements that favored local control and fragmentation persisted. Title I's chief instrument was a formula grant that was keyed mainly to the incidence of poverty: once the total federal appropriation was decided, each state's allocation reflected its proportion of the national population of those who were poor, and the allocation within states followed in the same fashion.[6] Though the formula decided how much money states and localities would get, it decided nothing about how that money would be spent—save that it was to be spent on the education of children from poor families. Conservative legislators, Southerners chief among them, would only support aid that was distributed in this way. States and localities would control how the money would be spent—that was one political price of passage for the 1965 ESEA.[7] States and localities would submit proposals that offered assurances that the money would be spent as intended and would violate no one's civil rights, but how the money was spent would be decided by the same local educators whose schools had offered a thin educational diet to poor or black children. America's deep ideological divisions over state and federal authority were written into Title I; the legislation itself contained large political and structural barriers to federal influence on how Title I would be used.

Experience has also revealed huge educational barriers to Title I's influence. The most fundamental was that though Title I aimed to improve teaching and learning, public education never developed the common instruments that influence teaching and learning; it lacked the educational wherewithal—the infrastructure—that would make it possible for governments to guide what happened in classrooms. One of these instruments is common curricula, which were left instead to local school districts to oversee: each school or school system chose its texts, and most left instruction to teachers.[8] Hence, neither the central government nor the states could use a common course of study to encourage teachers and students to do more effective work. Each district, and in many districts each school, had its own curriculum.

Another common instrument is examinations that are tied to curricula. One advantage of such examinations is that they link assessment of students' academic progress to what they study, which was impossible in schools in the United States. Another advantage is diagnostic: these tests would make it possible for states, localities, or the central government to determine how well students in a school, district, state, or nation were learning the curriculum and where they needed more work. In the absence of common curricula, it was impossible to have such tests. Instead, psychologists devised norm-referenced tests, which rated students' performance relative to others who took the test; norms for achievement were created from the population of test takers rather than from the curriculum students were to learn. The norm-referenced tests were carefully designed to screen out any particular curriculum, to ensure that students who studied any particular curriculum had no advantage. This situation meant that localities, states, and federal authorities had no way to determine whether students were learning what they were supposed to.

Still another instrument is teacher education that is grounded in the curricula that teachers teach, so that professional education is tied to the instructional content on which teachers and students work. Teachers' education was grounded in no curriculum that they would use with students and hence was generic. For that reason among others, it was pitifully weak preparation for classroom practice. Another instrument is the recruitment and selection of teachers from candidates who have succeeded with those curricula and exams as students. These elements of educational infrastructure are common in most developed nations' school systems, but they were never developed in the United States, with the exception, for a time, of the New York State Regents and the Advanced Placement (AP) program.[9]

The existence of such an infrastructure does not ensure excellent education; that depends on how well designed the infrastructure is and on how educators use it. But if designed and used reasonably well, the elements of infrastructure as sketched above are important in part because they enable other things. Chief among these is a common language concerning teaching, learning, and academic content. Teachers who work with such an infrastructure have instruments that enable them to set academic tasks that are referenced to curricula and assessment. They have a framework that helps to define valid evidence of students' work. And perhaps most important, they have a common vocabulary with which to identify, investigate, discuss, and solve problems of teaching and learning—and thus the elements of common professional knowledge and skill. They have the means to work together as professionals, to solve the sorts of problems of educational improvement that Title I has recently tried to solve. Such an infrastructure also enables the development and expression of knowledge salient to practice.

The absence of such an infrastructure posed large problems for U.S. education. If teachers wanted to offer academically demanding work, they had to devise an infrastructure of their own: curricula, student assessments, and ways to learn how to do the work. Some did just that, but given the enormity of the task, most settled for less ambitious and more pedestrian work, based on what they happened to know and what texts their school or district happened to use that year. If any school, local school system, or state school system wanted a substantial instructional program, its educators would have to devise it themselves and try to sustain it through changes in school staff, policies, and local circumstances. Most important for our purposes, if Title I or any other school improvement program was to have substantial effects on instruction, the program and the schools in which the program worked would have to adopt or devise at least some elements of the missing infrastructure and find ways to sustain that infrastructure. In a nation whose schools were radically decentralized, and which lacked a common infrastructure, any effort to improve instruction would have to take on the fundamental weaknesses of the U.S. system if it was to have much hope of success.

The political governance arrangements and traditions of U.S. public education inhibited even discussion of such infrastructure; the very idea was unknown in 1965. But it meant that Title I faced an extraordinary challenge: it was to improve instruction for children from poor families in a school system that lacked common instruments to influence instruction. The absence of such instruments was, of course, not an oversight but a central feature in the design of public education.[10]

Title I's purpose was to improve education in a system that had been carefully designed to impede central political and educational influence on schools. Could Title I refashion the politics of American education to enable governance that would bring sufficiently strong and salient instruments to bear on educational practice?

There were other, related, political and educational barriers to the success of Title I; among the most important was the existence of race and class inequality in the very institutions that were supposed to be improved. In 1965, the Southern states were operating racially dual school systems, in which "Negro" schools were poorly funded, were often in bad physical condition, and lacked decent books, let alone libraries and laboratories. In many rural districts, both black and white schools were educationally weak. Schools in the North, especially the urban North, spent more, on average, than their Southern counterparts, but schools in black or poor neighborhoods typically had less money and worse facilities than schools in more privileged parts of the same cities; out-of-date books if, indeed, there were books at all; crowded conditions; and weak teachers.[11]

Few of those school systems had any experience with school improvement, for none had tried it. The improvement of school performance for children from poor families simply had not been on local school systems' agendas; in fact, it was barely on anyone's agenda. Only a few researchers had investigated the matter; improvement had no part in the curricula of education schools; and there were no specialists in school improvement, no offices in school systems that were devoted to the matter, and no research on the results of efforts to improve schools. There were not even publicly available data to judge which schools were weak, for there were no national data on student performance; school superintendents and school board members insisted passionately that such data and the comparisons they would permit would violate local control.[12] Legislators from the South denounced such things as socialist, or worse.

Finally, even though Title I brought federal aid to public education, that did not mean that states or localities could manage federal funds. Few states had anything that remotely resembled a strong education agency; in fact, Title V of the ESEA appropriated funds to strengthen state departments of education, many of which were so weak as to be ineffectual.[13] Many state education agencies employed only a few professionals, and these posts were regarded as opportunities for retirement on the job for former local superintendents. Very few state departments had any staffers expert in curricula, teaching, or teacher education, which, taken together, were the core of education. Some local school districts had curriculum departments, but most decisions about teaching and curricula were delegated to the schools. The only school systems that had experience with federal programs were those that received funds to offset the impact of military bases.[14]

Title I codified ideas about schools' power to remedy economic and social inequality. The program's underlying ideas about teaching and learning built on the assumption that palpable educational resources such as better books and equipment would readily translate into better education. But Title I's design meant that these ideas could build on no substantial foundation of common instructional instruments, state and local capability, or knowledge about how to improve education for children from disadvantaged circumstances. Title I lacked specific goals for performance, save better education for the children of poor families. The durability of governance structures that favored local control of schools meant that states and localities would get the money but would not be accountable for the quality of education that participation in Title I was meant to improve. Advocates of central authority won the argument about federal aid, but states and localities would decide how it was used. The 1965 ESEA managed the old political divisions in this new arena by building them into itself. Title I was a near entitlement for states and localities; several analysts noted that it was a funding stream, not a program that offered substantive guidance for teaching and learning. It was a real breakthrough, yet it also was quite limited, for it became law in a governance system that had been artfully designed to constrain central power in domestic affairs. The federal government would be politically accountable for Title I, but it had little influence with which to improve local education, and it was not even required to learn about program operations, except in studies conducted once every five years.[15]

We mention these problems in part because in what follows we explore how Title I has changed and how it has changed education. Given the political problems that we have just sketched, it seems that much has changed. Washington was a modest presence in education in 1965, but by the first decade of the twenty-first century it has become a center of decision-making for schools. Title I began as a weak program that brought new money to poor children's schools, but it is today a major force that has brought stiff federal requirements to schools in most states and localities. It began by shoehorning a national priority into decentralized schools but has wound up as the vehicle for extraordinary assertions of federal ideas and influence.

These political changes are especially noteworthy, for though Title I aims to help the poor, most Americans are not poor and are often suspicious of those who are. Why did they support a 1960s program that helped people they did not know or trust? Why, many years later, would they support a revised Title I in No Child Left Behind (NCLB), which requires states and localities to eliminate achievement gaps that reflect the educational advantages that white students and those from affluent homes have over black or Hispanic students and those from poor homes? Why would affluent and white Americans support legislation that would wipe out their children's educational advantage over students who are poor, Hispanic, or black?

The answer is not that affluent white Americans have bent to the social influence of the poor, for the poor have little influence. Critics argue that the poor are essential to keeping others' wages down and reminding the rest of us why we must work, but even if that is so, it does not bestow influence like that of doctors, attorneys, or corporate leaders. To be poor, economic depressions aside, is to have little social influence.[16] Nor do the poor have the political influence that might lead other Americans to attend to their concerns. The poor do not participate as actively in politics as others: they vote less often and are less likely to contact government officials, to take part in protest, or to contribute to campaigns.[17] The poor have little to spend on politics at a time when money talks.[18]

The poor also have little influence because they are less likely to organize to exert it. In principle, they have strong incentives to do so, but poor people are less likely to believe that organization helps or to know how to organize even if they thought it would help.[19] Few political candidates are poor, and poor peoples' movements in the United States have been few and far between. Most of these movements were organized by people who were not poor and were supported by wealthy donors and cosmopolitan foundations.

Programs to ameliorate poverty are at the mercy of these political weaknesses. If such programs benefit the rest of us, they do so more subtly than jobs that are tied to building roads or military contracts. To the extent that politics concerns the provision of such concrete benefits, gaining support for antipoverty programs has been an uphill battle.[20] Though this state of affairs rankles advocates, government seems unable to devise programs to help the poor unless they also offer something to more advantaged Americans.[21] Absent a large and well-organized poor peoples' movement, coalitions that spread benefits and unite sentiment behind programs for poor people are essential.

Title I originally did exactly that, as it slathered money over more than nine in every ten school districts. The program became a remarkable political success, for its formula for distributing grant money turned the educators who had been opposed or skeptical into supporters.[22] There was a serious cost, however, for broad distribution of funds meant that money was not concentrated in the districts and schools that had the greatest problems; given a relatively fixed federal appropriation, the price of political support was a lack of intense investment where it most counted. As a result, the coalition worked for decades, but Title I has changed: can it hold support among the affluent majority and educators when it aims to reduce the majority's educational advantage, makes many schools look bad, and complicates educators' work in thousands of schools across the land?

These political questions have been on many minds as the battles over reauthorizing NCLB have recently begun. Though the answers are far from clear, they will be influenced by the program's educational performance. That has been a continuing problem, despite efforts to make fundamental changes in education. President Bill Clinton's Improving America's Schools Act (IASA) and Goals 2000 Educate

America Act in 1994 and President George W. Bush's NCLB in 2002 were the federal expression of a broad reform movement that sought to use academic standards, tests, and accountability to improve schools. A few professional associations and states began standards-based reform in the 1980s, and as the reform spread, IASA and NCLB followed. Those two statutes required states to adopt demanding academic standards that specified the content that schools would teach and to test how well students learned that content. They required states to hold districts and schools accountable for students' performance, to eliminate average race and class differences in achievement, and to either improve schools in which performance was weak or put them out of business. IASA put no deadlines on state and local compliance, but NCLB required schools to eliminate the achievement gaps by 2014.

The reform strategy was to build a new framework of standards, tests, and accountability around public schools, and all states now have these frames. They are best understood as a sort of exoskeleton, for one guiding idea for state and federal reformers was that though standards, tests, and accountability would cause teaching and learning to change, they would not interfere in schools' internal work. The argument was that if standards created clear academic goals, if tests measured the extent to which students and schools achieved those goals, and if accountability gave teachers and those who managed schools and school systems strong incentives to make schools work for students, that would leave educators free to devise the teaching and curriculum that worked best for their students and themselves. Policy would operate in the sphere proper to it, and practitioners would operate in theirs; education would become more effective and more equal, but professional autonomy and local control would remain more or less intact. Policy, from this view, would shape practice without refashioning governance.

The reforms brought some clear benefits, some serious costs, and many hard questions. The benefits include unprecedented attention to poor children's school performance and equally unprecedented efforts to improve it. Doing so is now widely agreed to be the nation's top educational priority; it could barely have been imagined in 1965 or 1990, and efforts to improve education for poor children would not have materialized without these policies. Moreover, the movement for reform has had some effects: math test scores on the National Assessment of Educational Progress (NAEP) have risen for students who are nine- and thirteen-years-old, and they rose more for black than white students.[23] Scores on the NAEP tests of reading rose for all nine-year-olds, but a good deal less sharply than in math, and reading scores rose even less for thirteen-year-olds. Black students made more reading gains than whites.[24] Yet the new policies were not the only or perhaps even the chief cause of that improvement, for these NAEP increases began before the passage of IASA and all but a few state reforms, and they have slowed since the passage of NCLB. It is likely that the public attention to schools and the need for improvement, and the persistent message that education for poor students was unacceptably weak, caught educators' attention and prompted change. But the policies have been an important part of that movement and have helped to focus attention on its aspirations.

There have been equally impressive costs. NCLB declares that the achievement gap must be closed by 2014, but it is difficult to find an observer who believes that it will be. In addition, though math achievement has improved on the NAEP and reading has improved slightly, state tests tell a different story, in part because they are the tests that count for schools and teachers, and in part because doing well on most of them does not require the demanding academic performance for which IASA and NCLB called and that proficiency on the NAEP tests is believed to represent.[25] Both IASA and NCLB delegated most important decisions about standards, tests, and accountability to states, because the bills would not have passed if the federal government had tried to centralize power over these decisions in Washington. Like the original version of Title I, IASA and NCLB wrote the old divisions over state and federal power into the legislation. Many states therefore devised or purchased tests that show marked improvement in students' performance; the tests had easy standards of proficiency, so that many students with modest knowledge and skills could attain scores that seemed acceptable. Many failing schools have improved little or not at all. Because of the very weak educational infrastructure, state tests often become a protocurriculum, and teachers in many schools now spend weeks in often mindless test prep drills with students. The gaps in achievement that these bills proposed to eliminate remain largely intact on the NAEP. And many commentators, including former advocates of IASA and NCLB, now argue that the two statutes promoted fifty different programs by lodging authority for tests and standards with the states, many of which set weak criteria for success.[26] Critics contend that IASA and NCLB failed to make standards and tests effective and that only national standards and tests can do the job. There is a growing sense that NCLB has not delivered. The assertion of federal authority that reformers celebrated in 1994 and 2001 seems less credible today.

The questions are no less daunting. Some are political, grounded in persistent disagreement over government authority and long-standing governance arrangements that express those disagreements: Can a special-purpose federal program that modestly supplements local and state funds drive fundamental change in such a vast and decentralized congeries of school systems and create a new system of educational governance? Does Title I have the political and fiscal moxie to make standards-based reform work nationally? Do states and localities have the educational moxie to turn the federal legislation into real educational improvement? Do state efforts to increase the appearance of success by easing standards on state tests offer grounds for national tests and standards, or do they create more reason to doubt that federal power can drive deep transformation in an educational non-system that is so deeply decentralized? Ultimately, can Title I policy change the politics of education?

The answers to these political questions will depend partly on education: the more impressive their effects on teaching and learning, the more likely the reforms will prevail politically. We have no certain answer to whether these reforms have the necessary educational moxie—no one does—but in the chapters that follow, our analysis leads us to doubt that the policies will achieve most of their aims. Standards-based reform is a distinctively American and educationally quite unusual attempt to improve schools, because the instruments that the policies deploy—standards, tests, and accountability—are not instruments of instruction. They are not the infrastructure that education in the United States lacks. Standards and tests are not a substitute for curricula; they might be used to guide a curriculum, but they are not instruments that teachers and students can fruitfully use to advance learning. Nor are tests and standards instruments for teacher education; if they were used to guide the development of curricula, and if those curricula were used in schools, then how to teach those curricula might be made the focus of teacher education, but there is no evidence of such developments. There are no curriculum-referenced examinations; though states claim that their standardized tests are referenced to state standards, there is little evidence on that point. More important, there is no curriculum that is referenced to the standards. The instruments that the recent policies deploy do not bear on teaching and learning and do not provide the means to devise instruments that might.

That complicates efforts to make the reforms work. Assessing how well they work is further complicated because the schools' operation and effects are entangled with large social and economic problems. Black and white students and advantaged and disadvantaged students enter school with quite unequal average test scores, and the differences persist or grow over the grades. The entering inequalities are due chiefly to social and economic disparities, not to the schools.[27] Is it reasonable to expect schools to erase the educational effects of huge inequalities that are caused by economic, social, and political forces that educators do not control? If we say that it is the schools' responsibility, as IASA, NCLB, and state standards-based reforms do, then another sort of question becomes urgent: what resources would educators require—different practices, knowledge, will, and money among them—to eliminate average achievement differences between children from affluent and poor families? Mississippi, which has many poor families, spent an average of $7,173 per student in fiscal year 2006, while New Jersey spent $14,954 per student in the same period.[28] What would Mississippi need to spend, and what other resources would it require, to appreciably reduce the great average difference between the performance of its students on the NAEP tests that NCLB requires all states use, and that of students in New Jersey? And where would the money come from? States have primary responsibility for schooling in the federal system, a responsibility that IASA and NCLB intensify. Is it politically reasonable to hold states to the same standards of school performance? If we did so, it would mark a major change in the balance of influence between states and the national government that the Constitution's framers envisioned. But even imagining such a step is not possible in purely political terms, because states' economic, social, and educational capabilities differ so greatly. Given the vast differences between states like Alabama, Mississippi, and Louisiana, on the one hand, and New York, New Jersey, and Connecticut, on the other, federal aid to the poorer and weaker states would have to be packaged in something resembling the Marshall Plan to create a level educational playing field on which the two sorts of states could be held to the same demanding standards.

These are tough questions, but the fact that they are being asked may advance efforts to improve schools. It is a sign of how far Title I has come, and of its constructive influence, that some of these questions are on the educational and political agenda, and others lurk around the edges. When the ESEA became law, most supporters believed that better education would follow more money and that students' learning would improve. Experience has shown that things are not nearly so simple and that school improvement is neither easy nor quick. Changes in Title I and other policies have highlighted these things; though they are difficult problems, they are the right problems to work on. It is, however, a sign of how far Title I has to go that the questions it helped to open up are so deep and that there is such uncertainty about the answers. Title I has been a real success in some respects, but that success opened up terrific problems.

We investigate these matters here. We already mentioned one question that we will address: How has Title I changed? How did the weak program of 1965 become the aggressive program of 2002? The other question is, why did the new program provoke so many perverse effects, and encounter so much difficulty and controversy? Our investigations rest on the view that the relations between policies and programs like Title I and the practices that they seek to change present a dilemma. Policymakers define problems and devise remedies. Yet policy ultimately relies on practice: it depends on the people and organizations that have the problems to solve those problems. The likelihood that policies will be realized in practice therefore depends on the fit between aims and capability. Capability is contained in the instruments that policies deploy; in the instruments that practitioners can use; in practitioners' will, skill, and dispositions; and in the environment and organizations in which policy and practice subsist. The more aims outstrip capability, the more incompetence they create in practice. The less competent practitioners are to realize aims, the more likely are practice failures, perverse effects, and trouble for policy. Those practice failures, in turn, limit policy's ability to sustain political support.

We do not mean that policies should only pursue aims that are close to current practice. We mean instead to draw attention to a simple point that has large implications: the capability to make something constructive out of policies and programs is not fixed. It expresses a relationship between the aims of intervention, on the one hand, and the human, social, and fiscal resources that are available to achieve those aims, on the other. Other things being equal, when aims escalate, the capability to achieve them diminishes, unless it is enhanced. The success of innovative policies and programs depends, among other things, on the existence of instruments that offer either the required capability or the means to develop this capability and on whether practitioners and others in the environment possess or can improve capability. Though our attention is focused on Title I, these ideas are salient to educational interventions of all sorts.

Achieving congruence between aims, instruments, and capabilities is much more easily said than done. For the further policies try to push practice beyond what exists, the less practitioners, policymakers, or others in the environment can know how to do what policies propose. The more ambitious a policy is, the less likely that anyone could specify in advance what new capability would be required, in what types and combinations, to enable it to work well in practice. Policies can be understood as theories, or ideas about how things could work, but the further those ideas push practice from what exists, the less everyone will know about how to change practice to achieve new aims. The more ambitious policies are, the more success depends on instruments that can support change in practice including the opportunity to learn how to use these instruments to make the changes. If those instruments are forthcoming, the chances that policies can succeed in practice improve; success in practice can reinforce policies and strengthen the political arrangements that made the policies possible. If instruments and opportunities are not forthcoming, the chances of practice failure grow, because of the distance between the capability that ambitious policy aims require of practice and the extant capability. In such cases, policy creates incompetence in practice, which increases the chances of practice failure. That can be damaging for practitioners, but there is a risk for policy and policymakers as well, for practice failures can be traced to the policies that provoked them. In cases of this sort, practice failures can threaten the legitimacy of policy, the political influence of the sponsoring policymakers, and the influence of the coalitions that were associated with the policy. The contagion or spillover from policy success or failure in practice is an important avenue for practice to contribute to policy and politics.

We unpack and apply these ideas in the chapters that follow. We focus on Title I because its educational importance and political endurance are unequaled; because it is at the heart of recent efforts to transform schools; because the program has been beset by the old American divisions over central, state, and local authority; and because it is an excellent case with which to explore the problems of school improvement. Because our analysis of the relations between policy and practice, sketched here and expanded in Chapter 2, is central to our analysis, this book also can be read as a study of the ideas' usefulness in the analysis of educational programs and policies. But this is neither a comprehensive study nor an evaluation of Title I. We use evidence of Title I's operation and effects in its historical context, but we do so to probe the relations between what is done in Washington and state capitols, and what is done in practice. This is an interpretive essay that aims to offer a fresh analysis of efforts to solve America's most difficult school problems and of the relations between policy and practice.

CHAPTER 2

Policy and Practice

The relations between social policy and practice present a dilemma: public and private agencies identify problems and offer solutions, whether for welfare, drug use, or weak schools, yet the key problem solvers are the offending, needy, or damaged people and organizations that policy aims to correct. Governments typically have more power than those at whom social policy is directed and can devise instruments—incentives, ideas, money, leadership, rules, and more—to encourage implementation. Yet these help only if used well by those who are said to be the problem, and whose capability therefore is likely to be modest, and others who may assist. Though policymakers define problems and devise remedies, they are rarely the ultimate problem solvers; they depend on the people and organizations that have the problem to solve it. The latter depend on policymakers for some resources—ideas, incentives, money, and more—to help to solve the problem. Practitioners and policymakers often are at odds; yet the success of policy depends on finding mutually agreeable ways to manage this dilemma. This view highlights the tension between those who set the direction for action and those who interpret and carry it out. The tension is found in the relations between government policy and practice, but it arises at all levels of society, in government and private agencies, in capitals and classrooms. We use the terms *policy* and *practice* to refer to these roles, whether they occur in government or outside it. We develop the ideas here and sketch their application to Title I.

Research on the relations between policy and practice in education began during Lyndon Johnson's Great Society. The early studies often seemed to assume that well-designed policies would contain the resources that were needed to shape practice. Implementation was viewed from the vantage point of government, which later led to the appellation "top-down." Since the main issues were how control, compliance, and management influenced policy outcomes, research focused on compliance.[1] Researchers recognized that some local discretion or adaptation was unavoidable, but they doubted that discretion would add value to policy and thought that adjustments could weaken it.[2]

Doubts about these ideas arose in part from evidence that education policy did not have the expected effects. An early evaluation of Title I reported that it had no average effect on learning.[3] Though some schools spent the money on reading, others spent it on music instruction or field trips. Practice shaped policy by influencing how it was interpreted on the ground and thus how it turned out.

In light of such research, Richard Elmore titled ideas about the potency of policy a "noble lie" and argued that policy should be made by "mapping backward" from practice, so as to rest design with the practitioners who would use the policy.[4] Paul Berman and Milbrey McLaughlin took a similar view in the RAND Change Agent Study, in which they portrayed teachers' motivation and their opportunities to adapt programs to local needs and circumstances as keys for implementation: "Projects begun with broad-based support were not only more likely to have been implemented in a mutually adaptive way, but they also stood a better chance of attaining a stable continuation."[5] Practitioners' discretion was unavoidable; hence, policy could not design practice. McLaughlin later wrote, "policy cannot mandate what matters."[6] Practice was too complex and policymaking too remote for policy to prescribe for practice. That nicely represented what came to be known, inelegantly, as the "bottom-up" view: practitioners' world was their own, not easily reached by policy, yet crucial to its success.

In the view from practice, the key issues are not control and compliance but how practitioners' situations influence their use of policy.[7] Practitioners know things that policymakers could not, and they use that to adapt policy to their circumstances. McLaughlin and other researchers saw teachers' adaptation of policy as the result of professional judgment about policies' utility: "one ironic consequence of this street-level policy making and professionals' priority for client service is that reformers often may not get what they want, but get what they need as policy is put into practice."[8] Other studies expanded on these ideas: most influentially, Michael Lipsky's *Street Level Bureaucracy,* which argued that policy was effectively made in practice.[9]

These ideas gained indirect support from research on the effects of schooling. In response to researchers' reports that differences among school revenues, and the resources that money bought, had modest and inconsistent effects on school-to-school differences in average achievement, scholars began to study practice. They investigated the effects of instruction, organizational arrangements, and teachers' knowledge and skill and reported that teachers' and students' knowledge and academic practices, as well as school organization, mediate between the money and other resources that schools deploy, on the one hand, and learning, on the other.[10] This implied that the effects of resources depend on their use: different schools and teachers did different things with the same resources, with different effects on learning.

The headline news in the late 1960s and early 1970s was that school resources had weak and inconsistent effects on practice. That shook inherited ideas about the power of policy and helped to generate new ideas about what it might take to influence practice. The more fundamental point, which made no headlines, was that if the effects of resource allocation or regulation depend on practitioners' use of them, then policy depends on practice. If so, the classical instruments of education policy, funding and regulation, were not as potent as had been thought.[11]

Policy and practice seemed opposed in these lines of work: policymakers tried to secure compliance from implementers who reinterpreted, ignored, evaded, or buffered themselves from policy. This can be viewed as conflict over goals but also as an issue of democratic norms: some saw policy as the authoritative expression of representative government, which seemed to support a view from the top, but others saw it as an imposition on those who did the real work of social service. Advocates of the former view noted that policymakers knew things about goals, instruments, and policymaking that were crucial to policy formation and that practitioners were unlikely to know, while advocates of the latter view argued that practitioners knew things about clients and their situations that policymakers did not but that were crucial to make policy work.

However, understanding the relations between policy and practice entails more than political positions, in part because "top" and "bottom" can be rubbery terms. Title I of the 1965 ESEA is a federal program, so a view of its implementation from the top should begin and end in Washington, DC. Yet the program devolves extensive authority to the states, which allocate funds, screen local applications, and assist and evaluate local programs. The federal government is the top agency for states, and states are the federal agency's bottom of first resort. But those agencies in Albany and Sacramento also are the top for local education authorities (LEAs), even as the school principals' top in those LEAs is the central office, and the teachers' top is the principal. State Title I offices' problems of control and compliance vis-à-vis LEA central offices closely resemble the problems of control and compliance that LEA central offices have with schools. The problems that researchers identify with the top of policy also are problems for organizations and individuals that researchers identify with the bottom. In such situations, tension between policy and practice pervades the same agencies and individuals, rather than being aligned only with top and bottom. LEA central office workers who set direction concerning Title I for principals, teachers, and students also work as "street-level" bureaucrats in relation to those who set direction for Title I in state agencies. These public managers are both central controllers and street-level bureaucrats, trying to influence those for whom they make policy while also trying to cope with those who make policy for them. In such cases, policymakers and practitioners converge in the same person and office, and individuals and agencies experience the dilemma from both sides. A focus on political position obscures that, while the dilemma of policy and practice illuminates it.[12]

There are extreme cases: the central government is subordinate to no higher domestic agency, and students exercise no positional authority over others on whom they depend for services. In such cases, giving or enacting direction is aligned with political position. But many others are at neither extreme: they try to influence those who depend on them for resources and guidance while at the same time attempting to respond to those who seek to influence them by offering new aims, guidance, and resources. In these cases, the relations between policy and practice are better understood as an expression of the dilemma with which we began, rather than as positions in government hierarchies.[13]

The last two decades saw the development of several lines of analysis that departed from positional studies. One focused on the historical development of policy change and situated the problem of policy and practice squarely on the shoulders of political leaders who are unable to make binding policy commitments, because policies enacted at one time often unravel when their sponsors leave or change their minds, or attend to different interests. Solving this problem with durable policies appears more likely when broad policy regimes shift and reconfigure "interests, institutions and ideas,"[14] since regime shifts dismantle previous political relationships and create new ones.[15] If policies do endure, they often do so by creating new political coalitions that reconfigure politics, lend the program sustained political support, and disassemble the foundation of old coalitions and program opponents. This moves beyond tops and bottoms and focuses instead on broad political dynamics, where policies may create and support constituencies that in turn support policy and refashion politics.[16] While recognizing policies "cannot be implemented unless technical conditions are favorable," this approach attends primarily to politics and less to practice and the challenges that arise when policies require significant new capability.[17]

A second line of analysis has focused more specifically on practice by examining the role of knowledge and ideas in the relations between policy and practice. Janet Weiss called attention to the role of ideas in her study of mental health policy.[18] Several studies in education similarly investigated how educators' knowledge and interpretations shaped implementation of the ambitious policies that began to proliferate in the late 1980s.[19] One such study argued that practitioners' knowledge mediated the relations between policy and practice; implementation was portrayed as a species of learning, policy as a sort of instruction.[20] Several studies portrayed policies as ideas, and practitioners' knowledge and understanding as key features in their response to policy.[21] Other studies probed how communities of practice shape practitioners' understanding and thus their response to policy.[22] Another focused on the role that language played in mediating the comprehension of policy and, through that, practitioners' response.[23] Dvora Yanow's book *How Does a Policy Mean?* portrayed putting policy into practice as a continuing process of interpretation, one in which the meanings that implementers assign to policy play a central role in how things turn out.[24] James Spillane and his colleagues captured several threads in this line of work when they wrote that "reforms are complex ideas," and that "artifacts used to communicate these reforms encode representations of a set of ideas about the reform. . . . Implementation [thus] involves cognition . . . [and] requires thoughtful use of these artifacts."[25] The relations between policy and practice are here transformed into thought, knowledge, symbolism, and the vehicles of thought. The key influences on implementation are ideas, knowledge, and the influences on them including language and social organization. The primacy of thought replaces that of political position in these studies, which seems fitting at a time when education policy placed unprecedented demands on practitioners' knowledge and skill.

We begin from these arguments about the role of ideas in policy and the politics and structures that give those ideas currency. Where others see government position as primary, we see the dilemma. Those who set direction for action identify problems and propose solutions, but these can help only if used well by those who are given direction and who often are said to be the problem. This dilemma can be difficult to manage even in seemingly simple situations, as when teachers try to help students improve weak compositions. Teachers may see students as the problem, but students are the key problem solvers, for only they can learn to improve their compositions. Teachers can offer examples, assign exercises, coax, and insist, but they depend on students to use these things or respond to these approaches. Teachers have more power and knowledge, but students' will and ability are their own. Like others who direct, teachers depend on the people with problems to solve them. Teachers who set assignments that students are unprepared to perform risk resistance or revolt and loss of authority. If students will not or cannot do as teachers say, teachers are likely to settle for what students will do.[26]

The dilemma makes room for both policy and practice to shape politics. Policies create politics by providing resources and benefits that attract constituencies who then use those resources to engage in and shape politics.[27] Different policy designs can promote or discourage individuals' incentives, motivation, and resources for political participation.[28] Yet practice may also contribute to politics, for policies can create incompetence in practice. The further they depart from extant practice, the more difficult are the entailed changes in practice, the more incompetence the policy creates, and the more such policies require the acquisition of new capability and the unlearning of existing capability.[29] Yet, the more ambitious the policy, the more difficult it is to mobilize the resources that could forestall incompetence in practice, because the further policy presses practice into the unknown, the more scarce the needed capability becomes, and the more likely is practice failure.[30] Practice failure can erode trust in practitioners, but since the problem can be traced to policy, contagion can threaten the legitimacy of policy and shape political arrangements.[31] Shortly after Title I began, for instance, evidence that Title I had failed in practice threatened the program. Organized interests capitalized on that evidence to advance their political agendas and move the program toward more targeted instructional assistance and away from general aid. Practice shaped politics, which shaped policy.

The dilemma thus calls attention to both tension and mutual dependence in the relations between policy and practice. Mutual dependence arises in incentives to collaborate, to mobilize resources, to improve practice, and to make policy succeed, while tension arises in the risks associated with policy efforts to change practice. Such things sometimes play out in anticipated action and adjustment before policy spills into public view; if so, practice influences policy as it is being made. Often, they play out after policy is made, in implementation. Either way, the more policy puts practice at risk of failure, the more it can damage the interests and political legitimacy not only of practitioners but also of policymakers. The potential contagion of practice failure to policy is a key feature of their mutual dependence. It also is a key source of change in policy, since the prospect of failure can concentrate the minds and energies of policymakers and practitioners.

There are incentives for those who set direction for action to restrict the incompetence that they create in practice and to help make policy succeed. But these incentives are not necessarily controlling, since policymakers create incompetence for a variety of reasons. Teachers may be so unaware of students that they inaccurately estimate their students' capability, just as policymakers can be so ignorant of practice that they inaccurately estimate the demands that a policy will impose. Or they may set very ambitious goals to stir practitioners to act, in the same way that teachers sometimes do with their students. Or policymakers may wish to set goals that will cause practice to fail. Some critics assert that conservative lawmakers supported NCLB in the belief that its aims were so ambitious that the schools could not meet them and that the ensuing failures would further erode the schools' legitimacy and increase the appeal of school choice. Policy design reflects political considerations, and policy outcomes include politics as well as practice.

Management of the Dilemma

If tension between policy and practice is unavoidable, it can be managed in different ways. How it is managed depends on the distance between policy and practice and on the actions and resources that narrow or widen that distance. Those actions and resources are of four sorts. One is the aims of policy: some embody modest ideas about what policy should accomplish, while others embody ambitious ideas; some are relatively clear while others are ambiguous. The further aims depart from extant practice, the greater the resources that will be needed to realize these aims. The more ambiguous the aims are, the more difficult it will be for policymakers to know how to craft suitable instruments and for practitioners to figure out what to do in order to achieve these aims.

Three other sorts of resources bear on the distance between policy and practice. One is the instruments that policymakers and managers deploy; we see them as the capability that policy brings to relations with practice. Instruments include money, mandates, incentives to comply, flexibility to adapt policy to local conditions, and ideas that inspire or inform practitioners' understanding and action or that contain evidence about implementation and effects, among other things.[32] Instruments are socially created tools that are intended to encourage assent to policy or to help realize aims in practice, or both. Yet there is no science of implementation, and there can be deep differences in ideas about how best to achieve a goal. Instruments are often designed as much to satisfy the interests and ideas of legislative factions or interest groups as to improve implementation.[33]

A second set of resources is commonly referred to as capacity, though we prefer capability; this refers to the resources that practitioners and others bring to relations with policy.[34] Such resources include interests, practices, ideas (which comprise knowledge, values, and skill), will, and money. These elements of capability mirror several of those for policy instruments; that is no accident, for when policy instruments are effective, it is partly because they help to mobilize the capabilities that enable practitioners or organizations to improve services and solve problems.

Resources also arise in the environment of policy and practice: the governance structures, political organizations, and socioeconomic context in which policies emerge and subsist. Policies are designed in environments, instruments and capabilities are formed in and operate through them, and practitioners work in them. Environments influence policy and practice by acting on aims, instruments, and capabilities.

Policy Aims: Ambition and Ambiguity

Other things being equal, the more ambitious the change that policies seek in practice, the more difficult it is to manage the dilemma of policy and practice. Some policies only extend current practice: for example, they add five minutes a day to the ten already spent on composition, they include a new wetland in existing shoreline preservation, or they increase the income threshold for Medicaid eligibility. Because they call for modest change, they create little incompetence in practice. Other policies call for change that has little technical content: they shift school schedules or require patients to communicate with nurses rather than doctors. Their difficulty varies with the extent to which the changes depart from practice. Still others have much more ambitious aims, like replacing computation with conceptual mathematics or creating new environmental regulation. As they depart more sharply from practice, such policies create more incompetence, make implementation more difficult, and require more capability to revise practice.[35]

The implementation of ambitious policies also is influenced by their relative ambiguity. A policy that calls for more conceptual work in mathematics could do so by briefly stating that objective, contrasting it with computational work, and justifying the change with reference to the nation's need for scientists. That would be quite ambiguous, because conceptual mathematics can mean several different things; the difficulty of implementing such an ambitious policy would be increased by uncertainty about what conceptual mathematics is. Alternatively, the policy could spell out in detail the desired mathematical content and offer examples of conceptual work in each portion of the content. Such a policy would still be difficult to implement, but the difficulty would not be chiefly attributable to ambiguous aims.

Some policies are ambiguous because the organizations that implement them are so varied that uniform and specific aims would not work. In such cases, ambiguity is tied to local discretion, since the capability required to implement varies in practice. Other policies are ambiguous because they envision states of affairs so novel that they can be imagined but not specified in much detail. The capability required to implement lies nowhere and must be invented. In many cases, ambiguous aims arise as coalitions use vague phrases to cover differences that they cannot resolve. Giandomenico Majone and Aaron Wildavsky wrote that "in most policies of interest, objectives are characteristically . . . vague (because that is how we can agree to proceed without having agreed also on exactly what to do)."[36]

Federal education policy often has used ambiguity to manage both state and local variability and differences within coalitions. That affects relations with practice, for "the more general an idea and the more adaptable it is to a range of circumstances, the more likely it is to be realized in some form, but the less likely it is to emerge as intended in practice."[37] The ambiguity that attracts policymakers makes it difficult for practitioners to know what is expected of them; ambiguity can therefore enable policy while inhibiting practice.[38]

Ambiguity of both sorts has marked federal education policy since the 1960s. The aims of Title I of the 1965 ESEA embodied several ideas about what should be accomplished, and these aims reflected deep conflict between policymakers who hoped to improve education for disadvantaged students, and policymakers who sought to restrain central influence. As a result, the program's aims were so ambiguous that Title I seemed to be both a radical departure and a modest initiative. On the radical side, it aimed to improve schools for poor children, which implied federal influence on states and schools; federal officials tried to encourage school improvement, to advise states and localities, and to evaluate their progress.[39] Yet everyone was poorly informed; there was little knowledge of how to improve schools; teaching and learning were weakly understood; and state and federal intervention had been rare. Practitioners at all levels of the federal system faced large tasks with small capabilities. The more one viewed Title I as a policy to improve education for disadvantaged students, the more significant the distance between aims and practice.

These problems were multiplied by the structure of Title I. The program's formula grant came close to being general aid, for it was designed in part to please opponents of federal aid by limiting central influence.[40] The federal government had to decide how much to spend, to apportion this funding, and to mail out checks to funding recipients, while localities had only to spend the money on a broad category of school resources for a particular purpose and to fill out applications. For both federal and local government, these actions were more familiar than school improvement. Congress knew how to appropriate funds, and local educators knew how to spend on schools. Distributing funds was a bit novel for the U.S. Office of Education and required learning, yet handing out money was familiar federal work. It pressed everyone beyond extant capability but not so far as to make it very difficult to manage. In this view, the program's aims were at a modest distance from practice.

The implementation of Title I has been an exercise in managing this ambiguity about its aims. The program's first three decades saw cautious federal efforts to improve schools with something close to general aid. There was modest improvement, but ideas about the problem that the program should solve began to change in response to evidence on unequal school performance and new ideas about the schools' purposes and problems. These new aims for Title I were written into major federal statutes, as Presidents Bill Clinton and George W. Bush made Title I the core of federal efforts to reshape schools with standards-based reform. The original legislation's ambiguous ideas about improved schools for poor children were replaced with what seemed to be more specific requirements for students' academic progress.

Great ambiguity remained, however. One source was familiar from the past: key decisions about what Title I's new aims would mean in practice were delegated to states and localities. IASA and NCLB did expand federal influence, but states and localities were the operating agencies and retained great influence. In the 1965 bill, that ambiguity was displayed by targeting Title I funds to school districts with high concentrations of children from poor families while delegating most important decisions to states and localities. In 1994 and 2002, the ambiguity was displayed in aims that mixed much more ambitious, centrally inspired school improvement with the continued delegation of most operating authority and major decisions to states. For example, the criterion by which schools are judged to have achieved "proficiency" varies among states because both bills permitted states to choose their own tests and set their own proficiency standards. What appeared to be unprecedented clarity in the new Title I's focus on student test scores dissolves into a blur as states decide what tests to use and how to define proficiency.[41] The federal legislation set two aims—to improve achievement and to eliminate race and class inequality in achievement—that called for marked departures from practice, yet it enabled states to enact those aims in varied ways. Thus, the legislation created, potentially, fifty differences between aims and practice as well as ambiguity about which of these aims and practices would be satisfactory.

Another source of ambiguity in the new Title I's aims is the meaning of student achievement and the ways to improve it. When standards-based reform moved aggressively into the weakly understood and contested domains of instruction and its outcomes, it opened up great ambiguity about what defensible measures of achievement were and how to improve teaching, learning, and weak schools. One case in point concerned the use of standardized norm-referenced tests to assess schools' performance. The uncertain validity of tests to measure schools' performance was long known to researchers, but it was not salient to policy in earlier decades because no one used tests to hold schools accountable.[42] By 2002, however, tests were in the foreground of the debate about school performance because IASA and NCLB required students' scores to be the criterion for judging accomplishment of Title I's central aim. Ambiguity that researchers had known about for decades became highly salient to policy and exploded in public debate. Knowledge about tests and their use suddenly became a central issue as disputes erupted about whether tests can measure schools' progress well enough to decide whether they have achieved "proficiency." This ambiguity signals a great distance between aims and practice, owing to weak knowledge about how to measure school outcomes.

School improvement is a related case in point. The new Title I created great pressure for school improvement, yet knowledge about it was weak and quite insufficient to enable specification of the most effective ways to teach multiplication or composition, let alone how to do so for a great range of students in a great range of circumstances. The weakness of knowledge was familiar to researchers, but it had not before been salient to policy because no policy had explicitly made school improvement the criterion of its success. The seemingly precise aims of IASA and NCLB created great uncertainty, for so little was understood about how to achieve them. Whether policy aims are ambiguous depends at least as much on knowledge of how they might be achieved as on how clearly they are stated. The recent changes to Title I are a troubling combination of great ambition and weak knowledge, which created huge ambiguity. Here again, ambiguity creates great distance between aims and practice. Though ambiguity often is useful to policy formation, it can damage efforts to realize policy in practice.

Ambiguity is not inherently troublesome, however. Many policies with ambiguous aims delegate the problem solving to implementers and leave it at that. Ambiguous aims might have been less of a problem for the new Title I if pressure to improve test scores and schools had been modest. But the recent legislation coupled ambiguous aims to intense pressure for results; that turned weak knowledge about teaching, learning, and school improvement into highly salient incompetence in practice. The further policy aims depart from conventional practice, the more acute the dilemma of policy and practice becomes, for such aims reduce practitioners' capability and increase the risk of practice failure. Herbert Simon and his colleagues wrote over half a century ago, "If the people to be regulated do not know what they are supposed to do, they cannot do it."[43]

That leads us beyond aims, for the means to achieve them lie elsewhere—in the capabilities that practitioners possess and in the instruments that policies deploy or that exist in the environment.

Instruments: Capability That Policy Brings to Practice

Policies create a gap with practice by moving at least a bit beyond it; to put policy into practice is to close the gap. That depends in part on the instruments that policies deploy; they may be funds, mandates for action, incentives to comply, offers of local discretion, and ideas to inform practice. Since instruments are politically created, they reflect the views and interests of those who make policy. Though often crafted to encourage assent to policy and to change practice, they also have been devised to constrain policy.

Instruments vary in strength—their influence in practice—and in salience—how closely they connect with what must happen in practice to achieve policy aims. Strong but not salient instruments are likely to be less effective, for they create problems by telling practitioners to do something but leaving them to figure out what and how. Strong incentives to achieve aims that are beyond practitioners' capability are a case in point. Instruments that are salient for practice but weak also are less likely to be effective, for they connect to practice but exert little influence. Technical assistance to produce performances that implementers have no incentive to produce is a case in point.[44] Instruments that are both strong and salient are more promising, but they are more difficult to craft, in part because they typically require more knowledge to design and use. That requirement grows as policy departs further from practice, but the required knowledge also becomes more scarce.

Strength and salience do not inhere in instruments but vary with relations among the ambitiousness and clarity of aims and capability in practice and environments. Instruments that are strong and salient for a policy that departs only a bit from practice will not be equally strong and salient for a policy that departs much further. The federal Impact Aid program helps schools that serve families at federal installations, and its three instruments are sufficiently strong and salient: money, local discretion to spend it as officials see fit, and occasional oversight. Government compensates for a burden imposed, but it seeks no change in practice and thus creates no incompetence. In contrast, Title VI of the 1964 Civil Rights Act (CRA) sought to change Southern school officials' behavior in using race to assign black and white children to separate schools; the key instrument was the granting or withholding of federal funds from state and local agencies. Desegregation required dramatic change in practice, but funds were salient because money is essential to schools' operation. It also was relatively strong, for once Title I began, federal funds became a part of school budgets, and jobs and operations depended on this funding. The instruments that were sufficiently strong and salient for

Impact Aid would have been quite inadequate for Title VI of the 1964 CRA.

The more ambitious and ambiguous policy aims become, the more difficult it is to devise salient and strong instruments. The curriculum reforms of the late 1950s and early 1960s urged very ambitious change in classroom practice, but they were ambiguous; few knew how these curricula should be taught or what it would mean to teach them successfully. Some of the nation's most distinguished academics collaborated to produce new curricula in mathematics, physics, biology, and social studies; the curricula were bold departures from most then-current practice, and they called for new approaches to teaching and learning. Yet teachers got little help in learning how to use the new materials effectively. Summer workshops were offered for some teachers who could apply and take the time, but there was room for only a few of the many who needed help. Most teachers had no opportunity to learn how to use the new materials or how students might respond. There also were no other instruments to enable teachers' learning; there was, for example, no curriculum for teachers that helped them learn how to use the student curriculum well. There were no examples of students' work, no analyses of their thinking, and no examples of how accomplished teachers used the materials.[45]

We noted earlier the quote from Herbert Simon and his colleagues: "If the people to be regulated do not know what they are supposed to do, they cannot do it." They went on to write that in such cases, "agencies must engage in great amounts of public educational activities."[46] This is true, but devising those activities requires knowledge that is quite difficult to come by for novel policies, precisely because they are novel. It would have been difficult to create such instruments for the new curricula, for it would have required expertise in teaching with materials that had not been used before, which meant that no one had that expertise.[47] Academics wrote the curricula and let teachers cope.

The strength and salience of policy instruments are relative; they depend on the instruments' relationship to capability in practice and the environment and to policy aims. The strength and salience of Title I's original instruments depended on which idea about the program one held. If Title I was seen as general federal aid to schools, then the chief instrument, the formula grant, was adequately salient and strong. If Title I was meant to improve education for children from poor families, however, its aim departed sharply from policy and practice, and the formula grant was much weaker. This aim itself has been a significant influence on both policy and practice: the importance of improved education for children from poor families grew with time, and practitioners have increasingly focused on it. Yet that idea alone, even with the federal grants, did not dramatically reshape practice. Title I's formula grant was written as a virtual entitlement; once the formula was set and funds appropriated, state and local grants were fixed. States had to write proposals and offer assurances, but their grants depended less on the proposals' merits than on the incidence of poverty and a legislative intent that nearly all districts should receive funds. Title I offered an appealing idea and money but few other incentives to change practice and little help.

Compared with the 1965 version, IASA and NCLB's instruments seem strong. They require that states set clear academic standards and tests aligned with the standards, and they hold schools accountable for students' performance, all of which go far beyond the earlier Title I. Yet the strength and salience of these instruments must be considered in terms of the policies' aims as well as historically. From the perspective of recent policy aims, the instruments are much less salient than they are strong. One problem is that teaching and learning must change if Title I is to succeed, but NCLB's instruments do not reach these practices very well. Academic standards can be a useful frame for practice, but few teachers can turn them into lessons that advance the learning that the aims announce. Standards and assessments can exemplify policy goals but not in the detail or with the salience to instruction that would enable most teachers and students to use them effectively.

Accountability for students' achievement was meant to offer incentives for schools to attend to standards and tests, but such incentives are more likely to be effective if they are salient to instruction. The incentives that IASA and NCLB attached to accountability do not operate on instruction; they operate on state governments; and through state governments, on district governments; and through district governments, on school managers; and through school managers, finally, on teachers. There are no direct incentives for teachers and none for students, even though students are the people who learn—or not. Moreover, the target of these accountability incentives is not instruction but students' test scores.

The federal incentives to change instruction operate outside of instruction. They affect teachers through many layers of government, and if incentives reach students at all, it is through those indirect means. That blunts the incentives' salience for instruction and reduces the chance that they will much improve it. In such multilevel accountability, it would be impossible to attach incentives for performance to a particular instructional design, unless that design was part of the accountability scheme itself. That might have made more sense educationally, but it would have been seen as politically impossible and technically quite difficult, at least on NCLB's rapid compliance schedule.

NCLB's strong but not salient instruments sharpened the dilemma—of relying on those with the problem to solve it—and elicited some responses that do not help to improve instruction. If policies attach consequences to performance without making it possible for practitioners to respond competently, they increase the chance that practitioners will try to reduce risk by complying without improving practice. Many states adopted tests that were relatively easy, thus enabling the appearance of success. The tests often are used as a sort of curriculum, but this approach is likely to leave many students with narrow and superficial knowledge. Teachers and school managers tried to reduce the risk of failure by boosting outcomes without improving learning, by prepping students for tests, helping them to cheat, altering scores, or inflating average scores by keeping low-performing students away.[48] Such responses are to be expected if policies set implausible aims; or if they set plausible aims but fail to deploy instruments that are strong and salient enough to support their achievement; or if instruments are strong but not salient or strong and salient but operate on incapable practitioners. In such cases, teachers can be expected to reduce risk rather than improve performance because they lack the capability required to improve. We expect practitioners to act roughly rationally, given any set of aims and instruments; it is rational to try to reduce risk if one is required to do things that one cannot, especially if one may be penalized for failing to perform.

Instruments are the capability that policy brings to its relations with practice. They vary in strength, or their influence in practice, and in salience, or how closely they connect with what must happen in practice to achieve policy aims. What practitioners and policymakers can and cannot do, however, is not a simple function of aims and instruments. It also depends on their capability.

Capability: Resources That Practice Brings to Policy

Capability is essential to implementation because it consists of the resources that implementers and others bring to policy. Yet capability is relative: what is sufficient for a policy that departs only a bit from conventional practice is unlikely to be sufficient for a policy that departs much more dramatically. Capability varies not only with policy aims but also with instruments and extant practice.

Capability has individual and social sources. Individual practitioners bring values, interests, dispositions, skills, and knowledge to their encounters with policy. Values bear on capability because policy aims or instruments can attract or offend practitioners' values or those of others in the environment. The inclusion of evolution in the curriculum deeply offends some educators, parents, and politicians who believe that this teaching introduces incorrect or evil ideas, while its absence from the curriculum deeply offends others who accept science. Such values influence capability by enhancing or weakening the will to implement policy or by impeding or enhancing acquisition of the skills and knowledge needed to implement.

Values can vary with environments. Aversion to the teaching of evolution is more likely in the U.S. South, while support is more likely in urban areas. Similarly, policies that reduce speed limits are more likely to be accepted in urbanized states than in the American West, where they are thought to infringe on basic liberty. Even when programs seem to have no prominent value content, values can still come into play: adding ten minutes of daily writing may reduce recess or music, requiring practitioners to adjust their priorities not in principle but in the daily conduct of valued work. Such conflict can reduce practitioners' will to do as policies propose.[49]

Interests are another source of capability. A policy that requires firms to cease dumping polychlorinated biphenyls (PCBs) in rivers may cost them money or market share, and requiring educators to test students and track their progress is similarly costly. Even if manufacturers or educators agree with the policies, implementation can damage their interests by reducing profits, cutting products, or changing work. That can diminish the will to implement, just as policies that enhance practitioners' interests can increase it. Rewarding corporations for protecting the environment, by supporting pollution-reducing practices, is intended to enhance their will to advance policy by enhancing their interest, just as paying teachers to learn more about their subjects could increase their will to improve instruction, by showing how more knowledge could advance their interest in student learning. Such interests also can vary with environments: towns that are on polluted rivers far downstream from the pollution source are likely to have a greater interest in creating and implementing remedial policies than those at the source, where families depend on polluters for jobs, and towns depend on them for taxes.

Knowledge and skill are a third source of individual capability. Teachers use their knowledge of academic subjects and teaching skills to help students learn, but when a policy urges a substantial change in practice it can create incompetence by requiring practitioners to do things that they do not know how to do.[50] Some offer to educate practitioners, to improve their knowledge and skill to reduce incompetence.

Dispositions are a fourth source of capability. Teachers with similar values, interests, and knowledge often approach their work quite differently: some are warmly engaged and eager to work, while others are diffident. Some managers are aggressive in pursuit of their objectives, while others are cautious. Such differences contribute to capability by influencing the will to work, the motivation to learn, and engagement with practice.

The social sources of capability arise in organizations and environments. Affluent districts and schools in affluent neighborhoods typically employ more qualified teachers, who have more resources and use them more effectively than colleagues in poorer schools and districts. Schools with better leadership, which are more often found in affluent communities, make better use of teachers and other resources. Schools in less affluent communities have more staff turnover, which reduces capability, in part by impeding the development of stable knowledge among practitioners.[51]

Environments also affect collective capability. State and local school systems have very unequal capabilities owing to large differences in wealth, parents' education, and community resources. Title I is a modest federal supplement for states and localities: the entire federal contribution is now about 7.8 percent of total local revenues, and Title I is about 3 percent of those revenues.[52] Title I's influence on practice thus depends on what local schools bring to bear. The states and localities that need Title I the most bring the least capability to implementation; the program's operation and effects are shaped by the very inequalities that it aims to ameliorate.

Organizations and environments also influence capability by shaping the exchange of knowledge about practice and the interests and values that inform practice. For instance, the size and complexity of service delivery organizations affect practice by affecting the exchange of knowledge about practice; the larger and more complex they are, the more difficult it is to exchange knowledge. Other things being equal, it is likely to be less difficult to implement a school improvement policy in a medium-sized subdistrict of New York City than in the entire city, for communication, learning, and oversight would be more difficult for the entire city.[53]

Organizations can structure themselves to address this matter. School systems in some other countries use inspectors to monitor and improve instruction, and the inspectorates can institutionalize knowledge, skill, and the disposition to improve practice. If they do, they become repositories of capability. The absence of such organizations can inhibit capability: in the United States, quality work in teaching has not been required to maintain teaching or administrative posts, and there are no inspectorates; such organizations would have violated traditions of local control and weak government. To the extent that it exists, instructional expertise is concentrated among classroom teachers. The lack of such collective capability makes it more difficult to improve teaching and management.

Organizations also can be devised to create capability and mediate between policy and practice. Several nongovernmental organizations each created a Comprehensive School Reform Design (CSRD) to help high-poverty elementary schools to improve teaching and learning. The CSRDs mobilized skilled staff–devised designs for better education, and built educational know-how that helped many schools to improve; that helped to put state and federal standards-based reform policies into practice. In these cases and others, such organizations create, mobilize, and direct capability that can contribute to the success of practice and policy, but would otherwise be absent. They mediate between policy and practice, connecting them in ways that otherwise would be unlikely to occur.[54]

Our analysis implies that capability is task-specific. When policies propose to change practice, they create incompetence, but the "incompetence is not, of course, a trait like having brown eyes. It is a description of a relationship between a task or function in the situation up to a given, though ultimately arbitrary, standard of some sort."[55] Some policies set relatively narrow tasks for practitioners: federal Impact Aid requires practitioners only to accept money and spend it on education. Capability centers on accounting and has nothing to do with teaching or learning. Other policies set very broad tasks for practitioners: President Clinton's and President George W. Bush's revisions of Title I set ambitious new tasks for educators, for they required the elimination of race-, class-, and gender-based inequality in student performance. The needed capability spans teaching, learning, school management, school improvement, and assessment, among other things. Both Impact Aid and standards-based reform focus on education, but they require quite different capability from practice.

Capability arises not from a single attribute—skill and knowledge are most often mistaken for the whole—but from combinations of individual knowledge, values, interests, and dispositions, along with social attributes. All of these attributes interact. Practitioners are likely to find it more difficult to acquire or use knowledge when policies negatively affect their interests or values or when they are not disposed to engage with practice. Values can help to create interests, as when lobbying for charter schools yielded legislation that created networks of charter sponsors, educators, and parents, which became significant in state politics and support for charter schools. Capability subsists in such interactions and is maintained, enhanced, or degraded by them.[56]

Organizations can enhance capability by enabling and institutionalizing the exchange of knowledge about practice and the interests, values, and knowledge that inform practice. Or they can constrain capability by inhibiting such an exchange. This sort of capability seems to be a form of social capital that grows when organizations enable and institutionalize collective practice and shrinks when practice is kept private.[57]

The underlying point is that capability is relational, like the other resources that we have discussed. It waxes and wanes in interaction with the aims that policies set, the instruments that they deploy, and the environments in which policy and practice subsist. One can speak accurately of capability only if one speaks in relational terms, and one can shape capability only in relation to those other resources. IASA and NCLB created major problems of capability in practice by setting very ambitious aims but not deploying instruments that could build the needed capability in practice and the environment of public education.

Environment

We take this resource last because environments act on all the other resources—instruments, aim, and capability—that shape management of the dilemma in the relations between policy and practice. Ideas are one crucial feature of the educational environment. They were important for Title I, for the program owed its existence in part to changed ideas about education and poverty. Michael Harrington's early 1960s book, *The Other America,* brought national attention to poverty, portraying it as the consequence of institutional and political forces that could be corrected, not as the result of poor people's failings. That idea shaped policy by making poverty appear to be a problem that politicians could solve; they began trying, soon after the book was published, with President John F. Kennedy's War on Poverty and later with Title I of the ESEA. The civil rights movement, which gathered momentum at the same time, also shaped policy formation by changing many Americans' ideas about racial justice and helping to turn racial inequality into a problem that politicians might solve. Title I was in part an effort to solve this problem. It is difficult to see how the program could have been created had these ideas not come into play.

Ideas continued to shape Title I. Ideas about the purposes of schooling changed in the 1980s to focus on demanding academic standards and schools' accountability for students' performance. Ideas about the problem that Title I should solve also changed, from vague ambitions for school improvement to closing the achievement gap. The new ideas helped to shape policy and change the politics of education by fundamentally changing Title I; in the next decade, it became the key instrument for Presidents Clinton and George W. Bush in their efforts to impose standards-based reform on the nation's schools, and its aim was to close the achievement gap.

The environment also can be understood as the circumstances that bear specifically on a policy or program. In this sense, it is a specialized subset of organizations, political structures and processes, economic arrangements, fiscal practices, and culture. The boundary of any subset, and thus the salient environment of a policy, depends on the policy in question. Teacher education is part of the larger environment of education, but it is not part of the environment specific to a policy that changes Title I fund allocation. It is part of the environment of other policies: most U.S. elementary school teachers learn little about the subjects that they will teach, due to the weak professional education that higher education and state government support. That limits the capability teachers bring to ambitious curricula or demanding academic standards, and that limits the implementation of policies that promote such standards and curricula.

Considered this way, environments regularly affect policy design and implementation. Goals 2000 and IASA were written in close consultation with chief state school officers and other education groups. The bills had broad support from these groups, but that was partly because the bills delegated most key decisions about implementation to state and local education agencies. The groups' support was essential to legislative success, but that support required a policy that the groups could accept. Private organizations shape the relations between policy and practice as they influence policy formation.[58]

The environment of education also can be understood as the larger political, social, and economic circumstances in which policy and practice subsist. One important feature of those circumstances is the paradoxical role that schools play in U.S. social policy. Several European nations directly address social inequality with health care, education, income, and tax policies, but the United States has restrained its social policy to modest welfare, health and unemployment insurance, and old-age pensions.[59] Public schools were thought to guarantee equal opportunity and reduce the need for other policies.[60] Yet economic liberalism and hostility to government kept schools and governments weak: states delegated core educational functions, like tests, curricula, and writing texts, to private firms, thus outsourcing the technical and professional capability that most national systems retain. Hence, the educational capability of the state and local agencies that operate school systems and schools has been quite limited. They have few staffers with expertise in curricula, learning, teaching, and teacher education; states delegated most instructional decisions to localities, and most localities delegated them to schools. In the 1980s, California, a huge state that is larger in size and economy than many nations, launched a major statewide reform of mathematics teaching and learning; yet the state education agency employed fewer than three professionals to guide and assist hundreds of school districts, thousands of schools, and tens of thousands of teachers.

The capability of local school systems and schools has been further limited by the relationship between governments and social and economic conditions. Schools are governed, financed, and operated by states and localities. To the extent that the spatial allocation of population and wealth are congruent with jurisdictional lines, school government will reflect race and class divisions. In the United States, intense residential segregation by race and class has turned many neighborhood schools and increasing numbers of school districts into racial and economic enclaves. At the same time, regional economic differences have created enormous economic and social inequality among states and regional groupings of states. The growing congruence of race, social class, and wealth, with jurisdictional boundaries, has had a huge impact on the fiscal and educational capabilities of states and localities. For Title I, the key point is that students from poor families arrive in school with, on average, less of the knowledge and skill required to do well than more advantaged students, and their schools typically have less of the educational resources that would help to redress this inequality.

Schools have been central to the ideas that guide U.S. social policy, but their capability to deliver on those ideas is quite limited. Schools play a paradoxical role: strong in principle, popular belief, and policy but weak in practice. Access to schools was seen as the key to opportunity, and the United States created access earlier than most nations. Yet schools were modestly and unequally supported, so there was less to access than met the eye. Schools' capability to equalize opportunity was incommensurate with policy and popular belief.

These features of the environment bear directly on Title I. The program aims to improve poor children's schools, but it is a very modest supplement: more than 90 percent of school funds are provided by state and local sources. Schools are provided unequally, so the modest federal supplement rests on educational programs that are significantly weaker in less advantaged schools and districts, where most Title I students are. Title I builds on a significantly stronger educational resource base in higher-spending districts than in lower-spending districts.[61] Title I's operation is compromised by the problem it aims to solve.

There are many ways to manage the dilemma that we have been discussing, and our analysis of Title I in the chapters that follow discusses some of them. After several very difficult early years in which the program faced serious threats, revisions and other changes created a rough parity among the configuration of the program's aims, the instruments that it deployed, and practitioners' capability. But ideas about the problems began to change in the 1980s, and Title I's aims became more ambitious. That change took firm shape in IASA and then NCLB, which set much greater aims for the program: increased achievement for all while eliminating average achievement gaps between black and white students and between affluent and disadvantaged students. These policies augmented the instruments that were to support implementation but not enough to maintain a rough parity among Title I's aims, the instruments that it deployed, and practitioners' capability. Aims far outstripped capability and instruments, and increasing conflict has marked the relations between policy and practice.

The lack of parity is at the heart of NCLB's problems; it is unlikely to become more effective educationally or sustainable politically unless its aims, instruments, and capability can be made more commensurate. The problem does not reside with the goals alone but in the configuration of goals, instruments, and capability.

That does not mean that all political conflict is avoidable if nice symmetries can be achieved. One virtue of the dilemma that we discuss is that it highlights the presence of incentives for both conflict and cooperation. The recent policies recognize that state and local school systems served poor children badly, and from that angle it made sense for state standards-based policies, and NCLB, to use tough instruments to mobilize educators' will to improve, to identify weak professionals, and to spur performance. Yet if educators are to improve weak schools, it also makes sense for policy to offer them the assistance, encouragement, and trust that they need to do the job. Advocates of the first view tend to see advocates of the second as apologists for those who failed poor children and would defeat policies like NCLB by allowing weak performance. Advocates of the second view tend to see partisans of the first as inflexible enforcers who are likely to defeat school improvement by driving practitioners into mechanistic compliance. The difference is built into the dilemma that frames relations between policy and practice, and it was expressed in conflict, during legislative drafting, over how tough or helpful NCLB should be. It has been expressed during implementation in conflict over how aggressive or helpful governments should be. It is expressed in continuing debate and conflict on these points among those interested in and engaged with implementation. And it is expressed in current debates concerning the reauthorization of Title I.

Such conflict is difficult to avoid because each view has a portion of truth. The people and organizations that have been the problem often are complicit in social damage and, from that perspective, cannot be trusted to do the right thing; it makes sense to treat them with some skepticism and to call them to account. Yet they also are the chief available agents of improvement, so it also makes sense to give them the help and trust that could enable them to improve. In principle, policymakers and practitioners could devise ways to do both, for, short of creating entirely new systems of service provision, policies would be more likely to improve practice if they blended pressure to change with support for change.[62] But in practice, that is very difficult to accomplish, in part because the political groups that shape policy often deeply divide on this matter, and the divisions are very difficult to overcome. That certainly has been the case with NCLB.

CHAPTER 3

Recovering from Practice Failure

The travails of Title I began soon after it became law, with evidence that it had failed in practice. This threatened the program's guiding ideas, its legitimacy, and perhaps even its existence. Title I's design might have been seen as surefire protection against such threats, for it sent money to virtually all House districts[1] and to more than 90 percent of school districts, left most important decisions about the use of the money to localities, and severely limited federal influence. Yet it also set a federal priority on better education for poor children and put money behind this priority. Given the dilemma of relying on those with the problem to solve it, such an ambitious but vague aim could be trouble, for it was married to policy instruments, educational practice, and an environment that had little capability to improve schools.

Yet nearly all advocates and many observers expected Title I to work. They believed that adding resources would help remedy racial and class inequities in buildings, books, and other palpable resources. More money would flow, as the prosperous Great Society rolled on. Research had linked schooling to economic success by the mid-1960s, and Lyndon Johnson, Health, Education, and Welfare Secretary Anthony Celebrezze, and Education Commissioner Francis Keppel all made that point.[2] Johnson said, "poverty has many roots, but the taproot is ignorance: Poverty is the lot of two-thirds of the families in which the family head has had 9 years or less of schooling. Twenty percent of the youth aged 19 to 24 with an eighth grade education or less are unemployed—four times the national average. . . . The burden on the Nation's schools is not evenly distributed. Low-income families are heavily concentrated in particular urban neighborhoods or rural areas. Faced with the largest educational needs, many of these school districts have inadequate financial resources."[3]

A growing war in Vietnam consumed both the expected budget surpluses and much of the president's extraordinary influence. Title I was left to fend for itself, with its vague ambition, its original appropriation, and little capability in practice, government, or the environment. As the Great Society began to peter out, an NAACP Legal Defense and Education Fund (LDF) study claimed that Title I funds were being misspent: some localities used the money to buy band uniforms and other such things, not better education. To make things worse, the federal government had not monitored practice and rooted out abuse. On the heels of that report, a study commissioned by the Department of Health, Education, and Welfare (HEW) reported on Title I's effect on students' test scores.[4] The 1965 ESEA did not mention such scores, but the HEW study made explicit the assumption that more money, and the better education it bought, would boost achievement. It found no such link.

If the Great Society had rolled on with huge congressional majorities, large budgets, and popular support, these reports of practice failure might have been less trouble. But with the collapse of the Johnson administration, intense political conflict in the late 1960s, and growing Republican hostility to Great Society programs, the two reports were a real threat. One seemed to show that the key ideas about the program's effects had been mistaken—more money did not yield improved learning—and the other seemed to reveal state and local failures to properly use the funds and a federal failure to manage the program. The reports raised deep doubts about the program and made it vulnerable politically at a time when liberal ideas were in retreat. Title I's future as a politically successful initiative could depend on repairs of the practice failures; without the repair, practice failures could infect the policy and change the politics.

Management Failure and Program Design

The LDF report questioned Title I's integrity and effectiveness.[5] Ruby Martin and Phyllis McClure charged that some schools had grossly misused funds and that others offered weak programs.[6] They implied that federal authorities left schools to their own devices. Some Title I supporters saw federal funds as general aid, but Martin and McClure saw it as an antipoverty program and tried to push it further in that direction. They described local schools that treated Title I as general aid—that is, using it to pay salaries for staff who provided no Title I services and to buy intercoms, swimming pools, and band instruments for entire schools.[7] Title I supplanted existing programs rather than supplementing them, as local managers used the funds to pay bills that previously had been paid locally.[8] Martin and McClure portrayed a program that worked badly, even ineptly.

They also implied that Title I offered weak inducements for localities to properly target program funds and expressed doubt that a poorly targeted program could be effective. Because eligibility was defined so broadly, program benefits were spread thin.[9] That helped to create a large constituency among educators and in Congress, but many low-achieving children got weak services or none at all.[10] As it spent money in nearly all districts, Title I even followed small pockets of poverty into relatively affluent schools and districts.[11] That cut against efforts to target the money on schools that, from a national perspective, had the most serious problems. The formula grant that won Title I many friends in public education and Congress also weakened its influence in the most needy schools and districts. Early estimates of Title I's average expenditure varied from nearly $120 per student per year down to about $95.[12] With average national per pupil expenditures around $700 at the time, this was no revolution.[13] Large as the program seemed in Washington, compared with other federal education initiatives, it was modest when divided among thousands of districts and tens of thousands of schools.

The targeting problem that Ruby Martin and Phyllis McClure highlighted was not chiefly due to local malfeasance; rather, the problem was built into Title I. Indeed, the broad and thin allocation of funds was the key to the program's political success. The requirements of the program's political viability were at odds with the requirements of its educational viability.

The point is so fundamental to our story that we will make a brief foray into Title I's origins to explain it. When Lyndon Johnson became president, in the wake of John F. Kennedy's murder, he renewed the War on Poverty, mobilized support for federal aid to schools, and used his extraordinary political skills to gain legislation for which the civil rights movement had pressed. Title VI of the 1964 Civil Rights Act banned discrimination in the use of federal funds, which was a key to federal school aid, for it meant that federal money would not be used to support Jim Crow schools. This broke the civil rights barrier to federal aid.

Pressure from the civil rights movement stirred some in Congress to think that they should improve conditions for disadvantaged Americans, but other barriers to federal aid remained. Catholics had no reason to support aid to public schools; conservatives opposed a federal role; civil libertarians and many Protestants opposed aid to religious schools; and there was no educationally feasible design.[14] Francis Keppel, the commissioner of education, worked with Congressman Carl Perkins, Senator Wayne Morse, and others to solve these problems. They devised a categorical program that delivered federal aid to states and localities in a formula grant that was tied to the incidence of poverty. They aimed to bind many interests to shares of aid and to frame the aim as better schools for poor children. NAACP leaders denied that such legislation was a plausible response to their concerns, but Johnson, Keppel, and congressional leaders promoted the bill as a response to pressure for social justice. It offered federal aid to schools whose students most needed help but, to gain support, spread aid over most school districts and House districts. The bill's authors aimed to join the presumed interests of the poor to those of professionals, politicians, and liberals.

Keppel and his allies also used the "child benefit theory" to include religious schools, an idea that was based in part on a 1947 Supreme Court decision, *Everson v. Board of Education,* in which the Court had held that public financial aid to religious schools was legal if it supported educational and not religious activities.[15] Keppel designed the bill so that federal monies would benefit education for parochial school students but would not aid their schools because it would be spent only on improved education for specific eligible students; hence, it would not violate the establishment clause of the First Amendment.[16] That helped to satisfy private schools while appeasing those who worried about the separation of church and state or who were hostile to Catholics. The draft bill left it unclear whether just parochial schools or all schools had to focus aid on particular children, and that ambiguity helped to make a winning political coalition, for it allowed public educators and others who favored general aid to see new resources with few strings attached, at the same time that Catholic educators could see their schools benefit from a historic compromise. Keppel's draft married the conflicting interests and ideas that had prevented federal school aid.[17]

Despite the formula's basis in poverty counts, the result was hardly a pure antipoverty program. Those who wanted federal aid did not select schools because of compelling scientific evidence that it was the best way to fight poverty. When policy was made in 1964 and 1965, only a school program was on the table; no one asked how it compared with direct income transfers, jobs, housing, or other options. Commissioner Keppel's task was not how best to solve the poverty problem but how to get federal aid to schools. John F. (Jack) Jennings, a congressional aide who worked on Title I for decades, said that "The War on Poverty was the ascendant discussion at the time, and so the theory was that you could gear aid to poverty as a way to get something enacted. . . . [I]n political terms . . . this is the way to break the log jam over enacting federal aid."[18]

Title I resembled Medicare in several respects. Medicare extended coverage to a group that was seen as needy—the elderly—but it entailed no fundamental change in professional practice nor any distrust of professionals. It extended conventional practice to new clients and helped to create a broad constituency by linking hitherto disparate interests: elderly Americans and the health care industry and professions. It required no fundamental change in the practice or organization of health care, so professionals could relatively easily accept it. They could bring conventional services to new clients, their dominion would grow, and Americans' health would improve.[19] Apart from administrative arrangements, no new medical infrastructure would be needed.

Title I similarly linked the interests of the poor and nonpoor. It did more than extend existing benefits to unserved clients, for most children already were in elementary school. Instead, it helped schools to add services for children, but the services would be only a larger or better dose of what students already had. Given profound differences in the allocation of educational resources, providing more resources to children who attended poor schools helped address the visible problem of resource inequity. Moreover, it did not require major changes in practice or organization: poor students would get better education by way of expanded conventional services.[20] Teachers would do the same sort of work; only they would do it more, or better, with certain students. There would be no revolution in practice, and educators would make nearly all of the key educational decisions. Here, too, it meant that no new infrastructure would be needed.

Though that formula was politically winning, it was why Robert F. Kennedy and Kenneth B. Clark, the distinguished psychologist, doubted that Title I would work educationally. They saw educators as the problem, because they could not or would not respond to the educational needs of children who were poor, or black, or both. Title I's architects did not see it that way; inadequate school funds and poor children's educational disadvantages were the problem. This perception fit nicely with what most Americans believed about how schools worked. It was politically useful, for, contrary to Kennedy and Clark's view, it allowed supporters of federal aid to believe that the very schools that had failed poor children would help them to succeed.

The appeal of Johnson's health care and education initiatives owed a good deal to their combination of radical and conservative features. Commissioner Keppel's bill brought the federal government into schools in an unprecedented way, for, like Medicare and Medicaid, it set new priorities for professionals. That was radically new in a nation whose schools were locally controlled and whose politicians sometimes equated federal influence with Communism.[21] But that was combined with the conservatism of the formula grant, which many took to be federal aid without federal control and encouraged some local administrators to misuse the money. The legislation embodied both federal influence and the primacy of state and local government, which enabled conservatives to support Title I while opposing federal intrusion.[22]

The bill also accepted professionals and practice as they were. Like LBJ's health care initiatives, Title I fought poverty: its categorical focus on poor children appealed to liberals and advocates for the poor, yet it did so by offering direct assistance to educators, not poor children's families. If educators would help the poor, that added significant political support, and if they could not improve schools, who could? There was no effort to build the sort of educational infrastructure that we discussed in Chapter 1—curricula, teacher education, or examinations—that could help, nor would that have been likely; those things were the prerogative of each local district. It was wise to rely on institutions that many Americans trusted instead of trying less familiar things like income transfers, but these were the same institutions that had failed so many black and poor students and that had little capability to improve. Title I linked interests that other schemes could have driven apart. Congress could act nationally without rocking boats locally. It could make a big difference for schools and poor families, yet not weaken professionals. Liberals gained federal aid while conservatives saved local control. Title I managed the tension between central power and state and local influence by embedding it in the program.[23] As a political matter, everybody seemed to win.

Managing Title I

But that success created a situation in which the executive branch lacked the capability to manage its own program and in which schools and state and local governments were in the same boat. U.S. political institutions were designed in ways that reduced the chance that national programs like Title I could work coherently across states and localities. ESEA's mere existence was remarkable, but to exist is not to be effective. The U.S. Office of Education (USOE) was poorly equipped to manage Title I, lacking administrative means to distribute funds, let alone offer guidance. With little capability of its own, the USOE initially distributed journal articles, to explain "the details of the legislation and how it worked" as "information guides" for state education authorities (SEAs) and local education authorities (LEAs).[24] A government that had no guide of its own was no match for those it was to regulate. John Hughes, then a USOE official, wrote that the National Education Association (NEA) and "hardware agents" sent schools proposals to use Title I for "increased teachers' salaries, improved facilities, and new hardware."[25] USOE staff did solicit comments from professional associations and state and local officials and visit districts. Yet compared with established organizations, they had little capability to gain attention for their priorities.[26] That weakness was compounded by weak state school agencies, whose staffers saw themselves as educators who should consult with colleagues, not oversee them or enforce laws.[27]

Even the USOE staff were at odds about the federal role: some older staffers viewed Title I as general aid and opposed ambitious change, while some newer employees argued for a stronger federal role to improve poor students' education. When reformers in the USOE tried to set bold guidelines and regulations to support the program's antipoverty aims, they met stiff resistance not only from local schools but also from colleagues. The resisters cut provisions to concentrate funds on a "limited number" of Title I children.[28] USOE traditionalists had several such successes;[29] even limiting the number of draft copies of guidelines sent to states and localities.[30]

Under White House pressure to put the program in place quickly, the USOE sent checks. That was no small thing, for roughly a billion dollars had to be sent to about twenty-five thousand school districts in fifty-four states and territories in fifteen months.[31] Early work focused on such tasks and on approving state proposals that promised to obey the law.[32] Staff grew, were reorganized, and got stronger for a few years.[33] The mid-1960s economic boom helped, as did support for antipoverty programs and remarkable leadership by Frank Keppel and Harold Howe. As things improved, the USOE even explored how program design and content might influence children's education.[34] Still, Title I had a weak start, and the USOE gained the capability only to get the money out and to offer general advice. That was far from what would be needed to change schools. Keppel and Howe were extraordinary, but their achievements were much more impressive when looking back at a history of weakness than when looking forward to better teaching and learning. In its early operation, Title I acted more like general aid than a school improvement program.

The LDF report was less an effort to correct local failures than to redirect Title I away from general aid toward aid that focused more specifically on educational services for poor children. Local misspending was useful for that endeavor. The report presented no evidence on the incidence of the problems it reported, and as far as we can find, no one asked whether misspent funds were a tiny problem or the tip of an iceberg.[35] Yet the report was influential. The government presented no evidence on the matter. Ruby Martin was a respected former federal official, and Phyllis McClure had worked with the bipartisan U.S. Commission on Civil Rights. The report was brief and well composed, had vivid examples, and was sponsored by an organization that had battled segregation. The LDF had no mass membership, but it was tied to the NAACP, and in 1969 everyone knew how many Americans that organization could mobilize.

The report presented a paradox: it pressed Title I to improve education for poor children, yet it argued that government had mismanaged Title I.[36] Federal oversight and administration were woefully inadequate; the USOE was "reluctant and timid in its administration of Title I and abdicate[d] to the States its responsibility for enforcing the law"; and states, localities, and schools were portrayed as self-seeking and noncompliant.[37] Yet if things were that bad, how could the USOE, states, districts, and schools solve their problems?

The Response to Practice Failure

Practice failure is rarely dealt with purely as a technical or professional matter, for policy typically mixes the professional and technical with the political. The response to the reports of practice failure certainly was at least as much political as technical and professional, because the reports of practice failure threatened the success and legitimacy of the policy that Title I represented. There were, however, two very different political elements. One arose in the tension between guns and butter that had been created by Lyndon Johnson's foreign and domestic policies. When it became clear that Johnson could not have both, and that the 1965 ESEA was not the down payment on a vast federal investment in education, that meant that Title I's political success would continue to be educationally risky, for spreading money widely also meant continuing to spread it thinly: the more the program succeeded politically, the more it risked failing educationally by missing needy children, or by spreading resources too thin to make a difference, or by failing to help schools connect new money to better instruction. Rep. Carl Perkins, then chairman of the House Education and Labor Committee, probably had that in mind when he said, in 1973, "the greatest obstacle to obtaining better results and better achievement has been the inadequacy of funding."[38]

Yet there was little hope to solve that problem in the late 1960s, for Title I was in a radically new political situation: Richard Nixon was president, and he was cool to Great Society programs.[39] This was the second political aspect of the program's problem. Both in his campaign and in the White House, Nixon urged a domestic agenda that would move federal school aid from categorical to block grants and would support states' rights.[40] He proposed special revenue sharing in 1971, to give states and localities more flexibility to spend the money. In 1973, he proposed to consolidate funds from Title I and other ESEA titles and to give these funds to states with few strings attached.[41] This move would delegate decisions about Title I to states; some Title I supporters thought that the reports of practice failure provided a rationale for Nixon's proposals.[42]

In fact, Nixon's proposals had different sources: animosity to Johnson and his policies and different ideas about government and its proper role. If liberals worried that, absent specific mandates and enforcement, states and localities would neglect poor students' educational needs, conservatives worried that government intervention would supplant local control, discretion, and liberty. Nixon's proposal drew on research to justify less targeted aid but did not turn on research.

Moreover, the decisive influence on the proposals' fate was neither research nor political principle; practical matters trumped all else. State and local officials might prefer less federal authority, but if that meant less money or different allocations, few would agree to the change. It was just such fears that reduced support for Nixon's proposals. If many members of Congress aim for local control, they also aim to do well by their constituents and to get reelected. Less federal authority might advance the first objective, but less federal money would not advance the second.[43] Title I supporters compared the revenue-sharing proposals with the original formula and told members of Congress how much money they would lose if Nixon's program passed.[44]

It did not. But the proposals' failure did not cool worries about Title I. This was not the sort of program that President Nixon would have created, but if it could not be changed to suit his political ideas, it would have to be managed better. There were two efforts to do so in the years between Richard Nixon's and Ronald Reagan's first inaugurations. One was to improve program administration, to repair the practice failures that Martin and McClure had brought to light. Another was to revise management to create better information about Title I's operation and effects. These efforts had important positive consequences for Title I, but they did not dampen concern about reported failures in classroom practice. Hence, two studies of Title I's effect on learning also were undertaken to determine whether classroom practice had, in fact, failed, and the government sought to make the program more effective educationally. We discuss the managerial reforms here and the educational problems in Chapter 4.

Improving Management Practice

One way to repair the practice failures was to ensure that Title I funds were spent on the education that the legislation envisioned, and another was to create clear state and local accountability for the use of federal funds. If these steps to correct failures of managerial practice worked, they could help to save a threatened program.

Program Focus

One element in the revision was to target Title I funding more specifically on services for the most needy children. That was appealing politically, for it did not disturb grant allocations to districts and would maintain broad political support. It was appealing administratively because it made program beneficiaries clearer and promised better management. It also made sense educationally because many believed that improving poor children's access to the sorts of tangible resources—updated books, well-credentialed teachers—that more advantaged children enjoyed would improve poor children's education. Cynthia G. Brown, a long-time civil rights advocate, said that "we had this horrible problem of minority access to quality education. . . . We couldn't see the fundamental problems of quality and the difficulties of poverty when we had this surface issue of racial discrimination. And so we . . . thought that student achievement was poorer because of racial discrimination."[45]

Brown and others saw school resources as what educators had long used to make schools better; that parents and citizens used to judge schools' quality, for which they paid taxes; and that Southern schools had kept from African American students.[46] "There were so many difficult access issues, and so many difficulties about Title I not reaching the kids it was intended for you couldn't start looking at achievement results of the program if the money wasn't reaching the kids, and good programs weren't being established."[47] More teachers, books, and money made good sense in school systems that lacked more developed means to create and judge educational quality.[48]

Better targeting also appealed to state and local officials who were being pressed to spread federal funds around their districts. They wanted to maintain Title I's categorical focus and clear targeting to shield themselves from such pressure. Richard Gousha, vice president of the Council of Great City Schools, testified in the 1973 congressional hearings about revenue sharing: "There are tremendous pressures in every major city, in our city . . . there would be pressure to divert funds from the most disadvantaged. . . . It would come from citizenry, and I think it would come from some of the professional organizations. I think the categorical nature and the reasonably rigid guidelines make certain that the program is delivered to the kids who are most disadvantaged in our city. . . . I don't want to see too much flexibility in delivery of that program."[49]

Others disagreed. Many school administrators would have wanted to decide targeting themselves, and members of Congress who saw the program as general aid preferred minimal federal requirements. Once the program began and funds flowed, however, recipients and their representatives found Title I useful. With the program under attack, a Title I that was somewhat more targeted to disadvantaged students seemed much better than no Title I. The resulting compromise was a more focused program that was more plainly aimed at educational improvement but that still had a broad political base.[50] Districts got the funds that made the program a political winner, but services were more focused on needy children within them.

Finance, Administration, and Politics

Better administration and fiscal integrity were crucial companions to targeting, for they could help to deliver resources where they were needed and ensure that money was spent appropriately. Despite his distaste for the Great Society, when Nixon took power his administration became responsible for the government, and more reports like Martin and McClure's would be trouble. But if administration officials wanted to improve Title I's management, they could not simply tell state and local officials what to do.[51] HEW had to induce the very state and local agencies that were the problem to improve their performance. The solution was a small set of new instruments— administrative and fiscal standards—that more clearly specified the terms on which schools could use Title I funds. The standards were a structure around which the program could be organized and fiscal integrity improved.

Though these instruments made important changes in the program, they did not touch a political third rail by revising the distribution of funds among districts. They created specific definitions of proper fund use, provided criteria for administration, and thus set a foundation for stable and predictable operation, without upsetting the alliances that had coalesced around the program. They also were instruments that the federal government, states, and most LEAs could use without a revolution in capability.

Relying on those with the problem to solve it thus meant persuading state and local officials to use the new standards and managerial practices that would ensure Title I's good name. One approach was to "supplement not supplant" local funds—to guarantee that Title I added services to total local outlays and not to spend money replaced by Title I in other schools. Regulations had required this before the Martin-McClure report, but the report found apparent violations. The federal government moved the requirement from regulation to law, when the 1969 amendments more clearly specified what compliance entailed and encouraged strict enforcement.[52] Practitioners had a clearer view of what the program required them to do and stronger incentives to do it.

Comparability, a second instrument, sought to ensure that Title I built on roughly the same base in all schools within a district.[53] If it was to offer truly "supplementary" assistance, Title I schools had to have no fewer local funds than those available to more affluent schools in the same district; otherwise, Title I students could not catch up. There were two reasons for concern. One was typically great revenue inequality among districts within states, which meant that poor children in poorer districts attended schools with fewer educational resources than poor children in more affluent districts. Comparability could not solve that problem without remedying intrastate fiscal inequality, which was seen as politically and fiscally impossible. The other reason for concern was fiscal inequality among schools within districts. Districts typically spent less state and local money in schools that enrolled many students from poor families, in part because teachers in these schools were less experienced and thus less expensive. Districts often also spent less on books and supplies in such schools, because they were in neighborhoods in which discrimination was a well-established habit or because parents were less likely to press for quality. In these schools, Title I funds could be used to fill in for what districts did not spend.

Advocates for Title I knew of this problem before the 1970s, but state and federal auditors had not had measurable criteria to decide whether districts were allocating non-Title I funds comparably.[54] Advocates for the poor pressed for specific and strict comparability standards, but some state and city school officials claimed that such standards would interfere with teachers' contracts or require teacher transfers; those contracts and "transfer rights" were exactly the source of many inequalities among schools within districts.[55] After some negotiation, the USOE devised criteria that required localities to allocate their own funds in similar fashion throughout a district and not to use Title I to make up for local fiscal inequality.[56]

Maintenance of effort was a third instrument; it required LEAs to sustain state and local school expenditures from one year to the next. Some advocates worried that without this requirement, districts would pare back their yearly commitments to education and use Title I funds to compensate for the difference. This standard required schools to sustain rather than reduce aid to programs for the poor and to schools receiving Title I assistance. Districts that failed to maintain yearly fiscal commitments would be penalized by reduction or elimination of their Title I grants.

The new instruments had promise. They could set clearer aims for the allocation of Title I funds and thus set standards for more effective managerial practice. Better management could provide disadvantaged children with supplemental assistance and ensure fiscal accountability. These things could improve confidence in the program. The new instruments' appeal was enhanced because they did not upset any important political interests: they implied no broad new federal authority, and they ignored such politically difficult problems as fiscal inequality among districts or states.[57]

Changing Practice

But these promising features would amount to little if federal officials could not persuade their state and local counterparts to put the standards into practice. It was an achievement to develop and specify them and to mobilize political support, but it was quite a different matter to put these changes into practice. Without incentives to use the new instruments, the knowledge and skill to implement them and to oversee and support implementation, the entire effort might come to naught.

Incentives

Audits and program reviews created incentives for states and localities to use the new instruments. Federal audits were an established way to determine whether funds were used appropriately, and audit exceptions were a well-understood way to identify inappropriate spending. The HEW Audit Agency investigated state and local Title I administration, using well-established tests and indicators. If there were problems, the reports recommended changed administrative practice or repayment if money had been spent inappropriately. HEW had the capability to do audits. It pushed local practice far enough beyond extant habits to encourage compliance but not so far as to require a revolution. The incentives for compliance matched the program's importance to states and localities: there was a rough symmetry between instruments and capability.

Yet collecting on repayment, if that was in order, was not the HEW Audit Agency's job; that task fell to the USOE. There was no judicial precedent for collection, especially if federal requirements were ambiguous.[58] Education officials had often settled previous audit exceptions informally, requiring only a promise that questionable expenditures would stop, with no penalty.[59] Hence, collection on Title I audit exceptions began poorly. Some states asked federal officials about audit exceptions they had received but got no response until years later, when federal officials tried to collect.[60] Federal officials developed procedures to act more systematically on reports of misuse and to collect misspent funds.[61] It took only a few well-publicized exceptions and requests for repayment to set a new tone for federal-state relations.

Program reviews also encouraged compliance.[62] They had begun in the late 1960s and expanded with efforts to revise the program. Teams from the USOE's Division of Education for the Disadvantaged visited states and localities, examined fiscal practices, investigated use of Title I funds, and made suggestions about compliance.[63] The teams sent reports to the chief state school officer, who was expected to submit a plan of action to the USOE if changes were in order. If the changes were serious and the state refused, a hearing was held. If states and districts failed to cooperate, or if there were egregious transgressions, the USOE could withhold funds after an appeals process. As state and local budget constraints grew in the 1970s, Title I funds seemed more attractive, and the incentive to comply was more persuasive.

Practice

Incentives helped, but practice had to change. State and local officials could not comply unless they knew how or could quickly learn. Improved management would require more administrative skill, new record keeping, and know-how. State and federal officials also would have to oversee local management and program operation; yet they were not well situated to teach these things. The USOE had little managerial depth; the staff additions of the mid-1960s made only a modest beginning on improved management, and there were pitifully insufficient staff to help fifty states and thousands of school districts. States were similarly limited. The American tradition of weak government, and the historic devolution of most decisions to localities, impeded better management.

The USOE tried to increase know-how by building Title I staff, but that was a continuing struggle. The program staff grew quickly when Title I first began but then shrank by nearly two-thirds; by early 1970, only three "desk officers" monitored Title I for the nation.[64] Pressure associated with the Martin-McClure report prompted a staff increase to fifty by the end of 1970. Staff replacement and reorganization also bolstered Title I's capability in Washington, as the USOE drew more professional administrators and policy specialists into its ranks and sent inherited staff to less influential divisions.[65] Capability grew greatly over 1964, but given the work that the new standards posed, the gain was modest. Title I had only fifteen desk officers for the entire nation in 1972.

Practice did change. One reason was that ESEA's Title V underwrote improved SEA capability. USOE funds for state management were written into this title of the bill, and Washington managers saw that they needed state allies who supported Title I. USOE official John Hughes and others encouraged the creation of state Title I offices that hired administrators with strong ties to their federal counterparts.

State education governments also grew, and that growth in capability helped the USOE to create a national administrative infrastructure. That, in turn, helped Title I managers to work around opponents of federal regulation, like the chief state school officers. Title I managers also improved guidance to help states and localities learn how to meet federal standards.[66]

Greater state capability helped, and the new instruments did not require vastly more know-how, which also helped. Audits and oversight helped USOE managers to learn from Audit Agency staff, who had the know-how. It also helped that compliance focused on conventional educational resources, for managers could more easily track dollars than more elusive instructional resources. Following the money was a less ambiguous basis for monitoring, since the clearer the evidence, the easier to discern compliance.

Finally, the new instruments worked because they required narrow intervention in schools and fit with the incentives Title I offered. Federal officials had funds that states and localities wanted, but they were a small part of state or local funds. It was crucial that incentives and benefits be commensurate with Title I aid: if states and localities could meet requirements, they could use federal monies and Washington could have some influence on state and local behavior. State and local capability to implement the requirements was an incentive to comply. If federal officials had insisted that states and localities do more, like overhaul instruction, federal leverage likely would have been insufficient, in part because the incentives that they offered would have been incommensurate with the task, since the capability for such change was very limited.[67]

If the management changes were feasible, they were not simple. Details of the revised instruments were unsettled, even in the late 1970s. There were disagreements over how to measure, track, and enforce compliance. Auditors and program reviewers sometimes contradicted each other, USOE divisions disagreed on appropriate indicators of compliance, and compliance was far from uniform.[68] Even relatively straightforward tracking of funds was complex. Some states and localities could circumvent or creatively interpret the new requirements, and mixed signals and associated flexibility offered some localities an opportunity to avoid the new standards.[69] Still, worries about fiscal abuse and bad management began to dissipate in the mid-1970s.[70] Arguments about compliance now occurred within a new framework of legitimate and effective administration and posed no serious threat to Title I.

As she looked back much later, Phyllis McClure, coauthor of the NAACP report that helped to trigger these changes, said, "we got a lot of that [fund misuse] cleaned up [in the 1970s] and then in the 80s, the audit process really started to work. . . . [T]he fact that the federal government was actually requiring states to refund money made the program really hunker down, made the central office really lock onto what the schools were doing with the money, made the states much more conscious. So there was much more top-down control over the program because the authorities didn't want to have to get socked with these audit exceptions."[71]

The new instruments helped to focus Title I and to ensure that money got to the right places for the right purpose. Title I had been nudged a bit more toward being an antipoverty program for schools, and it had clearer goals: to deliver money to eligible schools and students and to ensure that the money was spent on the activities that the legislation envisioned. Instruments that enhanced these aims were devised and enforced, and a management infrastructure that bridged national, state, and local governments grew up. Local behavior changed, roughly in line with federal priorities, and fiscal abuse appeared to diminish. Federal policy was somewhat revised in practice. These things helped to achieve fiscal integrity, to set limits on local use of federal funds, and to deter attacks on the program. The practice failures in management and finance had been repaired, and by the late 1970s there was a sense that Title I "worked," as a way both to define and deliver funds and to mobilize political support for the program.

These renovations changed the politics of education. They modestly expanded federal influence, as federal oversight and fiscal controls came to states and localities. They also more firmly set the political agenda to include attention to the problems of poor students, and they encouraged and supported the growth of state and local government units that managed Title I and supported its aims. But if these changes were important, they were no revolution: federal influence grew while retaining local discretion, for the new instruments concerned only a narrow range of local behavior and only Title I funds.[72] Schools could solve the problems that policymakers set because they had been set in ways that fit extant capabilities and political arrangements. Federal influence grew with only a slight diminution of local control.

More important, Title I helped to build a new set of interests in and around public education and to encourage the growth of educational values that had been much less evident in 1964. The federal program, its priorities, and its funds for constituents, schools, and poor children helped to create and sustain new networks of political, professional, and financial interests, all tied to improved schools for disadvantaged children.[73] That helped to advance a significant social purpose, to temper some deep ideological differences, and to bridge chasms in the U.S. political system.

One key element in all of this was that management practice changed, and one reason it did was that the new aims, instruments, and capability were roughly commensurate. The new aims did not create profound incompetence: some managers knew how to navigate the new requirements, and others learned without heroic effort. Workers in relatively weak agencies could learn to manage fiscal transfers among governments, and there were palpable incentives to learn; states and localities did not want to lose money, and federal officials wanted no more scandals. Practice improved at all levels of government, and confidence in Title I grew. Only a decade after it was in such deep trouble, changed practice made the program a political and administrative success. Whether it worked educationally, however, was another matter.

CHAPTER 4

Could Federal Policy Change
Classroom Practice?

Despite better management, Title I's other practice failure—reports of no improvement in student achievement—remained. The G. E. TEMPO report had raised deep questions about the program, but the report's effects were amplified by other major studies, which found that school-to-school differences in educational resources had little or no effect on school-to-school differences in average student achievement. Worse yet, the resources in question were the very things that Title I supported: money, along with the teachers, books, and other familiar things that the money bought. If researchers said that these resources had no effects, why should politicians believe that they would work—that they would be strong and salient for practice—when Title I delivered them to schools? The research also was troubling because it revealed a large gap between the average achievement of poor and minority group children and that of their advantaged peers, and it showed that the gap grew over the grades. That large and growing inequality was taken to mean that schools were not what Horace Mann had termed "the balance wheel of the social machinery." Title I was expected to help restore that balance; yet the research claimed that public schools carried on and perhaps compounded inequalities that society inflicted on children.

The program was between the devil and the deep blue sea. It had scored an important success by creating more commensurate relationships among its aims, instruments, and capabilities in program management and finance, but Title I aimed to improve education, not local financial management, and students' education had been found to be weak. Washington could hardly ignore that, but the schools lacked much educational infrastructure, and the program lacked the instruments that could most directly influence teaching and learning. The situation vividly presented the dilemma: only local schools and school systems could solve the problem that Title I had defined and set for them in 1965, but as long as they failed to solve it, the failure could spread to Washington and threaten both the program and its political sponsors.

The 1970s saw several efforts to deal with this problem by trying to add policy instruments to Title I that might influence practice. One was government acceptance of attempts to improve education in Title I schools by focusing services on eligible children through "pullout" programs. Another was federal sponsorship of research to discern whether Title I had in fact failed to improve learning. A third was an effort to improve Title I by improving state and local Title I evaluations, to generate more comparable and valid evidence on its operation and effects. The studies brought some good news about the program's effect on student learning, but also some dismaying news about the strength and salience of Title I's instruments and capabilities in operation.

The Politics of Bad News

The first bad news about Title I's lack of effect on classroom practice had come from federally funded research that was intended to help Title I to improve. Soon after ESEA became law, HEW Assistant Secretary for Planning and Evaluation William Gorham and Deputy Assistant Secretary Alice Rivlin launched a study of Title I projects to discern differences in program design and quality, to relate them to students' performance, and thus to improve the program with evidence of what worked best. But the study, done by G. E. TEMPO, turned up no evidence of more effective programs. That news became public along with a small eruption of disappointing studies of Head Start and other Great Society programs. Instead of providing helpful advice about program improvement, the evaluations provoked fundamental questions about whether Title I could significantly improve poor children's education.[1]

It was difficult to conduct the study: such research was unfamiliar, school managers were not eager to report data to federal evaluators, and much of the data that researchers sought did not exist. Traditions of state and local control made educators wary of the federal study, but even when evaluators got access, the data often were quite poor. Schools did not collect evidence on teaching, curricula, and special programs; few collected more than routine data for reports on attendance, spending, and the like. Researchers had not studied school effectiveness, and few systems had tried to improve schools' performance, especially schools that served many poor children. Title I was politically possible because it accepted a limited federal role and deferred to state and local authority, but the weakness of those authorities included technical incapacity that impeded efforts to learn about the program.[2]

Even when evaluators got the data, analysis was difficult. Most school systems used Title I as a funding stream with few restrictions, and local projects varied dramatically. Some focused on remedial math and English, others on health or nutritional needs, others on field trips. Some were not primarily instructional. Those differences made defensible comparisons of projects difficult, especially when taken with demographic differences among localities. The political design of Title I that insulated localities from much federal influence coupled with weak knowledge about how to improve education and the lack of any coherent approaches to improvement, created a formidable barrier to collecting evidence that might help the program to correct problems.

Still, G. E. TEMPO weighed local projects' aggregate achievement against each other, assuming comparability despite variation in aims, methods, and student populations. Title I students did no better than students without Title I. No program type seemed more effective than any other—it was, in fact, difficult to distinguish program types.

That cast doubt on Title I's ability to become an effective antipoverty program. The study offered no support for the idea that distributing additional resources to schools and districts, to spend as they chose, would improve students' learning.

The aim of the study was sensible: to learn from experience, to discover what worked and what did not, to understand why, and to use the results to improve the program. But the quality of the work had been seriously impeded by the fragmented political structure of schooling in the United States and by the weak capability of local school systems. These things also impeded the operation of Title I. Absent an education system that could support the collection of evidence and the production of useful analysis, efforts to learn from experience to improve Title I would face serious barriers.

If such reports of Title I's noneffect had been confined to one study, it probably would have had a less dramatic impact. But the G. E. TEMPO study came on the heels of James Coleman's much larger study, which also told a dismal story about the effects of educational resources. The 1966 Equality of Educational Opportunity Survey (EEOS) usually is seen as the first major study of school effects; it was sponsored by the USOE, pursuant to an obscure subsection of Title IV of the 1964 Civil Rights Act, which required a national survey of inequality in education.[3] Alexander Mood, a statistician who then was assistant commissioner for educational statistics in the USOE, invited Coleman to lead the study. They agreed that Coleman would study not just the extent of inequality but also its consequences for student achievement.

Much to Coleman's surprise, he found that within regions of the United States, inequalities in library resources, teachers' experience and education, per pupil expenditures, and science labs and other facilities were not strongly related to students' race and class. More surprising, school-to-school differences in those same educational resources were weakly related to differences in schools' average student performance: variation in these resources had weak or no association with average student achievement. The strongest predictor of students' performance was their parents' education and social background; in comparison, the influence of educational resources was weak to nonexistent.[4]

The EEOS seemed to suggest that more investment in conventional resources might not produce more student achievement, which seemed to imply that Title I would not be effective. Coleman's findings had not come out of left field; many previous small studies had showed that the school resources that conventionally were thought to be potent actually were weakly and inconsistently related to student performance.[5] Project Talent, a huge longitudinal study of secondary schools done in the late 1950s, found similar results in a tighter research design.[6] Yet the earlier studies were not major government projects, and they were done well before a large federal program put the central government behind efforts to improve schools. They made no news.

Coleman's report did, and it was taken to mean that schools "made no difference." It meant no such thing. The EEOS asked not whether schools made a difference but whether they were differentially effective: were differences in schools' average student performance related to differences in school resources? Schools certainly made a difference; after all, students learned algebra and French and literature in school, things that few would learn without school. Many learned to read only in school. The question was whether some schools were more effective at teaching these and other things and, if so, why. Coleman reported that they were not: given that nearly everyone learned in school, school-to-school variations in how much students learned were weakly related to school-to-school variations in money, books, laboratories, and teachers' attributes.

This report was quite limited, however, for Coleman also found that more than 80 percent of the variation in students' achievement lay within, not among schools. On average, student achievement was much more similar among schools than within them, but the design of the EEOS meant that Coleman could not relate resources and achievement within schools. If the report seemed to imply that allocating more resources to schools that enrolled poor children would be unlikely to improve achievement, it could not probe the relationship within schools, where most of the variation in achievement lay.

Despite these qualifications, which few understood at the time, the EEOS seemed to have foretold the practice failure that G. E. TEMPO reported, for Title I allocated just the resources that the EEOS found were differentially ineffective. The studies implied that Title I's primary policy instrument, the formula grant, held little promise of being sufficiently strong or salient to change practice. That was especially shocking because Title I's strategy was consistent with settled ideas about how schools worked and with long experience in state and local support of schools. The 1965 bill defined the educational problem as deficiencies in poor students' experience before school, combined with deficient school resources; the formula grant would deliver resources to improve schools' capability to compensate for students' weaknesses. The very districts and schools that had failed poor children would, in this view, change and improve.

That seemed plausible in 1965. Like taxpayers who voted to support local schools, many politicians assumed that schools were relatively easy to improve because the resources that influenced children's achievement—money, books, teachers—were easy to identify and manage. Title I fit with familiar ideas about public education; after all, it had begun based on the belief that youngsters would learn readily if they had upright teachers and decent materials in suitable facilities. Horace Mann and other crusaders for common schools thought that young minds were both curious and pliable and would thrive if given even a modest opportunity.[7] These ideas were central to the Enlightenment beliefs about the plasticity of mind and the power of environments and to the low-church Protestant passion for individual Bible reading, which together helped to ignite American enthusiasm for schools as agents of personal salvation and social improvement.[8]

Precisely because Title I fit with the ideas that informed decades of state and local school aid, it was easy to believe that funds from Washington could make a difference in Peoria. HEW Secretary Anthony Celebrezze said: "Because the tax base is low, funds for education are inadequate and the schools and children suffer."[9] Title I was only the most recent of many initiatives that rested on these beliefs. The idea that more money would work for students' benefit was hardly new; it had long informed practice in Shaker Heights and Scarsdale. What was new was the effort to put federal money behind the ideas, for students from poor families.

There were dissenters. Sargent Shriver, President John Kennedy's brother-in-law, who headed the Office of Economic Opportunity, was not eager to see Head Start in the schools, partly because he and his staff thought schools would stifle it. Senator Robert F. Kennedy argued that Title I gave federal authorities little leverage and doubted that it would do much good. He contended that left to their own devices, schools would take the money but do little for those with weak influence. Many school systems were strapped for cash and faced pressure from advantaged parents: would they not more readily spend new funds on those who had more clout?[10] Kennedy rejected the idea that the schools that failed poor children would turn themselves around with the mere addition of funds; he saw external leverage as the only hope to make schools work well for the poor.

Kenneth B. Clark also had doubts. He wrote that low achievement was due to teachers' often unknowing racism, including the view that "culturally deprived" students could not get beyond the basics. Clark saw schools' weaknesses—including attitudes and practices that kept teachers from using educational resources to poor students' advantage—as the problem.[11] Resources would not work for poor children unless the schools changed. Kennedy proposed that schools be required to make public their Title I evaluations. If evidence on schools' performance was public, parents could see it and use it to press for change; knowledge could induce schools to attend to the politically weak.[12] The idea was controversial, but RFK's influence got it quietly written into the bill.[13]

Kennedy's and Clark's ideas came into their own several decades later, with efforts to hold schools accountable for students' performance. But the big news in the late 1960s and early 1970s was the report that investment in schools had few effects. The G. E. TEMPO study, the Coleman report, and Christopher Jencks's *Inequality* marked a watershed, for they undermined the long-standing belief that added resources would add results. In just a few years, research generated more worries about Title I than its authors could have imagined; it began to seem that better schools for poor children would require more than added money.[14] The formula grant appeared insufficiently strong or salient to build the capability to enable Title I to improve student learning. A funding stream began to seem to be no substitute for an educational infrastructure.

Politics amplified the trouble. As the Great Society began to come undone, Republicans read the research as a sign of possibly fatal flaws in President Lyndon Johnson's social engineering, and they pressed for more evidence on Title I's effects. Soon after he was elected, Richard Nixon accepted Daniel Patrick Moynihan's idea that America needed better research on how its schools worked more than it needed more money for schools. Nixon got bipartisan support to create a National Institute of Education (NIE) to do that research, but Democrats worried that it could further undermine liberal programs; some saw research as a threat, perhaps even an enemy of such social programs.[15]

The problem that the research opened up persisted, in part because the studies fueled doubt in Congress. In 1973 House hearings on Title I reauthorization, Rep. William A. Steiger, a Republican from Wisconsin, told a witness from the NEA: "I don't find, for example, any substantive analysis of the impact of Title I. . . . What has it done? What kinds of results have you found in terms of the effect on children of the use of elementary and secondary education money?"[16] Rep. Romano L. Mazzoli, a Democrat from Kentucky, also pressed a witness from the New York State Department of Education: "the difficulty for me . . . is determining if there is some empirical way to show just what improved education does for our children . . . how you justify to a largely jaundiced, jaded, reluctant public that these programs, this infusion of money . . . is, in fact, productive. What does it do?"[17]

These were not mere rituals of appropriation, nor was doubt confined to Congress. One advocate recalled that in "the mid 70s . . . when Title I was being reauthorized . . . we were really afraid that it was going to be lost because we didn't have any results and we really didn't know how to organize schools to get high achievement for low income kids."[18] Christopher Cross, who worked for Albert Quie, the ranking Republican on the House General Subcommittee on Education, said, "$10 billion had already been appropriated for that program. . . . Eight years had passed since the enactment of ESEA, and Congress was beginning to feel that it was now time for these programs to prove that they had accomplished at least some of what had been promised."[19]

John F. Jennings, then a Democratic staffer on the House Subcommittee on Education, told a researcher that "success came to be measured by achievement. Democrats who in 1964–65 had looked at Title I as a poverty program had to try to find achievement data with which to defend it. We were forced into wanting data."[20] Title I's educational and political problems interacted. Without appropriate instruments and capability to improve student learning, political support for the program grew more fragile.

The threat was real, for if the studies were roughly right, Title I would not be effective educationally, even if the problems that Martin and McClure had brought to light were solved. If it were ineffective, either the program would have to develop new and more potent means to improve schools or admit that it could not. The first would require imagination and stronger instruments, with more technical and professional capability than the USOE had. It also would require more political clout in order to reconfigure politics and governance arrangements among the federal government, states, and localities. The latter implied either general aid or a phase-out.

Social science had helped to create a skeptical climate of opinion about social programs in general and Title I in particular. But if research was a proximate cause of these developments, Title I itself was implicated, for it had helped to put a new question on the national agenda: what was educationally best for poor children? That question had barely been raised in national debate before 1965, but once Title I became America's answer, debate was unavoidable. If the studies mentioned here had not raised questions about the effects of Title I, others would have, because discussion of how best to educate poor children began to take on a life of its own in education, politics, and research. That was among the program's chief accomplishments, but it carried a risk: if learning did not improve, Title I would fail the very test that it had helped to create.

Improve Education with Pullouts?

That risk was especially great because federal influence on classrooms was so limited. As they tried to improve learning in Title I schools during the 1970s, federal officials were caught between pressure to make the program more effective educationally and the need to keep it viable politically. Given reports of Title I's failure to improve classroom practice and growing worries about the quality of education in Title I schools, it would be risky to do nothing; more reports of practice failure could only threaten the program more. Yet if Title I managers tried to improve instruction, the danger grew that they would venture into territory like curricula and teaching, which were off limits to the central government. The result was several federal efforts to improve instruction without intervening in instruction.

The efforts were as contorted as that sentence suggests. The story begins with the rapid spread of what came to be called "pullout" classes. Their design was simple: separate work for part of the day for students whose performance was the weakest and who were thought to most need remedial work. The classes usually offered basic skills instruction for thirty to sixty minutes, several days a week, taught by a teacher or aide at a slower pace to fewer students than in regular classes.[21]

Federal policy did not require schools to adopt pullouts. Yet, pullouts spread quickly in part because they helped to create a clear audit trail that would enable the federal management reforms to work.[22] Schools that received Title I could test students and target the lowest achievers to receive special assistance in settings that were purely for Title I. While Title I regulations did not require pullouts, they did "require that Title I children receive an identifiable program." It was easier to demonstrate compliance with pullouts than it was to provide "extra services to Title I students within regular classrooms."[23] If Title I was offered in regular classes, there would be considerable ambiguity about who was benefiting, and there could be challenges to benefits for non-Title I students.[24] Pullouts allowed federal officials to rely on extant audit structures, and local schools could rely on existing testing programs to decide students' eligibility.[25] Separate classes made it easy to show that Title I supplemented rather than supplanted regular funds, which made it easier to enforce law and regulations. As an administrative matter, there was a good fit among aims, instruments, and capability, but as an educational matter, it was less clear.

Would pullouts be an effective instrument for the improvement of education for disadvantaged students?

On the affirmative side, pullouts would not have become so popular if they had not fit with prevailing ideas about how best to educate children from poor families: in the 1950s and 1960s, researchers argued that these children were "culturally deprived"; they were said to lack the knowledge, skills, and dispositions that children from more advantaged families picked up at home and would benefit from more deliberate and didactic instruction that would help them to learn the basic skills on which more complex work could build. Pullouts also fit with practice: teachers were used to working on basic skills, many believed that disadvantaged children needed basic instruction, and pullouts did not require new practices.[26] Pullouts offered a plausible design for instruction that required little or no new pedagogical capability.[27] In addition, many teachers believed that students from poor families and African American children simply could not learn more complex material; that also fit with many teachers' established practice.[28]

Pullout classes promised better education that was politically acceptable. They enabled Title I to focus on instruction without seeming to direct curricula or teaching. Local educators could do what the federal program wanted—spend Title I funds on services for disadvantaged students—without major changes in their teaching, curriculum, or ideas about what disadvantaged students could achieve. Pullouts fit with the program's modest leverage: viewed from the Potomac, Title I was a large program that created a federal role in schools, but when parceled out among those schools it was a modest increment that required modest change in practice. Had Title I required great change, the demand on local capability would have been out of proportion to the scale of federal assistance; pullouts helped to balance demand and assistance.

Considered from the vantage point of 1965, pullouts were a step toward intervening in instruction and away from general aid; yet they meant that the federal role in instruction was quite restricted. They focused on individual children rather than entire schools, so auditors had to deal not with entire school programs or general funding decisions but with clearly limited activities on the margin of school operations.

Pullouts satisfied federal requirements without requiring direct federal administration. They addressed some of the problems Martin and Mc-Clure had identified in ways that worked for schools and federal auditors. They offered assistance to particular children and eased the task of federal enforcement; hence, they responded to advocates' concerns about program administration and quality without significant infringement on local control. And they did not require federal intervention in teaching or curricula; those were the most direct instruments to shape instruction, but they were taboo for federal intervention. Pullouts were an instrument that was consistent with modest program aims and extant practice and capability.

At the same time, there was little experience with efforts to improve learning and little scientific work on that matter. That lack of knowledge and experience left Title I's approach to educational improvement vulnerable to changing educational and political ideas. Just as pullouts began to take root, ideas about how to improve student learning began to change, because the very things that made pullouts a viable policy instrument became a source of worry. Pullouts focused mostly or entirely on basic skills: students who remained in these small classes often had years of low-level work in reading and math and were never offered nor achieved more advanced skills and knowledge. The relationship between pullout and regular classroom work also was often uncoordinated, so that what students did in pullouts had no discernible relation to their regular classroom work. The people who taught pullout classes often were community aides or others whose qualifications to teach were less than stellar; many could do little more than follow the basic skills worksheets. Finally, many pullout classes consisted of all or nearly all black students, which struck many as a new form of segregated education.[29]

These things became a source of increasing concern within the federal government and outside it, and they tended to reinforce doubts about Title I's educational quality. When Mary Berry, an assistant secretary of HEW during the Carter administration, testified on the 1978 reauthorization of Title I, she told House members that "children in the first grade seemed to do better when they were in regular classrooms than in pull-out settings just for Title I compensatory services. This is important because first grade children frequently receive Title I compensatory services in pull-out settings. So we have to consider whether or not we want to do something about having children taught in regular classrooms . . . as opposed to pullouts."[30]

Mary Berry was not alone in her ambivalence toward pullouts. In 1977, Marshall Smith and Brenda Turnbull, then officials in the USOE, tried to find a way to improve instruction while also inhibiting the spread of pullout classes. In internal discussions, they proposed legislation that would state that "pullouts are not required." Their proposed alternative was schoolwide programs.[31] Schools with 75 percent of eligible students could "relax statutory prohibitions to permit upgrading of the whole school's program through collaborative planning and implementation by the staff. LEAs would request waivers of regulations from States, which would require a school-based plan for serving all children."[32]

The idea was that schools would be more effective if they had coherent, coordinated programs of instruction. In schools that mostly enrolled Title I–eligible students, it should be possible to create programs that offered better education without shutting some students off from the rest—thus the appellation "schoolwide." Coherent and coordinated instruction was the aim; that was an idea to which Marshall Smith would return in advocacy for standards-based reform a decade later. But federal officials could not press for this directly in the late 1970s, since doing so would have had the government urging the use of particular curricula, requiring in-service education that taught teachers how to coordinate instruction, or creating programs of classroom oversight to ensure coherence and coordination. Since such things were politically taboo, federal officials tried to use an organizational device to achieve the same effect.

Smith and Turnbull argued that schoolwide programs would be administratively cleaner and less burdensome,[33] but their chief point was that they would be more effective. They believed that pullouts were hurting kids, and that schoolwide programs would give high-poverty schools different options:[34]

[I]n schools with high concentrations of poverty, the pullout approach . . . makes little educational sense. It inhibits the school-wide planning associated with success in compensatory education; it disrupts instructional continuity for children by splitting the teaching responsibilities among two or more teachers who often have little contact with each other; it ignores the great error [rate] associated with individual testing; and it denies services to the children from low-income families who are gifted and talented but who may be educationally disadvantaged relative to their potential.[35]

These ideas helped to win support for schoolwide programs more than a decade later but not in 1978. One problem was divisions within HEW: Richard Fairley, then director of the division that managed Title I, argued that the evils of pullouts were overstated: "where the services are provided—is less significant than what is provided, by whom, and to whom. If needs of specific children are to be met, these children will be set apart whether within the classroom or by walking to another location. . . . [P]ullout versus mainstream is a false issue."[36] Fairley's point, that the quality of services was more important than the setting, was on the mark, but how could the federal government deal with that when it was the province of local educators?

Another problem was division in Title I's constituency: teacher unions supported pullouts, but administrators and school boards opposed them. The civil rights and other advocacy groups that sought to speak for poor children also worried that schoolwide programs would make it easier for schools to spend money as they chose, and that set off alarm bells. It was just a few years since Nixon had proposed to turn Title I into a revenue-sharing program to cut restrictions on how it could be spent, provoking fear of discrimination and misuse of funds. It also was just a few years since administrative reforms of targeting and fiscal accountability had been implemented to prevent misuse of Title I funds. Some groups feared that schoolwide programs would relax the reforms and turn the program toward general aid.

Another development that contributed to federal skittishness about efforts to influence curricula was the controversy over *Man a Course of Study* (MACOS). This was one of the curriculum reform projects that the National Science Foundation (NSF) had supported in the late 1950s and early 1960s, in a broad effort to improve the quality of education in the United States. The Harvard psychologist Jerome Bruner led MACOS in a bold attempt to introduce the scientific study of variation in human societies to elementary schools. Yet, as the curriculum made its way into schools, opposition focused on "relativism" in the treatment of different cultures and the prominence it gave to evolution. Congressional conservatives picked up the cause; after speeches on the floor and committee hearings in which the NSF was raked over the coals, the House slashed the NSF's budget for science education.[37] It was a political bloodbath for the NSF that helped to create a political climate in which federal officials were even more than ordinarily cautious about intruding on local education.

In these conditions, even the proposal for schoolwide programs would face serious opposition. Yet the administration was worried enough about the educational quality of Title I and pullouts, and keen enough to improve instruction, to develop the idea, discuss it with interested groups, and include it in its 1978 Title I reauthorization proposal. House opponents added a matching requirement: districts that wanted schoolwide programs would have to chip in many local dollars. The proposal passed, but the matching cost was so steep that the idea came to nothing in practice.

These efforts to improve educational quality in Title I had little success. Washington was far from the classroom, and it was politically impossible to use instruments, like teaching and curricula, that were salient to classroom work. Even if that problem had been removed, there was no common curriculum that Washington could use to promote better work, and there was no common system of teacher education with which to improve education for children from poor families. Lacking these and other elements of an educational infrastructure in political conditions that prohibited the federal government from recommending curricula, federal officials tried to invent instruments that might improve instruction without intervening in instruction: organization and fiscal incentives fit the bill, for they were less intrusive than teaching and curricula, but they also were much less influential. The existence of Title I and negative evidence on its effects created pressure to improve education, but the program's design, accepted political ideas, the lack of an educational infrastructure, and the fragmentation of government left Washington few means to do so.

Improve Education with Better Knowledge?

The central government had one other string to its bow: knowledge. Better research might help to reframe the situation if it could clarify whether Title I had in fact failed. Better evaluation might be a policy instrument that could improve the program if it could show how well or poorly Title I was doing and why. Program development could help to show how to improve education and to make such knowledge salient to practice. Each could help to improve the program, which could be useful politically.

These ideas informed several federal efforts to improve knowledge for Title I. Congress mandated the Compensatory Education Study (CES) in the mid-1970s, in part to revisit the question of its effects on learning. Then the USOE's planning office designed a much larger and more ambitious study of Title I—The Sustaining Effects Study (SES)—to probe its effects on learning and to get a better estimate of the education it supported. The USOE also tried to create a system to improve the quality and use of state and local Title I evaluations.

Congress took the first step in 1974: as part of the reauthorization of Title I, it asked the newly created NIE to study the program. This bipartisan request was prompted by worries about poor evaluation results and by members' frustration at the lack of such basic information as who received what services.[38] It was not easy to secure agreement on the terms of the study. Some House members, mostly Democrats, worried that research would reveal additional scandals or educational failures that would be used against the program; they required assurances that the study would not hunt for such things. In addition, Rep. Albert Quie, the senior Republican on the committee, had proposed allocating funds on the basis of achievement rather than poverty. Quie's idea unsettled many, because it would change the purpose and operation of Title I.

After considerable negotiation, it was agreed that the CES would focus on a range of issues, including the influence of class size on achievement, the effects of individualized instruction, the feasibility of Quie's proposal, and the effects of compensatory education on students' learning. The resulting work was not a comprehensive study of Title I but a collection of smaller studies that addressed congressional concerns.[39] It is worth noting how far this early inquiry reached into classrooms: Congress and the executive branch joined to learn about what influenced students' performance even though this was a matter in which federal agencies were supposed to have no role. They were drawn to the inquiry by the program's mere existence and by the worries about its effects that its existence prompted. This is one small example of the slippery slope to federal intrusion in local schools that had worried conservatives in both parties in the run-up to the 1965 passage of ESEA. The study was one of several early moves in Title I's turn away from the general aid that conservative Republicans and Democrats favored, toward a focus on instruction.

With evidence from a few dozen school districts, the CES probed Title I's effect on learning. It reported, gingerly, that students in the program made academic gains that were close to what might be expected— that is, they learned nearly a year's worth of reading in an academic year. The CES did not report on the more fundamental and dangerous question: did Title I students gain more from participation than other similarly situated students who did not participate in Title I?

Had Robert Kennedy not been murdered, he likely would have been dismayed to learn that neither Congress nor the executive branch used the annual state and local evaluations that his amendment to the ESEA required, and that the evaluations offered parents little data they could use to hold their children's schools accountable. Most districts and states responded in a perfunctory fashion: few had the capability to collect valid data on school operations or program effects, and Title I offered few incentives to develop this capability. The reports were generally so poor as to be useless to learn about the program, let alone to improve it. Federal officials initially did little to change that; the government funded state and local evaluations but did not try to regulate their quality. But pressure for evidence on Title I's effects grew, and in 1974 the USOE contracted with the Resources Management Corporation (RMC) to plan improvement in state and local evaluations, to make them useful to assess the program's effects.

The result was the Title I Evaluation and Reporting System (TIERS); it would guide local program evaluation, help educators to do better evaluations so they could learn more systematically, and make Title I more accountable by offering better evidence on its effects. TIERS required data on student demographics, the number of students, the amount of parental involvement, characteristics of Title I staff, services provided to students, and test scores, in yearly evaluations.[40] Schools would select the tests, but TIERS required districts to use one of three approved models to analyze the data.[41] Despite that, it was a very general frame for evaluation, included little evidence on teaching, and thus offered no way to probe its influence on learning.

In 1976, the federal government created and funded Technical Assistance Centers (TACs) to help states and localities use TIERS, something that many had not done very well on their own. A few years after that, Jane David studied how TIERS affected evaluation and knowledge use in fifteen localities. She reported little evidence that improved evaluation prompted local learning about Title I and no evidence of any effect on program plans.[42] One reason was that local projects changed little, if at all, so they made few decisions about the program that an evaluation might influence. Another was that learning and accountability were at odds. TIERS was meant to improve local learning from evaluation, but it also was meant to improve the program's accountability by collecting better evidence on Title I's effect on student achievement for federal use. There was no penalty for reporting poor test scores, but such reports could trigger administrative action or congressional hostility.[43] Learning requires trial and error, but holding learners accountable for errors boosts the risk of trials and inhibits them. TIERS offered no incentive either to undertake trials or to reduce their risk. It assumed, naively, that educators would want to see the results of the evaluations and that they would take corrective action when they saw problems. But learning to improve schools is not easy: it can disrupt habitual work and comfortable practices, lead to costly program changes, or even terminate some activities. To take evaluation seriously could expose weaknesses and open a Pandora's box of educational and political problems. It would have been amazing if TIERS had much improved the use of evaluation.

A third reason for TIERS's poor track record was that it could work only within Title I's political design and administrative structure, which meant that local districts would receive funds regardless of evaluation quality. TIERS sought to get localities to do things for which the program offered disincentives; the formula grant that made Title I a political success kept local educators from taking TIERS seriously. The "federal-state-local division of labor was tight enough to establish a federal presence in local school systems but loose enough to allow for the play of state and local interests in the construction of Title I programs."[44] The fact that federal funds were to flow by formula allocation to the local level "reinforced local views that the federal money was rightfully theirs, immensely weakening the ability of the federal officials to bargain with states and localities over improvements in administration."[45] The formula grant was essential to continued political support; it was not intended to prevent educators' systematic learning, but it offered disincentives for it, and incentives were required. The features of the program that contributed to its political success inhibited its educational success.

Federal managers could create modest penalties for localities that did not do the evaluations, but there was no penalty for doing them badly or for not using them. There also was no penalty for failing to improve programs, nor were there rewards for improving them—that would be even more intrusive. A former federal official recalled that "In '78 we put something in the language requiring that the results of assessments be used to improve local programs, knowing that that requirement was not enforceable, but . . . in case locals were thinking . . . that this was all giant paper exercise for something that existed in Washington . . . we would have at least some way of putting on paper for them '. . . no, the idea here is for you guys to think and use information, and you might want to entertain the possibility of doing that, please.' But, we knew that wasn't enforceable."[46]

TIERS fell far short of its sponsors' aspirations because many LEAs did what was required, but few did what was hoped. Jane David wrote that district staffers used TIERS to satisfy Title I requirements. They saw evaluation as just another federal "string," a useless but painless bureaucratic hoop that offered little credible evidence with which to judge programs and few useful means to improve them.[47]

A last reason that TIERS was little help was that most schools and school systems had little capability to do research or evaluation. TIERS and the TACs aimed to solve that, but they did not address the underlying problem: school systems were organized to batch-process large populations and had little time or know-how to observe, analyze, and improve practice. Teachers and managers were not taught to do such things, and their work was not organized to enable it. Few central offices gathered useful data or made the data available to schools, and state agencies did less. These things apart, school systems offered no incentives to generate and use knowledge to improve instruction. Educators were rewarded for keeping orderly classes and schools and for delivering education in a disciplined manner, not for generating and using knowledge.[48] The same problems that had plagued G. E. TEMPO were little different a decade later; systematic learning was not a state and local priority, and the infrastructure that might help to improve instruction simply did not exist.

The General Accounting Office (GAO) published a devastating study of state and local Title I evaluation in September 1981.[49] "[R]egarding evaluation," it wrote, "ED [the Education Department] has not given states adequate criteria for assessing title I [*sic*] project quality. States have not effectively assessed the quality of Title I projects, and ED has not adequately monitored the states' activities in this area. Local evaluations of Title I projects have been deficient."[50] Neither the federal Department of Education nor state departments monitored program quality or student performance: "ED officials told us that their Title I monitoring emphasized compliance with appropriate procedures and not achievement or quality. . . . State Title I assessments . . . generally do not focus on program quality and are not adequate to detect Title I projects needing improvement."[51] The capability to perform valid evaluations was weak at all levels of government. As a result, federal, state, and local officials lacked an accurate and detailed picture of the education that Title I offered, what students learned, and why. Aside from the mandated state and local evaluations, Title I did not regularly collect such data.

There was one very illuminating exception: at about the same time that the CES began, the Planning and Evaluation staff in the USOE launched a very ambitious investigation of Title I and its effects. The Sustaining Effects Study (SES) was the most comprehensive study of Title I ever done—a longitudinal national survey in a representative sample of three hundred elementary schools between 1976–1977 and between 1979–1980. It included ethnographic studies of fifty-five of the high-poverty schools and about 120,000 pupils.[52] Students were tested in literacy, reading, and math, and their attitudes were assessed. Teachers reported on the instruction that they offered.[53] The duration and complexity of the study improved its quality, but they also meant that it was very complicated to pull off, and that analyses were not available until after the Carter administration had left office.

SES researchers faced several problems as they probed Title I's influence on learning. One was the criterion of effect: no state or national standards or curricula specified what students were to learn; that was another result of the lacking infrastructure, and it meant that there was no external criterion against which to judge learning. Researchers could not know whether the desired learning had been accomplished because there was no indication of what the desired learning was. Instead, they compared Title I students with students who were otherwise similar but had no Title I services. The trouble—the second problem—was that valid comparisons required either that the two groups be identical in all salient respects or that the differences be known, so as to enable statistical adjustment. But if schools assigned the neediest students to Title I, as required, there could be no valid comparison group; students not in Title I would, in some unmeasured way, be less needy than Title I students and thus likely to be more successful in school. Title I's effects would be understated by an unknown amount.[54] Similar problems plagued the SES's effort to discern the effects of multi-year participation in the program. Since selection for Title I services happened anew each fall, the students "who participated for multiple years were those whose achievement was persistently low, resulting in more understatement of the program's effects."[55]

The SES team devised an inventive remedy. They capitalized on Title I's limited coverage and asked teachers to identify disadvantaged students who were in Title I, more advantaged students who were not, and "needy" students who had no compensatory education but would have been in Title I had there been more money. The "needy" students would be as close as one could get to a true control group, given the program's design. Then the study team followed several cohorts of these three groups through three years of elementary school, testing achievement each spring and fall and collecting other evidence on students, schools, and instruction.

This helped, but it was not a cure. Title I's aim was to get educational services to the most disadvantaged students, and "needy" students might be in less educational trouble than those in Title I.[56] Only random assignment of eligible students to Title I and no Title I could ensure a valid estimate of the program's effect. Few argued for this approach, partly because the evaluations were not part of a program to build knowledge about Title I. Had they been, researchers probably would have at least proposed such experiments.[57] But evaluation got attention only every five years, when the program was to be reauthorized; that made it difficult to plan for sustained knowledge growth about Title I.

Despite that, the SES was illuminating.[58] Title I students began school trailing the more advantaged students, but they gained on standardized tests at the same rate as advantaged students. "Needy" students—those who were eligible for Title I but did not have the program because there was not enough money—also began school trailing the more advantaged students, but they lost academic ground compared with the other two groups, even in the early elementary grades. The gains were most consistent in both reading and math in grades one, two, and three, and in math through grade six. In primary grade reading and all elementary grades in math, Title I stopped the relative slide in rates of learning for its students; they were able to maintain their relative academic position vis-à-vis more advantaged students and to modestly reduce the gap in achievement with their more advantaged peers.

The researchers concluded: "the results [of all analyses] are all consistent in showing that Title I participation is associated with increased relative growth."[59] That was probably why, "while the academic achievement of most children stagnated during the 1970s and 1980s, that of more disadvantaged students rose, according to the National Assessment of Educational Progress (NAEP)."[60] The NAEP was a national system of tests, devised and administered by an independent agency, that was seen as the "nation's report card." Though it was not designed to assess program effects, changes in NAEP scores got close attention.

Title I students did not benefit equally, however. About one-quarter made large enough gains to be transferred out of Title I after one year; school staffs considered them no longer eligible because they had improved. That was a success for Title I, especially since these students then maintained their performance in succeeding years.[61] Yet these had been the least disadvantaged when entering the program; others, lower-achieving at entry, did not improve their relative position on achievement tests and remained in the program. The SES researchers concluded: "The poorest students do not gain [on more advantaged students] from participating in Title I, but they also do not fall further behind, as might be their fate had they not been in Title I."[62] Launor Carter, the study director, noted that "the better students profit the most from Title I."[63]

It is impressive that Title I students at all levels seemed to benefit. This is especially so in light of later evidence that "needy" students were not a comparable control group; analysis in the 1980s revealed that they were in fact more advantaged, began school with higher scores, attended more advantaged schools, and had some compensatory education. Hence, the SES underestimated the benefits of Title I; needy students who were truly comparable with Title I students but not enrolled in the program would have been even further behind, and Title I's effect in arresting that slide probably would have been even larger.[64]

That was good news, but to say how good would depend on the quality of education that Title I offered. If the program created high quality education but got only modest effects, we would have a different view than if it offered weak education and nonetheless got positive effects. But to figure out the quality of education that Title I offered, one must address a second problem: should Title I be considered a national program as a whole or as varied local projects? One reason to consider the entire program was Title I's framing idea: to use federal funds to improve schools for disadvantaged students. If the program had that uniform purpose, perhaps it was reasonable to treat it as a unit and to ask about its effects. Another reason for this approach is that Title I had become more coherent: by the late 1970s, it delivered instruction. The G. E. TEMPO study found extensive variation in what Title I delivered in the late 1960s: some projects provided help in reading; others provided meals; others provided hearing aids, music programs, or museum trips. By the late 1970s, most of that subject matter variation seems to have been eliminated: most Title I projects offered reading and math in pullouts.

A third reason to consider the entire program is that certain practices had become nearly universal. One such practice was that instruction for Title I students was heavily focused on remedial basic skills. The SES reported that there were small differences in reading instruction for Title I and regular students in the first two grades. However, "as grade increases, the regular students receive instruction in more abstract and advanced materials, while the Title I students continue to be taught more basic subject matter. . . . Thus, while Title I students are getting more basic instruction, they are losing out on other instruction. Unless the number of school days is increased or the school day is extended for Title I students, this result is inevitable."[65]

Elsewhere in the report, researchers noted that the gains for Title I students in reading were much more pronounced in the early grades than in the later grades.[66] The educational diet for Title I students continued to be relatively thin because it consisted of basic skills, while non-Title I students in the same schools had a progressively more rich educational diet. Title I students also received much more instruction in small groups in or out of regular classes. They were much more frequently taught by less experienced teachers, teaching assistants, and aides.[67] It was no secret that weak teachers were more concentrated in low-income schools,[68] but the SES drove home the result: Title I students who had less educated and experienced teachers gained less on tests of achievement. Teachers' experience was one of the few conventional resources that helped to explain differences in students' performance, in the multivariate analyses that SES researchers did. The assignment of mostly special teachers, teaching assistants, and aides to Title I was a surefire way to constrain growth in achievement.

One other common practice concerned eligibility: each year about 40 percent of Title I recipients were replaced by new low-achieving students. Students who gained academically were no longer considered eligible and were promoted out, so that each year the low-achieving Title I population was refreshed by new low-achieving students.[69]

Yet in other respects, Title I was not an educational unit; designing it so that it was not had been key to its political design, for the formula grant preserved state and local control at the expense of national influence. Title I set priorities and sent money, but districts and schools set programs. Given the country's size and diversity and the lack of an educational infrastructure, it was predictable that localities would use federal money differently, which G. E. TEMPO and the CES had already confirmed. Title I might seem coherent inside the Washington Beltway, but U.S. government was designed to defeat coherence outside it. The SES investigated whether Title I was a coherent treatment, using the surveys to identify patterns in teaching and learning and ethnographic studies to dig more deeply. The conclusion? Although most Title I projects offered reading and math instruction and "although the Title I program was a massive funding program, it did not represent a unified or coherent treatment. . . . Title I students were the recipients of diverse services. . . . Title I . . . was better defined as a funding program than as an educational treatment."[70]

If so, what resources did Title I deliver, and how were they used? The SES reported that on average in the middle and late 1970s, Title I added about $436 per student per year, a modest fraction of average outlays. Nearly all of this funding went to salaries for teachers, aides, and specialists.[71] But that only begins to unpack resource delivery, for Title I was a supplement; it could work only in conjunction with local resources. Local educators decided who would be in Title I, who would teach, how, and what curricula they would use. Title I was designed to build on local programs, not to replace them or operate separately. That was a fact of life for any supplemental program and a fact of politics for Title I: it had to defer to localities to avoid infringing on their control.

If Title I was not independent of local resources, then the quality of education in the program could not be judged apart from the local programs it supplemented. That was a problem: Title I's existence made it a target for evaluation, but its design made it difficult to treat apart from the schools it supplemented. It was designed to be a creature of local schools; given how it deferred to them, the best approach to studying the education that it offered would have been to probe how states, districts, schools, and teachers used it. Yet that would have led to inquiries into the nature of local school programs, what they made of Title I, and the effects on school management, teaching, and learning. That would have required close study of local programs, which would have been politically difficult and would have led to complex reports on varied uses of a federal supplement.[72]

In addition, since Title I was designed around the idea that added resources would improve teaching and learning, Washington policymakers wanted to know about the entire program's effect. To ask instead about how localities used the federal aid would have violated both inside-the-Beltway views about Title I's integrity and the power of conventional resources, and a reasonable wish to learn about the entire program's effect. Ambiguity about whether Title I should be considered a national program or a local supplement frustrated efforts to build knowledge that could promote strong, salient instruments and commensurate capability. The SES team saw the problem, but they had agreed to do the study that the government had requested. Their study treated Title I as though it was coherent and independent, while also collecting evidence on how local conditions shaped it.

Some of the most persuasive evidence on the program's variable implementation derived from a later study of the fiscal foundations on which Title I built. Jay Chambers and his colleagues reported that Title I's average contribution to local schools in the late 1980s and early 1990s was about $900 per student per year, about 20 percent of average local expenditures. That was a modest supplement, the tail and not the dog. More important, it did not add to a uniform base. Title I schools in wealthier districts spent 35 percent more per pupil than Title I schools in poorer districts: $6,725 as against $4,025.[73] Taken with school poverty levels, the effects were dramatic. High-poverty schools in wealthier districts spent nearly twice what high-poverty schools in less affluent districts spent: $7,126 against $3,849.[74] Affluent districts also spent much more on teachers' salaries and special needs.[75]

Title I teachers in wealthier districts also were better educated than those in less affluent districts, and poorer districts were more likely to spend Title I monies on much less educated aides.[76] Schools in less affluent districts were older, and, in addition, they were larger by one-third. Teacher turnover was nearly twice as great in high-poverty schools in less affluent districts than in similar schools in more affluent localities. Though all principals in high-poverty schools in more affluent districts reported that their teachers were "much above the district average" in quality, only half of principals in such schools in less affluent districts said the same.[77] In fact, schools in poorer districts had more poorly educated teachers and aides and fewer local programs, like Limited English Proficient assistance, special education, and attendance and health services with which to address students' problems.

The study concluded that Title I "builds on a significantly stronger educational resource base in high revenue districts," and "there are major disparities in educational programs related to district revenues. . . . [S]chools in higher revenue districts, regardless of poverty level, had more art/music/gifted and talented staff; teachers with more teaching experience, more formal education, higher salaries, and higher ratings from their principals; smaller elementary school classes, more health services, more instructional equipment, and larger facilities than schools in low revenue districts. Schools in high revenue districts also reported fewer problems with student absenteeism, student health problems, and discipline."[78] Different local revenue bases led to different Title I programs, as differences in local school quality led to large differences in the quality of these programs. Modest federal supplements built on much stronger programs in some districts than in others. The weaker the programs on which Title I built, the less likely that educators could make good use of federal aid.

The design of Title I combined educational plausibility with political feasibility. It was a federal program that aimed to solve a national problem, but it modestly supplemented local school programs. Those schools operated in a decentralized political system, in which states, districts, and schools within districts had very unequal resources and educational capability, and in which federal capability was weak. Title I could not avoid deep entanglement with that inequality.[79] Poorly educated aides and less experienced teachers became the program's workhorses, not because Title I conspired to send the weakest to the neediest but because it had to accommodate most local practices; they were the foundation on which it built. Giving senior teachers their choice of where to teach was an established practice, which many used to transfer from poor to more privileged schools.[80] Low-income schools also were ports of entry for beginning teachers and last resorts for weak teachers who could not or would not move elsewhere. Similarly, schools recruited aides from their neighborhoods because, given poor salaries and tough working conditions in high-poverty schools, it was difficult to find well-qualified teachers to work in them. Teachers also liked the help that aides offered, and aides were paid less.

Given the structure of American government and the politics of education, districts were relatively free to do what came habitually. This included assigning the weakest teachers to the neediest schools and focusing on basic skills. That made a thin educational diet for Title I students, a pattern that was most pronounced in the poorest schools and districts, in which teachers and students needed the most help.[81] Title I did not create that problem, but given its design, it could not avoid abetting it. That was the dilemma in another form: the program was a modest supplement to schools that were partly responsible for the problem that Title I was to solve, but ESEA made them the problem solvers and was given little influence on local personnel or educational practices. Schools with the least educational capability were the agents for improving education for poor students, so the solutions tended to perpetuate crucial elements of the problem. In schools with the least capability, a vast gap yawned between the aim of improved student learning and the instruments Title I deployed to achieve it.

The Politics of New Ideas about Teacher and School Effectiveness

Both the CES and the SES were progress of a sort for Title I, for they offered evidence on how education for disadvantaged students could be improved. Teacher assignment practices that sent much better educated teachers to the students who needed them most would help. So would a much larger supply of well-educated teachers who were determined to do good work in Title I schools, as would pressure to enrich the curriculum for Title I students so that it built basic skills but went well beyond them. Larger federal appropriations, so that all eligible children could participate or so that the same number of children could receive more intensive services, would expand the program's effects. Taken together, these things could appreciably strengthen Title I and, given the SES's analysis, would reduce race and class differences in achievement.

The evidence for these steps was pretty convincing, but it was purely notional: such measures were seen as politically infeasible. Standards for curricula and teaching were off limits to federal authorities, as was teacher education. More funds could have helped, but that alone often would not build the educational capability of weak schools, since many schools lacked teachers and managers who could use the money effectively. U.S. educators had only begun to consider how teachers might be better educated, let alone better educated to work in schools that served disadvantaged students.

Researchers began work on these problems in the 1970s and identified steps that schools could take to improve. For example, Congress had asked the CES to investigate whether time in school influenced students' achievement. William Cooley and Gaea Leinhardt designed a study and collected evidence and reported that it did not: more time alone did not boost students' scores, but time spent on academic tasks did matter. Teachers who spent more time on instruction, set academic tasks more clearly, and attended to students' task performance had students with higher test scores.[82] Increasing time by itself was unlikely to be beneficial, but improving the use of time had promise. That was informative, but it implied much more sophisticated instruments than Title I had at its disposal.

Several other researchers investigated teachers' effectiveness, and Jere Brophy summarized the results: more effective teachers planned lessons carefully, selected appropriate materials, made their goals clear to students, maintained a brisk pace, checked students' work regularly, and retaught material when students seemed to have trouble. They also spent more time on instruction, had coherent strategies, deployed lessons and other resources in ways that fit with the strategies, and believed that their students could learn and that as teachers they had a large responsibility to help. Though typically traditional and didactic, their lessons were well thought out, well organized, and well paced. These teachers used conventional tests and texts as parts of strategies to improve learning, and their students had higher scores than those of teachers who did not use such practices.[83] The latter group of teachers deployed resources in scattered and inconsistent ways, had vague objectives, and taught disorganized lessons. Their classroom work was not well paced, and these teachers either did not regularly check to see how students were doing, or, if they did, they did not make mid-course corrections. They did not exert themselves to make educationally fruitful connections with students, and when working with children from disadvantaged circumstances, these teachers would water down their instruction. These studies highlighted the influence of professional practice; they identified knowledge, skill, and behavior that was salient to students' learning. Teachers could not use resources they did not have, but added resources alone were unlikely to help, unless they were used well. That also was informative, but also implied much more sophisticated instruments than Title I had at its disposal.

The 1970s also saw a rash of studies of school effectiveness. The question was whether some schools made better use of their resources than others, and if they did, why. Ron Edmonds began this line of work by arguing that some schools produced unusually large test gains because teachers shared a purpose, believed that the school should promote student learning, and were committed to students' academic success. Principals' leadership helped to build and sustain these beliefs and practices.[84] Critics pointed out problems with studies of this sort, including large interannual variation in effectiveness[85] and dubious reasoning from atypical to ordinary schools.[86] Yet Edmonds offered an appealing depiction of the differences between strong and weak schools, and his work inspired other researchers. Stewart Purkey and Marshall Smith published a detailed analysis of these studies in 1983, in which they observed:

> Having expressed our reservations . . . we nevertheless find a substantive case emerging from the literature. There is a good deal of common sense to the notion that a school is more likely to have relatively high reading or math scores if the staff agree to emphasize those subjects, are serious and purposeful about the task of teaching, expect students to learn, and create a safe and comfortable environment in which students accurately perceive the school's expectations for academic success and come to share them.[87]

As with studies of effective teaching, Purkey and Smith stressed the importance of schools' academic climate, professional norms, consensus on aims, and a focus on academic tasks.[88] Yet these sensible ideas were a potential political problem, for ESEA tied school improvement to more money. The guiding idea was familiar from local tax levies to support smaller classes or more books: more is better. Yet research suggested that the effects of added resources depended on how educators used them, which depended on their knowledge, skills, and values, and on schools' organization and leadership. The things that counted the most for improved practice were the most difficult to influence, especially from Washington, while the resources that were easiest to manage—money, books, and other such things—were less likely to affect practice.

The research was promising, for it began to identify steps that educators could take to improve schools; if it could be widely used, it could help. But it was also troubling, because it heightened a tension between politics and education. Mailing checks to schools was good politics in a nation with weak government; it helped to get Title I on the books and keep it there. Yet Title I's existence provoked studies that began to show that funds alone were unlikely to much improve achievement. Some gains might be expected, for in any sizable set of teachers, some would put added resources to good use, but Title I was especially important for schools in which teachers were least likely to do that. It began to seem that better education would require more complex and subtle work than had been supposed in 1965. If so, Title I could become more effective only by way of instruments that were salient to school management and classroom practice and strong enough to change them.

For better and worse, Title I was created at a time of great change in ideas about how schools worked and how they might work better. Its existence and ambitions helped to provoke and draw attention to these issues, which was progress given America's long habit of offering poor children inferior education. Yet Title I was supposed to be the answer to this problem, and in 1979, after a decade and a half, there were more questions than answers. Just as the program solidified politically and administratively, the educational ideas on which it rested began to liquefy.

We already have explored much of the research that provoked that liquefaction, but one additional bit must be mentioned. James Coleman's 1965 EEOS revealed a large gap between the average scores of advantaged and disadvantaged students and between black and white students. The CES and SES confirmed it. The gaps were particularly worrying, for while many Americans believed, with Horace Mann, that schools would redress social and economic inequality, the evidence seemed to show that schools actually carried it on and perhaps compounded it. In 1965, there had been no clear idea of how much poor children's education should improve, and Title I was aimed at a vaguely defined problem: weak education for the children of America's poor. There was no settled idea of how weak their education was and no clear sense of what, beyond creating better schools, the result of Title I should be.

Research on the achievement gap clarified things. It revealed a much more specific weakness, for the gap was a dramatic fact and a plain target. Should it be the problem that Title I would get schools to solve? It seemed a little unlikely, for the same studies that announced the gap also reported that the gap began before school began, and that schools' had very modest differential effects on students' achievement. James Coleman wrote that schools with more of the educational resources that Title I might deliver did not have higher student achievement once social and economic differences among students' families were accounted for. The same research that highlighted achievement gaps that Title I might reduce cast doubt on whether schools could reduce them.

In addition, Title I had grave structural weaknesses: its design combined very broad and thin coverage, its instruments were not strong or salient for instruction, and its chief work was in schools that habitually sent the weakest teachers to the neediest students. Title I was not a strong treatment that needed a clearer aim; it was a modest supplement to unequal schools that was used in ways that fit with the conventional practices that were partly responsible for students' weak academic performance. Those weaknesses were daunting: Title I tried to combat the educational effects of race and class inequality, but in a society and school system that were solidly built on that inequality. As the program was constituted in 1979, it did not bring to bear instruments that were likely to yield more than the very modest progress on the achievement gap that the SES found. That study and others also revealed very modest capability in educational practice to make an aggressive attack on the gaps. These considerations do not necessarily mean that reducing the achievement gap was out of the question; but they do mean that neither the Title I program nor the schools in which it was most needed had the capability to make dramatic progress toward such a goal.

This does not mean that Title I was a failure. On the contrary, if we consider where America was in 1965 with respect to the education of disadvantaged children, Title I had made significant progress by the end of the 1970s. It delivered funds that were reasonably well targeted to schools with disadvantaged students. It helped to make better education for disadvantaged students a new educational priority. It moved local use of federal funds from diverse and often noninstructional services to instruction, and it did these things without losing political support. Moreover, it accomplished these things in a weak state, which had been carefully constructed in ways that impeded coherent action in domestic affairs. In these and some other respects, Title I performed well, and it did so in good part because the instruments that it deployed were roughly commensurate with the aims that it sought and the capability in schools and the environment. Despite its modest size and grave weaknesses, it also stopped the relative slide in achievement for many of its students and enabled them to make small relative gains in the early grades. That was both indirect evidence of how weak education had been for those students and a success for Title I. That element in its success was modest, but so was the program.

CHAPTER 5

Mission Revised

The aims of Title I began to change dramatically in the 1980s. The first formal steps were taken in 1988, when the ESEA was amended to compel states to require that weak schools improve students' achievement. But that change was provoked partly by a new view of the problem that Title I was meant to solve, which began to take shape earlier: in the new view the program was not just to improve education for disadvantaged students by adding educational resources but to improve results and reduce achievement gaps between advantaged and disadvantaged students and between black and white students. During the 1980s, Title I began a fundamental shift, away from a program that sent money to schools, toward becoming a program that pressed schools to boost students' achievement scores. In this chapter, we sketch some of the causes of this change, detail the nature of the change, and discuss some initial difficulties that the revised program encountered.

The program's new aims were in part a reflection of a remarkable shift in American ideas about what schools should do and what students should learn. Members of business and civic elites and some educators began to argue, early in the 1980s, that schools should demand higher academic standards and be accountable for students' performance. These ideas owed something to worries about the U.S. economy, prompted partly by Detroit's lagging competition with Japanese auto makers. Cross-national studies also showed that U.S. students did less well than students from East Asian and other nations, which boosted the new ideas, as did the "cognitive revolution" in psychology, which portrayed young minds as active sense makers that did well solving complex problems and poorly doing rote work. There also was a growing belief that schools would not change if left to their own devices, an idea that stemmed in part from the perception that Title I had not produced major change, in part to growing business interest in education, and in part to the view that the lack of a "bottom line" left schools with no incentive to do their best. A growing demand for "accountability" was one result.

The achievement gap also got more attention. James Coleman's 1966 report had highlighted social class and racial inequality in test scores, but it was the first national study to report average differences by race and social class. In the 1970s and early 1980s, evidence from the NAEP, the Sustaining Effects Study (SES), and other studies also highlighted large differences in average race and class achievement. Those differences were taken as evidence of the schools' inadequacy for disadvantaged students, and that began to inform views of Title I's effectiveness. The SES showed that Title I students had made modest gains in achievement and that what seemed a large program in Washington was actually a modest intervention in the schools. The NIE's study concluded that "compensatory education students spend an average of five and one-half hours per week in special instruction," which is between 15 and 20 percent of the time students spend in school.[1] Given its modest nature and scope, Title I was modestly effective, but the gains seemed small when viewed in light of the gap in achievement. As the gap gained visibility in debates about schools, Title I came to seem less effective. The broader school reform movement reinforced that view, for its advocates held that U.S. schools allowed most students to do pallid work and that the solution was more academic challenge.

These changes provoked a revision of the program's guiding ideas.[2] In 1965, the deficit was thought to lie both with the children of poor families and with resource shortages in their schools: social and economic disadvantage meant that these children came to school with less knowledge and skill than their more advantaged peers, and their schools often had less money than schools that advantaged students attended. Title I sought to address those deficiencies by adding funds, which local schools chose to use to offer remedial instruction in basic skills. By the end of the 1980s, that view was being replaced by the idea that the key deficit lay not with students nor with palpable resources but with schools that offered a thin diet of remedial education, rather than ambitious instruction. If students never got beyond the basics, they could not close the achievement gap, but a "thinking curriculum" would open more opportunities to achieve. Title I had been based on the idea that the key deficit resided in students, but the new view was that the chief deficiency lay with schools.

This shift was momentous for Title I, for it meant that schools would have to make deep changes. Educators would have to turn from basic skills to more ambitious work, which meant much improved capability. That would take considerable learning, and if schools were as deficient as the new ideas implied, educators would need help. The mere addition of funds was unlikely to work, for money alone teaches nothing; educators would need help to build new skills and knowledge. That implied either much stronger government or private agencies and program instruments whose focus on instruction was strong and salient enough to change teaching and learning in thousands of schools. These things were not nearly as clear then as now; many advocates for poor children and sympathetic policymakers thought that schools already did good work with more advantaged students, and that all Title I students needed was equally good schools.[3]

Yet there were two problems, which we discuss here and in Chapter 6. One was the capability to realize the new aims in practice, for just as the ideas that led to new aims began to develop, pressures grew to reduce the central government's influence in social policy, to devolve authority to states and localities, and to move schools to private control.[4] Ronald Reagan launched an era of improving schools while reducing government. It began with his proposal to turn Title I into a block grant, to cut federal education funds and staff, to shift decisions to states, and to encourage charter schools and tuition vouchers. Conservatives thought that more demanding education and less government were a sensible combination, for their explanation of schools' weak performance was timid professionals and bureaucratic bloat.[5]

Liberals saw the combination of stiffer standards and weaker government as a paradox, or worse.

Conservatives gained. Charter schools became a national movement, and eventually courts and a growing sector of public opinion accepted school choice.[6] Democrats took both ideas: Bill Clinton shrank government and cut budgets, using elements of Reagan's agenda to reframe Democratic policy to gain partisan advantage.[7] Home schooling grew, as did conservative efforts to influence state and local schools.[8] Yet as the federal government weakened, ambitions for Title I grew. The 1988 amendments pressed for more demanding academic work and schools' accountability for students' learning, but the program did not grow stronger educationally. The instruments deployed in 1988 were not commensurate in strength and salience with the new aims.

That brings us to the second problem: Title I focused more on improved instruction, but the instruments that were deployed in several revisions of the program did not deal directly with instruction. That was especially troubling, given the lack of an infrastructure that could support instruction or its improvement. Schools began to move higher on the national political agenda and become more central to domestic policy, but as Title I took on more ambitious aims and a more central policy role, and as the political stakes for its success rose, the program's capability to influence practice did not increase in a commensurate way. The new instruments were stronger and more focused when compared with the earlier program, but they were neither commensurate with the new aims nor salient to instruction. Efforts to make the program stronger actually made it weaker, for as new aims outstripped the capability to achieve them, practitioners' competence to deliver on policy decreased.

Better Schools, Less Government

These contradictory developments, which reflected shifting ideas and political arrangements in Title I's environment, began with the Reagan administration.[9] On the one hand, the administration pressed schools for more ambitious academic work, while on the other, it weakened the central government's capability to influence public schools. The first development was epitomized in *A Nation at Risk*. The report was phrased in the language of "basics" but called for more and better work on the "New Basics," which referred to more ambitious and demanding work: "Our goal must be to develop the talents of all to their fullest. Attaining that goal requires that we expect and assist all students to work to the limits of their capabilities. We should expect schools to have genuinely high standards rather than minimum ones."[10] The report became a touchstone for efforts to achieve higher academic standards. It helped to set a new agenda for school reform, to gain a larger role for schools in the new administration, and to stave off efforts to slash federal school funds. Though some in the administration, apparently including the president, disliked its support for public education, the report helped to build pressure for reform.[11]

The claims of *A Nation at Risk* were reinforced by cross-national studies, which began in the 1970s. As worries about the U.S. economy grew in the late 1970s, research reports that U.S. schools compared poorly with those in other developed nations began to pile up. An early 1970s study of high school students' reading comprehension in fifteen nations concluded that "The lowest country, apart from the three developing countries, is now the United States, and this corresponds to a retention in the final year of secondary education estimated to be 75%."[12] Students in Japan, whose auto industry was thriving in U.S. markets by the late 70s, consistently outperformed students in the United States. One researcher wrote in 1979, "At best, American average scores, as measured by international tests in mathematics and science, are well below Japan's, and the range of scores is also much wider. In short, the schools of America do not come as close in providing equality of training. The uniformly high quality of training provides Japan with an unexcelled supply of generally competent labor power prepared for company life and receptive to learning more specialized skills at the workplace."[13]

Critics argued that weak schools were one cause of poor economic performance and, in an increasingly competitive world, that America could ill afford weak schools. Some researchers suggested weaknesses in U.S. manufacturing and economic development provided the chief impetus for educational reform.[14] Reformers claimed that U.S. firms would do better in the world if teachers and students did better in schools. It was peculiar to trace the auto industry's woes to public schools, but the debate began to globalize American ideas about schooling and to lay even more emphasis on schools' role as an economic engine.

A Nation at Risk set the tone for many reports, in which unease about the U.S. economy and the country's place in the world was stirred up and focused on the school system. *A Nation at Risk* "spawned hundreds of other reports and commissions on education, most of them cast in its form, and guided by its substance."[15] There was some debate in the ensuing decade about the validity of the idea that U.S. schools were failing: David Berliner and Bruce Biddle charged that the claim was a "manufactured crisis," but theirs was one of the few challenges to the new ideas about the schools' failure.[16] Many of the arguments made in *A Nation at Risk* quickly became the new conventional wisdom. One was the idea that work was changing to require more thought and inventiveness and less routine. That had some roots in research, as did the notion that as knowledge grew more salient to work, the returns to educated labor grew.[17] These ideas also gained from the growth of computer technology, which fed the sense that work required more brains than brawn, and from a new view of learning as active judgment and engagement, not passive assimilation.

The new ideas took no account of the role that computers were playing in simplifying work, helping to downgrade skill requirements in a growing number of occupations and to reduce wages and education requirements. Nonetheless, educators and reformers argued that complex thought should be the schools' main work; knowledgeable teachers should engage students in a "thinking curriculum." Lauren Resnick, a psychologist who became a leading advocate of reform, wrote, "if a subject matter is worth teaching in school it is worth teaching at a high level—to everyone. A decision to pursue such an approach would transform the whole curriculum in fundamental ways. It would treat higher order skills development as the paramount goal of *all* schooling."[18] These ideas helped to shape a platform for more demanding and engaging schools, on which business leaders could work with governors, Republicans with Democrats, and educators with legislators.

As the 1980s reform movement raised aspirations for what public schools should do, it lowered perceptions of how well they were doing. As reformers called for more challenging academic work, policies that expressed this view took shape in California and Kentucky in the mid-1980s. Some other governors began to press for education reform: "a handful of governors," including Bill Clinton, Lamar Alexander, and Dick Riley "kept coming back to education and kept the NGA [National Governors Association] coming back to education. It was not a partisan issue and it was one that they could rally around."[19] In his recent study of federal education reform in this period, Maris Vinovskis writes: "the nation's governors became the most active and effective leaders of the school reform efforts in the late 1970s and early 1980s. . . . [T]he NGA played a key role in developing support for education goals and standards."[20] The potential advantages for the governors lay in both politics and policy. Better schools were an important element in economic development and social improvement, especially in Southern states, but the ideas made sense to other governors, as global competition played a larger part in state economies. As for politics, the governors quickly learned that school reform could be an issue that they could use to promote their careers and influence. The potential disadvantage, which seems to have been unappreciated during these years, was that the implementation of ambitious reforms could go awry; if the policies did not succeed in practice, the consequences could damage the sponsors politically.

Marshall S. Smith, then education dean at Stanford University, told the NSF Board that the key elements of effective school reform included consistency among high standards, more demanding tests, and schools' accountability for students' learning. "A carefully selected set of goals and a related system of indicators would give those within the system and the general public a sense of purpose and direction and a basis on which to evaluate progress."[21] He continued, "A common vision and set of curriculum frameworks establish the basis in systemic curriculum reform for aligning all parts of a state instructional system—core content, materials, teacher training, continuing professional development, and assessment—to support the goal of delivering a high-quality curriculum to all children."[22] He called it "systemic" re-form and developed the ideas in several articles with Jennifer O'Day. These pieces offered the nearest thing to a unifying intellectual frame that the reform movement had.

These developments opened up contrasting questions about Title I. One concerned content and arose with advocates of more ambitious academic work: if high standards were good for some students, why not for those in Title I? If to learn was to make sense of material, not to memorize facts and skills, and if all children were capable of "higher order thinking," perhaps the program's customary focus on basic skills was mistaken. Another question concerned organization, man-agement, and the federal government: should federal regulation of Title I be relaxed and states and localities given authority to tailor the program to produce results? If the first question led to using Title I to make more academic demands on students, the second suggested turning it into a block grant and weakening federal capability to man-age it. It was a wicked combination, as a less capable federal govern-ment pushed Title I to raise academic demands on students. But it might work for systemic reform, in which federal policy was seen as a way to drive fundamental change in schools, without reconfiguring politics and governance.

These and other reform ideas were organizational, not instructional. Organization became a stand-in for instruction in efforts to improve teaching and learning. One explanation is that there was no educa-tional infrastructure that could be used to guide classroom work, so there were no instruments with which policy might shape instruction. Another is that interfering with local control was one of the great ta-boos in American politics. Still another was that these reform ideas met with little response from Title I, its managers, or others deeply interested in the program. For Title I had developed neither system-atic means to learn from experience with school improvement nor scientifically defensible methods to authoritatively validate whatever was learned about the program; hence, its managers and others had little basis from which to make clear either what the program had ac-complished or whether proposals for change made sense.

Better knowledge alone would not have done the trick, a point that was nicely illustrated by how reformers and policymakers dealt with research on Title I's problems. One such problem was the excessive emphasis on basic skills in Title I classrooms. That worry focused chiefly on pullouts; though there was little evidence that pullouts were a problem, direct intervention in classrooms to reduce the emphasis on basic skills was off limits to Washington. There were only two sources of evidence on pullouts, the CES and the SES. The SES reported that "The typical mode of special CE [compensatory education] instruction was in a pullout setting . . . [which] seems to offer a positive learning environment; when compared to regular instructional settings, pullout was associated with smaller instructional groups, higher student-to-staff ratios, more student on-task behavior, less teacher time in behavioral management, a more harmonious classroom atmosphere, fewer negative comments by teachers, and a higher quality of cognitive monitoring, on-task monitoring, and organization of activities."[23]

The CES had reported earlier that instructional format, whether pullout or whole class, had no consistent effect on students' performance: whole class instruction was slightly more helpful for first-grade students in reading and math, but pullouts were slightly more helpful in the third grade in mathematics yet made no difference in reading. Most important, the study found that opportunity to learn—a measure of the intensity of focus on instruction and of the consistency between curricula and assessments—was more influential than any instructional format.[24] The quality of instruction, not its organization, was critical.

The evidence did not support the view that pullouts were a problem, but opposition to the practice grew through the 1980s. That made a certain sense: if direct intervention on instruction was off limits to the federal government, criticism of pullouts could be a proxy for criticism of an excessive emphasis on basic skills. The latter was a real problem, but there was no evidence that pullouts were the source of that problem. Criticism of pullouts was a way to deal with instruction by dealing with the organization of instruction, and it would become much more pronounced with the 1988 amendments to Title I.

In addition, some researchers, Title I managers, and educators were uneasy with separate education for poor students, many of whom were black. Brenda Turnbull, who worked in the USOE during the Carter administration, recalled that "we cited a whole lot of the NIE Title I studies [that is, the CES] which documented which percentage of kids were in pullout settings. . . . [P]ullout won in some of them and lost in some, in-class won some and in others were mixed. And it was inconclusive. But we had the argument that this segregates kids and that's just not right. And it can cause teachers, classroom teachers, to not feel responsible for the achievement of the Title I kid."[25]

Other researchers also worried about pullouts. Anne McGill-Frantzen and Richard Allington wrote that instruction in pullout classes was more basic and mechanical than in regular classrooms; in their account, Title I seemed an educational dead-end.[26] The study referred only to schools in parts of one state, but it signaled weak coordination between pullouts and the academic mainstream: if children in remedial pullouts missed what occurred in their absence, there would be no connection between the two sorts of instruction. That did not necessarily argue against pullouts; one could just as well conclude that instruction in pullout classes should be better coordinated with regular instruction. Yet McGill-Frantzen, Allington, and others portrayed pullouts as the problem.

Pullout classes also were implicated in concerns about interaction among federal categorical programs. Jackie Kimbrough and Paul Hill studied several dozen LEAs and reported that federal programs, including Title I, interrupted "core classroom instruction . . . [because] children were pulled out," that they "replaced core instruction," "clashed with teaching methods used in the core local program[,] . . . segregate[d] students for large portions of the school day," and "imposed administrative burdens on teachers and principals."[27] "[I]f districts are to avoid some of the more severe consequences of interference and cross-subsidy, they must begin to manage the overall district program in a fashion that integrates the core program with special programs." Yet, "few districts appear to make serious efforts at coordination." The authors urged better local management and more program consolidation.[28]

In all of these ways, a central instructional problem in Title I was framed as a problem to be dealt with not by changing instruction but by changing organization. A very different version of a very similar impulse occurred in the first Reagan administration, as it sought to improve classroom practice in Title I by reorganizing the program. In 1981, Ronald Reagan proposed abolishing the Department of Education, slashing Title I, reducing regulation, deregulating Title I's categorical structure, and including it in an education block grant that would give states and localities great discretion.[29] The "new federalism" would shift power away from Washington and move social policy decisions to generally more conservative state and local officials. The proposal assumed that those officials would trade less money for more control, and it asserted that classroom work would improve if federal regulation were reduced.[30] Some administration officials saw no disadvantage in this course of action, because they did not see Title I as an effective initiative.

Local officials demurred. The proposal was blocked by an alliance similar to the one that saved Title I in the early 1970s. Like Richard Nixon, Ronald Reagan had trouble finding House Republicans to sponsor his proposed changes to the legislation.[31] Title I sent money to nearly every House district, and even Reagan's secretary of education, Terrell Bell, opposed parts of the plan.[32] As one Republican House staffer observed, the proposal was too "insulated from the real world of political consideration or of school administration. . . . [T]he political reality was that it drove major constituencies right up the wall to the point that there was almost no support for it in Congress, even among Republicans."[33] The proposal's appeal was ideological, and that was no match for the appeal of money and settled operations. Congress ducked radical surgery, renamed Title I as Chapter 1 of the 1981 Education Consolidation and Improvement Act (ECIA), and weakened it. It remained a categorical program. The Department of Education also remained, as did the formula grant, testifying again to its political weight. Chapter 2 of the ECIA was an educational block grant, consolidating twenty-eight categorical programs and shifting authority for allocation from districts to states.[34]

Did this rather dramatic reorganization affect practice? Chapter 1 (we will return to referring to it as Title I when its original name is returned in Bill Clinton's presidency) did lose capability. Federal funds were cut by about 11 percent in both 1980–1981 and 1981–1982 and then by 5 percent in 1982–1983.[35] The administration weakened federal influence by reducing funds and staff for federal oversight and administration. Also weakened were the three instruments at the center of Chapter 1's fiscal accountability: maintenance of effort,[36] comparability,[37] and supplement-not-supplant.[38] Some requirements for technical assistance and for district use of federally prescribed evaluation models also were scrapped.[39] Departmental monitoring of state and local compliance was weakened by the reduction of program staff, especially in technical assistance, from ninety-five in 1981 to fifty-one in 1986,[40] by restricted federal on-site reviews of state and local programs and federal guidance,[41] and even by limited federal answers to state and local questions.[42] "[T]he prevailing view in the Reagan administration was, if the law didn't require it, the federal government shouldn't expand on the law. There was not a lot of regulation that went beyond the law."[43] Data collection on the program also was discouraged, for "the Department of Education was particularly gun shy in the 80's. [In] the first couple of years of ECIA, there was a very relaxed . . . management of the program."[44] No single change was fatal, but the combination eroded federal authority and capability by relaxing efforts to hold states and localities to federal standards.[45]

Despite these changes in organization and management in Washington, practice in states and localities changed little. Maintenance of effort, comparability, and supplement-not-supplant continued much as they had, even with weakened federal requirements and capability.[46] Federal changes were not reflected in state and local operations. One reason, analysts explained, was that "State officials attribut[ed] the stability of their policies to the institutionalization of these practices under Title I and to assumptions that allocating resources in this manner is fair."[47] They continued previous practice in part because they agreed with it; by the 1980s, there was a Title I "system" that spanned levels of government.[48] It was staffed by people who believed in it, often had grown up in it as professionals, and identified with it.[49]

They were "reluctant to disrupt services" because educators thought they helped children.[50] If Chapter 1 relied on professionals to improve schools, it could work only if it was their program, too—that is, if they had a professional interest in delivering services.[51]

Another reason practice changed little was that SEAs had modest managerial capability, even to carry out the modest responsibilities they had, much less to administer the new ESEA more creatively. In 1965, the average SEA employed seventy-five professionals; fifteen states had fewer than fifty on their staff.[52] The size and composition of state Chapter 1 staffs had changed little since then, and most of their work was application review and monitoring.[53] "No more dollars were provided to administer the Chapter 1 program in spite of the new requirements . . . and most states were still functioning with only 0.9% administrative funds."[54]

State and local officials also used federal requirements as political cover. The regulations enabled them to press for improvements they wanted but might not have been able to do on their own. Reagan's deregulation threatened to remove that cover, which elicited protests. One federal official said, "instead of jumping for joy, [state officials] practically demanded that there be more regulation . . . because it is easy to blame the feds for things you don't want to do. It is much easier to say 'the feds made me do it,' and we had taken away that excuse."[55]

Federal requirements also kept work predictable for state and local managers. They had learned to comply with Title I and to keep audit exceptions at bay. Uncertainty about the new Chapter 1 made them worry about being found noncompliant in audits, which was a disincentive to depart from more stringent extant procedures.[56] State and local programs continued as before, not capitalizing on less federal oversight. The program had worked less because of federal imposition than because state and local officials thought it helped their agencies and constituents and enabled them to do things that had suited their purposes. Changing the program would have rolled back a portion of the Great Society, as Reaganauts wished, but it would have upset many state and local apple carts, which states, localities, and Congress were unwilling to endure.

The other reason that practice changed little was that serious change often requires instruments and support, not just opportunities. But the very idea of "getting government off peoples' backs" that helped Reagan to win the election and maintain his popularity impeded the administration's efforts. It created opportunities by weakening Chapter 1 administratively, but it offered no support for state and local change. It was easy to weaken federal oversight after the electoral landslide but harder to help states and localities do things differently.[57] Neither alternative designs nor help to enact them were offered. Cuts in federal management actually impeded such things, as contact and communication with states and LEAs were reduced. State and local officials had not been unhappy with the program and had not pressed for major change; many liked it as it was, or did not dislike it enough to change it. Relaxed regulations and reduced oversight would not release creativity if no one felt stifled. Organizational change in Washington was remote from managerial practice in states and localities, just as the organization of pullouts was remote from the content of classroom practice.

A New Design

Despite the weaker federal education department, changing ideas about education helped to press a more ambitious approach to Chapter 1. Christopher Cross, who had served in several influential federal posts, said that "one of the successes [of Chapter 1] has been getting more resources into [Chapter 1] schools. A failure has been to assure that those resources were going for the right thing . . . improved performance."[58] The 1988 Hawkins-Stafford amendments to the ECIA set new aims for Chapter 1: teaching "advanced skills" in addition to basics and improving achievement for Chapter 1 students.

The amendments also sought to focus on schools rather than on individual students. They held schools accountable for student achievement: states and localities would track schools' success in boosting achievement, decide how much improvement was sufficient, help schools that improved, and penalize those that did not. They also revised and expanded schoolwide programs, with more flexible use of funds and educational programs, and made them available to high-poverty schools. The aim was to encourage schools with the most serious problems to succeed, by discouraging pullouts and encouraging schoolwide coordination of instruction. Concentration grants, to send extra funds to schools with many Chapter 1–eligible students, also were expanded. The aim was to make the program less marginal, with less thin funds, more instructional time, and more ambitious instruction.[59]

With these provisions, the amendments began to change the focus of Chapter 1 from individual students or groups of students to schools. Speaking of that time, one former federal official said that "Suddenly [Chapter 1] was viewed not as a program of compensatory services to certain kids but . . . about the school as a unit . . . of activity. How do you change a school and how do you . . . improve . . . the school?"[60] This began a momentous change, in which the school, not the student, was identified as the key problem. Title I had begun on the assumption that students' weaknesses and schools' insufficient resources were the problem, and that giving schools more money would enable educators to solve both. On this account, the task of policy was to get funds to schools, so educators could do more of the things that they already knew how to do, or could easily learn, to solve students' problems. Hawkins-Stafford began to break with that view, for it assumed that schools would not solve students' problems, if given more money and left to their own devices. That was the skeptical view that Robert Kennedy had expressed in the original debates about ESEA and Title I, and on that view, the task of policy was to make the schools change themselves, so that they would solve students' problems.

Schools' accountability for student achievement was the most radical of the new instruments and the sharpest departure from past practice. The amendments required districts to assess local program "effectiveness in improving student performance."[61] If a program was not effective, the LEA and the delinquent school were to develop an improvement plan, including "a description of educational strategies" and of "the resources, and how such resources will be applied."[62] If poor performance persisted, the state was to assist. States were to play a central role in determining how local programs' effectiveness would be assessed.

That was another fundamental change. Chapter 1 had held schools to account for the funds that they received but now sought to hold them to account for the results they produced. Key support came from Congressman Augustus Hawkins (Dem-CA), chair of the House Education and Labor Committee. "He represented a very poor, minority section of south central LA and did not see poor children's educational achievement improving."[63] The amendments also required districts and states to improve schools in which learning was judged to be inadequate. When Title I began, it aimed to improve education; though that was commonly understood to mean learning, the latter had been implied in the former and was not made explicit. With the achievement gap in mind, Hawkins-Stafford changed that; it began to turn Chapter 1 into a program that required schools to boost achievement.

Could schools change instruction? The legislation contained no instruments to do that; there was nothing about teacher quality, curricula, or other things that bear on teaching and learning. This was consistent both with the reigning political taboo on interference with local control and with previous federal efforts to improve instruction without dealing with instruction. It left accountability and whole school programs as the chief instruments that might influence classroom work. Accountability in Hawkins-Stafford thus presumed that schools performed badly because the staff lacked the will to do better; motivation, not skill, was the presumed problem. Identification of a school's weak performance would mobilize the staff's will to do better; they either already knew enough to change instruction or could learn. Federal policymakers could deploy this instrument without venturing into teaching, curricula, and other areas long thought to be the local schools' preserve. Whole school programs were expected to improve instruction by organizational means: end pullouts, increase coordination, and encourage schools to develop more coherent programs of instruction. The 1988 amendments sought to improve teaching and learning, in schools in which teaching and learning were weak, without acting directly on teaching and learning.

Another difficulty concerned the achievement gap: achievement is quite unequal as students begin school. There is a large gap between the average achievement of advantaged and disadvantaged students when they enter first grade, as there is for black and white students. Some studies found that the size of the gap persisted, unchanged, through the grades, while others reported a modest increase in the gap's size. Recent research strongly suggests that increases in the gap during students' school career are the result of differences in learning during summers, when students are not in school, not of differences during the academic year.[64] In any event, the achievement gap was for the most part not a problem that schools created but one that was visited on them by great social, economic, and racial inequalities. To make schools accountable for improving achievement for poor children is to require them to correct the educational effects of major social and economic problems. That objective had never been assigned to schools in the United States or, for that matter, in any other nation. Nor had it ever been on the agenda of any national system. It requires heroic assumptions about schools' capability to suppose that they could eliminate educational differences that arise from profound economic and social inequality. Hawkins-Stafford tacitly made such assumptions.

Another difficulty was the criterion of student performance for which schools would be accountable. Federal managers considered national performance standards for schools; they might have made educational sense but would have been unprecedented. There were efforts to create national standards, and even national tests, in the late 1980s and early 1990s; though the governors led this drive, it never got beyond discussion.[65] A national test for Chapter 1 would have been efficient, but it was thought to be politically impossible. The issue was so touchy that legislation and regulations stipulated that Chapter 1 could use only tests that localities used, not those that Washington preferred. Though Chapter 1 was a national program that sought national improvement, the politics of education ruled out national measures.

The only way to create a common standard of performance would be to statistically equate scores drawn from the varied tests that the LEAs used. The central government would try to use statistics and measurement to do what politics and education would not.[66] In the scheme that was finally devised, school average test scores were scaled against an expected student achievement growth curve; then a measure of expected growth, termed a normal curve equivalent (NCE), was computed, and each school's average gain in a given year was calculated by comparing its average score for the current year with the previous year's average scores.[67] The change in the school average scores would show whether learning had improved.

One additional problem, in this arrangement, was how much of a gain would be sufficient. Lacking a common curriculum or curriculum standards, there was no way to answer the question in terms of what students learned, even though, as an educational matter, that would be the appropriate approach. So the question would be answered with scores on tests that had been designed to be as independent as possible of any particular curriculum. Only in America was such a thing conceivable.

Washington was in no position to dictate a stiff standard, for the same reason that it could not devise national performance standards or a national test. This exercise was a preview of the issues that would arise when President George W. Bush proposed rigorous national testing and annual progress toward proficiency in 2001. Reformers and advocates in 1988 wanted stiff standards, but public schools were Chapter 1's chief constituency; they and most of their representatives in Congress did not want stringent enforcement, and in 1988 no powerful constituents pressed the other way. It was decided that an NCE "change score" of one or more, a bare minimum, would be "sufficient," and a score of zero, which meant that a school's standing in the percentile rankings had not changed in a year, would tag a school for improvement.[68] Though there was sufficient political will to write accountability into Chapter 1, there was not enough federal will, nor any of the educational infrastructure that were required to set or enforce demanding standards.

Still another problem was the lack of local capability to respond even to very modest federal requirements. Valid evaluation of schools' performance was part of this problem: few districts had the capability even to do valid evaluations, and the LEAs would need such capability if they were to comply with the accountability provisions of Hawkins-

Stafford. In response to local concerns on this point, Washington told those that wanted help to consult the TIERS TACs, but these centers had been modestly funded to begin with in the 1970s, and their funds had been reduced by the Reagan administration. They could not meet the demand; that was another problem of capability. A more serious problem was that districts that tried to implement the amendments needed to figure out how to reeducate or replace weak teachers and aides. Neither was a realm in which either districts or the TACs had much expertise, which meant that unless districts found alternative assistance in a system that had never attended to such matters, they were unlikely to improve.

Another part of the capability problem arose from the requirement that Chapter 1 schools teach "advanced skills." The aim—to reduce the almost exclusive emphasis on basic skills that the SES had found in Chapter 1 schools—was on the mark. It was premised partly on the view, common in the 1980s reforms, that learning complex skills and knowledge was more engaging and effective than rote recall of basic skills. Researchers argued that learning real tasks, whether in chess or at work, was complex and that learning was better when situated in meaningful tasks.[69] Yet the federal instrument was weak: LEAs had to describe the advanced skills students would learn, and how they would be taught, in their Chapter 1 grant applications, but the grants were allocated by formula, and districts were not required to deliver on the promises their applications made.[70]

As nearly as we can tell, there were few efforts to check on whether districts did what they promised. Shortly before the Hawkins-Stafford amendments, one researcher asked local Chapter 1 directors whether their programs offered advanced skills, and most reported that they did not. She recalled that the directors saw it as a question about compliance in teaching basic skills, which had been the program's emphasis for more than two decades. "[W]e dutifully asked the questions about higher order skills. . . . And you could just see [the directors] thinking to themselves 'Okay this is a trick question. I know the answer to this question. And the answer is "no." These are children who are deficient in basic skills. That's who we're supposed to work with.' It was [seen as] almost a compliance question—a trick question."[71]

Given the ingrained habits of practice, the instrument was a rhetorical gesture; ideas can make a difference, and these ideas did begin to call attention to the problem of an excessive emphasis on remedial instruction. Yet this element in the 1988 amendments added little or nothing to local instructional capability and thus little or nothing to local efforts to teach advanced skills; it was an indicator of changing ideas but was neither strong nor salient for practice.

If, despite the gesture, schools took the aim seriously, there would be a profound shift in Chapter 1 teaching, for the teaching of advanced skills was quite unfamiliar in most schools in the United States, not just in Chapter 1 schools. When teachers offered remedial work in basic skills, they needed to learn little or nothing new and could rely on conventional practice. This was one of the guiding ideas of the original Title I: schools would know how to use new federal money to solve students' problems, with little change in practice. But to teach advanced skills would require that teachers change their view of what students could do, learn many new practices, and unlearn many others. Most schools could not do that on their own with new federal funds, so the new assignment would sharpen the dilemma of relying on those with the problem to solve it.

These considerations are important for understanding the 1988 amendments, but they were largely a matter of principle at the time, for in practice districts did not need to take the exhortation about advanced skills very seriously. One reason was another aspect of the capability problem: districts used tests that had little to do with advanced skills; they chiefly measured basics, which created a disincentive to attend to advanced skills.[72] If districts did attend to advanced skills in classroom work, they could be penalized by the accountability tests, which did not measure many advanced skills and so could not reflect the schools' effort to do as the amendments asked. That problem was compounded by the system of equating tests, which included so much measurement error that schools that had done a relatively good job sometimes got scores that implied they had not, and vice versa.[73] That did not enhance incentives for schools to attempt advanced skills. There was enough political will to devise instruments that required modest improvement in students' learning, but there was little capability, anywhere in the educational system, to either define and measure the intended learning or to help schools to learn how to respond. Both are examples of the incompetence that the new policy aims created; this would become a much greater problem when subsequent legislation, the IASA and NCLB, made outcome accountability much tougher.

Schoolwide programs and concentration grants were the other instruments that Hawkins-Stafford deployed to improve learning. Schoolwide programs had been authorized but little implemented in the Carter years. Their reintroduction was justified by research that held that schools with concentrated poverty face many problems that were schoolwide, and that they were best dealt with by improving education in the entire school.[74] These programs aimed to reduce curricular fragmentation and to enhance instruction by focusing on instruction for entire schools, not on some of the individually eligible students. But the program tried to influence instruction by way of organization: the amendments lifted the prohibitive local matching fund requirement imposed at the end of the Carter administration and allowed schools with 75 percent or more of students from families living below the poverty line to use Chapter 1 schoolwide.[75] They still had to meet fiscal accountability requirements, but they no longer had to serve only children with low scores on particular tests.[76] They also could mingle Chapter 1 with other funds.[77]

These were major changes in funding and organization. Remedial work in pullouts had kept the improvement of learning on the margin of instruction. Even in high-poverty schools, in which many students got Chapter 1 assistance, the setting in which they got it was kept separate, in pullouts. Educational improvement was a sideline, even in the most needy schools, and the 1988 provisions sought to make it the entire school's business: Chapter 1 would include all teachers and students who worked in the grades in which it was concentrated. That was intended to make large changes in practice, for these programs would work only if all the teachers attacked the problem, rather than delegating it to aides and pullout teachers. Teachers would have to work together, not alone. They would have to work not simply to improve learning and teaching for the former pullout students but for many or even all students. That would radically redefine teachers' work: instead of improved instruction for a small group of students for a limited time each day, they would improve instruction for all students for much of the day.

The focus on whole schools fit with the evidence on too much remedial education in the SES, but that evidence did not necessarily lead to the end of pullouts or the creation of schoolwide programs. Chapter 1 managers could have pressed states and schools to reduce the remedial instruction that pervaded Chapter 1 schools and to replace it with more advanced work; that would have dealt directly with the main weakness of the existing program. But that also would have been federal meddling in local instruction. Pullouts were less of a political hot potato; the hope was that replacing them with schoolwide programs would solve the problem indirectly, by bringing Chapter 1 students into the instructional mainstream, rather than by directly addressing teaching quality. Schoolwide programs also fit with then-current research claims that effective schools boosted achievement by mobilizing schoolwide resources like leadership, common goals, and teachers' responsibility for students' learning, and with the Reagan-era view that schools needed more flexibility, not more regulation.

In the 1970s, Title I had tried to improve education with remedial work for disadvantaged students, outside mainstream instruction. Yet by the end of the 1980s, many saw schools as the problem, because they treated students as deficient and offered only remedial work in pullout programs. Hawkins-Stafford turned Chapter 1's problem on its head by legislating an end to the exclusive emphasis on repairing children's deficits and a start to repairing the schools' deficits. To do so, schools would have to identify and solve their problems, not their students', and schoolwide programs were a key instrument intended to enable that.

Taken with the proposal that schools teach more advanced skills and fewer basics, implementing schoolwide programs was a hefty assignment. Schools that qualified for schoolwide programs were among the most difficult in the United States, with the weakest teachers and most concentrated poverty. Chapter 1 teachers in these schools had not typically offered high-quality instruction, even though they worked with only a fraction of students, for only a fraction of the day, in settings that sheltered them from the entire school's problems. It would be much more difficult for all teachers to offer high-quality instruction for more students for most of the day, with new and more demanding curricula and pedagogy.

Yet this was to be done when Chapter 1 was a modest fraction of the budget, even in high-poverty schools. If many teachers were not paid by Chapter 1, why would they act as if they were? Could a modest federal supplement promote advanced skills throughout entire schools? If Chapter 1 had done so poorly at improving basic skills in schools with more focused and manageable pullout programs, why would schoolwide programs do much better on a much more challenging task in a much less focused program? Some years later, a federal official who supported the schoolwide program provisions told us that "We have all these wonderful notions of what a schoolwide program should be and how schoolwides should operate. The law has a lot of good language in it but I suspect, without some reason to behave differently, schoolwides will continue to be largely efforts to reduce pupil/teacher ratios with not a lot of thought to having a coherent education program for all children."[78]

Why did policymakers not try to improve teacher quality directly by encouraging the recruitment of better teachers to Chapter 1 schools and keeping unqualified aides from teaching? Because to do so would have required federal involvement in local personnel practices. That would have been politically difficult, even if teachers' and administrators' organizations had not opposed it. Federal intervention would have disrupted local collective bargaining, for teachers' contracts embodied improved wages and working conditions, including senior teachers' right to choose or influence their assignment. These provisions had been won from local school boards and administrators that resisted union demands. The contracts also were the unions' claim to existence. Officials in some teacher organizations wanted to improve education for disadvantaged students, but Title I was not the NEA's or the American Federation of Teachers' (AFT) bread and butter; local collective bargaining was. The AFT had organized and represented aides and was unlikely to put them out of work. To use Title I to supersede local bargaining would have required teacher unions to assign a higher priority to a modest federal supplement than to their own members. In this case as in others, this modest federal program worked by not attacking the local practices that formed the system that it supplemented. That made Chapter 1 possible politically while crippling it educationally.

Schoolwide programs avoided these difficulties by requiring no direct attack on weak teaching; they addressed pullouts as, in part, a proxy for weak teaching. The hope seemed to be that changing the organization of instruction would do the trick; here again, federal policymakers sought to improve instruction without using the instruments that actually bear on instruction: teaching, teacher education, and curricula. Research offered no support for the idea, but it might have worked if, instead of using schoolwide programs as a sort of mini-block grant, local educators used them to address poor instruction, by retraining or replacing weak teachers, among other things. Few did: only 24 percent of eligible schools had schoolwide programs in 1991, a few years after the amendments passed.[79] Almost half of the principals of eligible schools were unaware of their eligibility.[80] One researcher attributed this to caution: "We had visited districts, and Chapter 1 coordinators that said, 'I only told some of the principals about it. There were some principals who wouldn't make good use of the flexibility and I didn't tell them.' We had done the . . . survey of State coordinators, and found that some of them promoted the idea, held workshops and publicized it, while others allowed it to maintain a low profile."[81] A few years later, data from national surveys of Chapter 1 schools in 1993 and 1994 revealed very few differences between schools with conventional programs and those with schoolwide programs. Most germane to the argument in favor of conventional programs was the finding that both principals and teachers reported more collaboration and better working relationships in conventional than in schoolwide programs.[82] That did not support the idea that schoolwide programs made work more coherent.

That is not surprising given the ambitious work that effective schoolwide programs would require and the possible misuse of funds. Yet it meant that these programs were not a strong lever on local schools. Like other features of the new Chapter 1, success would depend less on what Washington did than on what the weak schools, districts, and states that were the problem made of the federally created opportunity to solve it. The dilemma that we wrote about in Chapter 2 was pervasive.

One reason that reformers expected schoolwide programs to work was the existence of concentration grants that would bring more funds to high-poverty schools. These grants were in the 1978 reauthorization and went disproportionately to large central cities; if poverty was concentrated there, so were Democrats.[83] Reagan's administration retired concentration grants in favor of more broadly appealing basic grants. Researchers laid some groundwork for the resurrection of concentration grants in reports that there were multiplier effects of high poverty and that remedies were needed.[84] This reinforced the idea that these schools needed more help,[85] but special grants to high-poverty schools would privilege them in the allocation of funds. The old formula was a politically winning way to broadly distribute monies, even where poverty was modest, but more concentrated funds would distribute funds either less broadly, by taking money from relatively advantaged districts, or more unequally, by giving more to the poorest districts.

The 1988 amendments funded concentration grants with new money. Even that met serious resistance, and only a modest effort passed. All districts that served more than 6,500 poor students, or had more than 15 percent of students who were poor, were eligible, which sent grants to a very large fraction of all Chapter 1 districts. Broad distribution was the price for some concentration. Schools in those districts could get grants if they enrolled 75 percent or more eligible students. One House staffer noted that the grants were "very politically difficult to enact. . . . It may not be the most concentrated form of direct aid, but Congress could not enact anything that was more concentrated. . . . We had to be politically realistic and enact something that would be funded, rather than putting something on the books that was ideal and would never be funded."[86]

There lay one of Chapter 1's great problems. The broad distribution of funds that had ensured political support for this program also impeded the more focused work that educators and advocates increasingly thought necessary. Chapter 1's great political strength was a key educational weakness, in this respect as in others.[87]

The Legacies of the 1980s

The 1988 amendments left Chapter 1 improved but also weakened. It was improved in that it focused more on the education of disadvantaged students: one federal official said, "Over its life, what it's done well is to call attention to the educational problems of children whom the education system has always done badly by.... [T]hat's its success."[88] More focus on instruction also was an improvement, as were more ambitious aims. In 1980, Chapter 1 had urged remediation in basic skills, but by 1988 it began to encourage schools to aim higher. In 1980, it was situated at the schools' periphery, in marginal pullout programs for thirty to forty minutes a day, but by 1988, it sought to improve performance for entire schools. In 1980, the program focused on delivering resources, but by 1988, it tried to improve students' performance. These were significant improvements.

Yet these changes occurred as the program was caught up in a wave of criticism of public education and rising expectations for it. Schools prospered in some ways, and future historians might portray the 1980s as the beginning of an educational renaissance of sorts, with new thinking about schools and more efforts to improve them. The decade ended with a 1989 meeting between President George H. W. Bush and the nation's governors. In Charlottesville, Virginia, they pledged to achieve "national goals" for education by 2000. The existence of such goals was itself remarkable, and the goals themselves were astonishing. They included high school graduation rates of "at least 90%"; educational improvement such that U.S. students became "first in the world in Mathematics and Science achievement"; and "demonstrated competence" for all students in "challenging subject matter."[89] The president and the governors said little about what would be required to improve teaching and learning and achieve these goals. Both the Charlottesville meeting and the subsequent work of the National Educational Goals Panel focused chiefly on tests and standards, implying that most of those who were involved thought that these instruments would be sufficient.[90]

But Chapter 1 also was weaker as a result of the 1988 amendments, for capability is always relative to the aims of policy, and Hawkins-Stafford and the national goals escalated those aims. Chapter 1 could not achieve higher standards and professional accountability unless it dealt with two huge problems. One was that most U.S. schools and school systems lacked the educational resources required to do "advanced" work with most ordinary students, let alone with disadvantaged students in the poorest schools. There was no educational infrastructure that might support such work, for U.S. public schools had not been built with such aims in view. They had been built to offer a modest minimum education to most and intellectually demanding education to only a small fraction of students.[91] The schools did not have the wherewithal to offer demanding education to much more than that small fraction. To build a system that could do much better would require instruments that addressed these systemic weaknesses and greatly enhanced capability, but the reframed Chapter 1 program had neither. By announcing ambitious goals but providing none of the means to achieve them, Hawkins-Stafford created massive incompetence for practitioners to deliver on policy aims.

If we look back to 1965 from 1988, Chapter 1 had made important progress, for it sought, much more frankly than in 1965, to solve the greatest educational problem of our time—race and class inequality. The program had a more explicit focus on learning and a more aggressive stance. But if we look forward to implementation, there was a painful paradox. The effort to improve student achievement and reduce inequality brought it into closer engagement with the schools' central problems, including the lack of infrastructure that could support broad improvement, very unequal funds, the least qualified teachers in schools that needed the most qualified, no coherent curriculum, and students who arrived in school very unequally prepared to take advantage of what schools offered. The instruments that Hawkins-Stafford deployed were neither strong nor salient for instruction, and they did not address these weaknesses. The 1988 amendments moved Chapter 1 toward the troubled heart of public education but did not equip it, or the institutions on which it depended, to solve the problems there.

The chief legacy of 1988, then, was a worrying gap between Chapter 1's aims and the capability to achieve them. That was familiar in post–World War II federal education policy: ambitious changes were announced, but the means to achieve them were cautious and limited. Another legacy was the increased tension between Chapter 1's educational and political designs. One key to the program's earlier success had been the relative congruence between these designs: after several unsettled early years, it targeted aid to distinct groups of students in settings apart from the instructional mainstream. The program focused on remedial education in basic skills, and schools were accountable for finance and management. Chapter 1's marginality was crucial to its political and educational viability, for its political design and chief policy instrument—the formula grant that distributed funds widely and relatively thinly—fit with an educational design that offered modest help to students in pullouts on the schools' periphery.

We do not argue that this was a good thing. We do observe that the congruence enabled a liberal educational program to survive in a weak state, in which the poor had no strong constituency and Chapter 1's main political support came not from the poor but from the school systems that had long failed to make a serious attempt to improve education for disadvantaged students. The SES showed that this marginal intervention modestly improved student performance, and it noted several things that could be done that would be likely to improve students' performance, including more demanding academic work. The scrutiny of other studies revealed a similar conclusion.[92]

If policymakers had observed Hippocrates' injunction to first do no harm, they would have considered the likely effects of the disruptions to the congruence between the program's educational and political designs that resulted from the creation of ambitious new aims without commensurate instruments. Instead, the program's modest effectiveness was recast as an educational weakness. Remedial education came to seem backward in an age of advanced skills and high standards. Pullouts were said to be crippling in their limited scope and lack of large impact on instruction. Accountability for resources came to seem inadequate in light of the achievement gap.

These changes are both troubling and puzzling. The original Title I was very carefully designed to be weak and to retain most educational influence in local districts and schools. The Hawkins-Stafford amendments did nothing to alter that weakness: no new instruments to strengthen teaching, curricula, or teachers' on-the-job education were added, precisely because of the political arrangements that were built into Title I and the political ideas that informed its original design. The new instruments added accountability on the apparent belief that the weak schools could be made to work better if there were stronger incentives for performance. Why did policymakers attack such profound problems in such a limited way?

Advocates of reform and the program's critics believed that Chapter 1 had not succeeded, and they urged a more ambitious program to remedy what they took to be poor performance of a less ambitious program. In our interviews, no one who had worked in or around the federal government said that the program had been designed to be weak and that, given the design and the myriad weaknesses of the schools, it had done remarkably well. In addition, state and federal politicians had begun to learn that political hay could be made from reforming schools, even though they knew little about schools or how to improve them. Finally, reform was in the air, and for those who sought to make or influence federal policy, Chapter 1 was the only lever; no other federal programs presented the opportunity to reach nearly all school districts. Weak or strong, Chapter 1 was at hand.

It was not well made for its new tasks. Chapter 1 fit with a system of weak government that the Reagan administration had made even weaker, but the new aims implied either a very strong state or some other commensurate means to deploy strong and salient instruments and cultivate greater capability in schools that educate disadvantaged students. That lack of symmetry between education and politics in Chapter 1 was one other legacy of 1988. The new Chapter 1 set much more difficult problems for educators to solve, but it did not offer instruments with the strength and salience that would enable practitioners to solve them.

Another legacy was that the program had two new problems to solve: one was to repair the schools' (rather than students') weakness, and the other was to close the achievement gap. One difficulty with the first problem was that though its solution would depend on dramatic changes in instruction, Title I was designed to specifically keep it from intervention in classroom work; another was that American political institutions and traditions meant that the program could not intervene directly or seriously in instruction. That connected to the second problem, for how could schools close the achievement gap if they were not directly and seriously encouraged to change instruction? In addition, few commentators or politicians bothered to point out that the gap was caused not by schools but by enormous social and economic inequality and that there might be reasons to attack those problems directly. Of course, officials in the Education Department had no authority to deal with those problems, even if they wanted to, and officials in the White House in the 1980s did not believe that government should be concerned with such issues.

These new views of what Chapter 1 should do helped to make it educationally aggressive but technically and politically feeble, a stew of great educational ambition, great political caution, and great professional and technical weakness. Federal officials set bold new aims, delegated most responsibility to the localities that had or were the problem, and then—to accommodate political realities—set performance standards so low that most could comply with little effort. This ensured that few schools and the sponsoring federal policy would seem to fail. As we will see in the next chapter, this set a pattern for coping with structural defects of such policies. Policymakers managed the dilemma by setting, or enabling others to set, low standards of success for practice, thus protecting everyone from the appearance of failure to which the design of the policy would otherwise lead.

Still another legacy of the 1980s was confirmation of earlier conservative fears that the 1965 ESEA would be just the camel's nose inside the tent, with much more camel to follow. But how much more, and how influential it would be, was yet to be seen. Another legacy still was to open a path for education politics to become more national, while educational operations remained preeminently local and state matters. In each of these legacies, Chapter 1 was both stronger and weaker.

The key policy instrument, unmentioned in the 1988 legislation, seemed to be hope—that schools, districts, and states would rescue themselves from their long history of weak work with children from poor, black, and Hispanic families, and rescue America from the educational consequences of large problems that lay largely outside the schools' domain. No one seems to have asked how a program that had such modest capability could provoke weak schools to make strong changes in students' performance, when politicians were so averse to federal influence in classrooms and schools had neither the incentives nor the required technical and professional capability. Those questions were left for the years to come.

It is easy to make these calculations in retrospect. For those who were at work on Chapter 1 at the time, the 1988 reauthorization presented an opportunity to push the program in what seemed a constructive direction. Even if it had been entirely clear just how much more difficult the amendments made education, many would still have urged the changes. The question for those acting in the moment was not whether refocusing Chapter 1 on advanced skills and schools' responsibility for students' learning would require more political will at all levels of government, much more knowledge and skill in and around schools, and more money to support the cultivation of these and other resources. Nor was it whether it made sense to settle those ambitions on Chapter 1 just as President Reagan's legacy of weaker government, tight budgets, and an increasingly conservative temper began to mature. They would have asked instead whether taking action then would open opportunities for more gains for progressive education policy a few years down the road. In 1988, many were convinced that it would.

CHAPTER 6

A Growing Gap between Policy and Practice

The policy ideas that sprouted in Hawkins-Stafford blossomed in the 1990s. Presidents Bill Clinton and George W. Bush required states to adopt ambitious academic standards and tests of student achievement that were tied to the standards, and to accept that schools were accountable for students' learning. Title I was the vehicle for these changes as well as the muscle: if states participated but did not comply with the key requirements, part of their administrative allocation from the program would be at risk; if they did not participate, they would not be eligible for Title I funds.

The Clinton and Bush policies owed a great deal to state adoptions of standards-based reform. The policy was not a gleam in any eyes in 1984, but California, Texas, Vermont, and Kentucky adopted versions of it in the next five years. The Charlottesville Education Summit not only announced national education goals but also established the Commission on National Goals, which enthusiastically publicized the goals and associated reform ideas, as did the governors and other groups. That helped to encourage more states, including Virginia, North Carolina, and Massachusetts, to adopt versions of the policy in the early 1990s. The state adoptions legitimated the reform, which helped to make dramatic changes in federal education policy possible.

The new federal policies also owed a good deal to growing interest in the improvement of education for poor children, and a sense that change was possible. President George H. W. Bush called for the creation of the

New American Schools Development (NAS) Corporation, a private effort to sponsor the development of designs for school improvement, and get them operating in disadvantaged schools. David Kearns, the former head of Xerox, led the effort.[1] A few teams of developers and researchers created Comprehensive School Reform Designs (CSRDs) in the late 1980s to improve high-poverty schools; Success for All and the Accelerated Schools Program were among the leading pioneers, and schools began to use the designs in the 1990s. School improvement had been an obscure topic in the 1970s, but by the mid-1980s, it had gained some attention among educators and researchers, owing to the work of Ron Edmonds and the writing of Marshall Smith, among others. By the mid-1990s, it was a national concern, with millions of dollars invested and much more to come. Many designers applied to NAS, fewer than a dozen were approved, and by the late 1990s hundreds of schools had adopted one or another design.

The new federal policies also reflected continuing discontent with Title I. Some of those who pressed for change in 1988 were not satisfied with the amendments; shortly after the amendments passed, an Independent Commission on Chapter 1, composed of academics, analysts, and advocates, began to meet.[2] The Commission's recommendations, issued a few years later, went far beyond Hawkins-Stafford; the Commission proposed that Title I should require higher academic standards, that schools be held accountable for student performance, and that fiscal inequality be eliminated. The report argued that Title I should be a key feature of federal efforts to advance standards-based reform. Despite dissent from George Madaus, a leading expert on testing, and Bella Rosenberg of the American Federation of Teachers, the Commission proposed that schools be held accountable for students' achievement.[3] Madaus wrote that "There are simply too many technical, practical, equity, and cost questions to which we do not have answers regarding the large-scale deployment of these new techniques."[4]

When Bill Clinton was elected president in late 1992, his transition task force in education dealt in detail with how federal action could advance the reform. The reports of the Commission and the transition task force set much of the frame for Goals 2000 and the Improving

America's Schools Act (IASA). When the administration's plans for the reauthorization of Title I were about to be released, one reporter wrote, concerning a draft outline, that "the Administration proposal resembles a plan released last year by the Independent Commission on Chapter 1, a panel of educators, researchers, and child advocates. Undersecretary of Education Marshall S. Smith, who is overseeing the drafting of the Administration proposal, was a member of that commission."[5] Those two bills, in turn, set a new frame for federal education policy and played a key role in pressing nearly all states to adopt a version of standards-based reform by the late 1990s. The new policy frame, and the expectation of dramatic change that accompanied these developments, helped to create the perception that states and localities were not responding strongly. That made it possible to draft and pass No Child Left Behind (NCLB) early in George W. Bush's presidency. Title I was the muscle behind NCLB, just as it had been for IASA.

The federal policies are paradoxical. They have been very constructive in promoting the aims that Title I first announced in 1965. They press schools to improve students' learning and to eliminate race and class inequality. They set a frame for education in which improved student outcomes are central, and they moved states to adopt that frame. IASA, Goals 2000, and NCLB strengthened a political and educational climate that encouraged educators to do more ambitious and effective work, especially with students from poor families. They helped to prompt more determined efforts to improve education for disadvantaged and minority students and pushed for unprecedented efforts to make those improvements; some of the most promising cases in point include several of the CSRDs, some charter school networks, and several efforts to recruit and better educate teachers to work in high-poverty schools. In these respects and several others, federal and state policies have had clear positive effects, as they moved federal policy closer to the heart of public education. That, too, was positive; after all, Title I aimed to improve teaching and learning, both of which are the heart of the educational enterprise.

Yet education has a weak and troubled heart, with serious blockage to improvement in and around it. The schools for which the policies sought dramatic improvement were quite weak educationally, with more than their share of poorly educated teachers and school leaders. Those weaknesses were in part the result of large inequalities in school finance and the educational resources that money can buy, and in another part the result of state and local policies and practices that systematically favor more advantaged schools and communities. Many students were so disadvantaged that they had health and nutrition problems, unemployed parents, and poor living conditions. As a result of these conditions, schools often had high rates of student and teacher mobility, which made it very difficult to develop and sustain coherent educational programs. The creation of such coherence was made much more difficult by the absence of the educational infrastructure—a common curriculum, assessments referenced to that curriculum, teacher education grounded in that curriculum, and school leadership capable of organizing schools around those elements of infrastructure—that can provide the materials for coherent teaching and learning.

The collision between these conditions and the new policies had the constructive effects that we just sketched, but there also were more troubling consequences. Most generally, the collision heightened the dilemma that framed Title I: by setting extraordinarily ambitious new aims for extraordinarily weak schools and school systems, it widened the distance between policy and practice, and created massive incompetence in practice. The great gains in achievement that the policies sought were not forthcoming; in fact, technical deficiencies in assessment capability have made it difficult to get a clear idea of whether there were any improvements. The collision also led many states, localities, and schools to practices of management, testing, teaching, and learning that are far from the intellectually ambitious and academically demanding work that the policies sought. These developments threatened the legitimacy of practice and, by contagion, that of policy, and this has had political effects. One of them was erosion of political support for NCLB; for example, Michael Petrilli, formerly a top official in the Education Department and an advocate of NCLB, wrote, "I've gradually and reluctantly come to the conclusion that NCLB as enacted is fundamentally flawed and probably beyond repair."[6]

The account that follows sketches the chief locations and consequences of the collision.

The Clinton Reforms

President Clinton's first initiative, Goals 2000, passed in March of 1994 and committed the nation to standards-based reform. The act's purpose was "to provide a framework for meeting the National Education Goals." That included:

(1) promoting coherent, nationwide, systemic education reform; (2) improving the quality of teaching and learning in the classroom; (3) defining appropriate and coherent Federal, State, and local roles and responsibilities for education reform; (4) establishing valid, reliable, and fair mechanisms for—(A) building a broad national consensus on United States education reform; (B) assisting in the development and certification of high-quality, internationally competitive content and student performance standards; (C) assisting in the development and certification of opportunity-to-learn standards; and (D) assisting in the development and certification of high-quality assessment measures that reflect the internationally competitive content and student performance standards; (5) supporting new initiatives at the Federal, State, local, and school levels to provide equal educational opportunity for all students to meet high standards; and . . . providing for the establishment of high quality, internationally competitive content and student performance standards that all students, including disadvantaged students, students with diverse racial, ethnic, and cultural backgrounds, students with disabilities, students with limited-English proficiency, and academically talented students, will be expected to achieve . . . encouraging and enabling all State educational agencies and local educational agencies to develop comprehensive improvement plans that will provide a coherent framework for the implementation of reauthorized Federal education and related programs in an integrated fashion that effectively educates all children.[7]

Other things being equal, the more ambitious the changes that policies seek in practice, the greater the resources that will be needed to realize them, the more difficult it will be for policymakers to know how to craft suitable instruments, and the more difficult it is to manage the dilemma of policy and practice. Goals 2000 was nothing if not ambitious. In addition to setting these aims, it offered assistance to states that adopted such policies: it authorized grants to states to help them develop standards and assessments, and it established the National Educational Standards and Improvement Council (NESIC). The NESIC was to identify areas in which voluntary national content and performance standards were needed, to certify such standards once they were developed, to certify state standards and assessments if states submitted them, and to help states that asked for help in developing ambitious standards and assessments.

Goals 2000 was to set the agenda for education policy, to guide and support the development of standards and assessments, and to help states develop these. Clinton's second initiative, the IASA, passed later the same year. Its purposes were consistent with those of Goals 2000, including "(1) ensuring high standards for all children and aligning the efforts of States, local educational agencies, and schools to help children served under this title to reach such standards; (2) providing children an enriched and accelerated educational program . . . (3) promoting schoolwide reform and ensuring access of children (from the earliest grades) to effective instructional strategies and challenging academic content that includes intensive complex thinking and problem-solving experiences."[8]

IASA reframed Title I as the muscle for the agenda set out in Goals 2000. If states wanted Title I funds, they had to implement the standards-based reforms that Goals 2000 announced and that were repeated in IASA: "Any State desiring to receive a grant under this part shall submit to the Secretary a plan, developed in consultation with local educational agencies, teachers, pupil services personnel, administrators, other staff, and parents, that satisfies the requirements of this section and that is coordinated with other programs under this Act, the Goals 2000: Educate America Act."[9]

IASA and Goals 2000 were, at the time, the most ambitious federal education legislation in U.S. history. They set two new aims for schools: excellence and equality. States were to improve learning for all students while also boosting performance for poor and minority students. Either would be extraordinarily ambitious, but the combination was astonishing. IASA required schools to eliminate average differences in school achievement among several groups of students, including blacks and whites, advantaged and disadvantaged, and boys and girls, even though the race and class differences arose outside schools, in social and economic inequalities whose reduction was effected by no other Clinton policy. At the same time, the legislation sought to create academic excellence by implementing high standards for all. Neither aim had ever been attempted anywhere in the world, nor had any nation ever attempted both at once. America, with its famously hopeful view of what schools could do, is probably the only nation in which such a combination could be taken seriously, let alone become law.

Policies like IASA and Goals 2000 create a gap with practice by moving far beyond it; to effectively put policy into practice is to close that gap. Doing so depends in part on the instruments that policies deploy. Instruments are the capability that policy brings to relations with practice. To accomplish their ambitious aims, the two bills sought to create something entirely new: a federal-state regulatory regime for instruction and its outcomes. The idea was to build a framework of standards, tests, and professional accountability around existing school systems and schools. It would shape behavior in schools by setting educational objectives, creating tests to determine whether students met the objectives, and creating incentives for school professionals to meet the objectives. It also would focus federal policy on schools' outcomes rather than on their resources.

IASA's key instruments were Title I grants, the requirements that states set ambitious academic standards, use tests that were consistent with those standards, and hold schools accountable for closing achievement gaps. These mandates set an ambitious agenda for national education policy and made the national government a key player in state and local decisions about school outcomes and processes. Yet

IASA delegated most authority to the states, offering a familiar political trade: states would get Title I funds if each built a new framework of standards, tests, and accountability around the existing system of schools. The central government would set the broad terms of reform, but each state would decide on its standards, its tests, what would count as success, and what the schedule for change would be.

That dealt with two very different matters in a single stroke. One was the guiding educational idea of the policy: standards, tests, and accountability would enable schools to dramatically improve their work. The signals about what to teach and learn would be clear and consistent—in the argot of the reform, "aligned." There would be strong incentives to teach to the new standards and tests. Advocates argued that if states adopted the reform, they would, by so doing, endow schools with new capability: clear academic aims, tests of how well students learned the content specified in the standards, and incentives to enable them to learn. At the same time, schools would have plenty of room to figure out how to do better work. The theorists of reform were confident that schools were the place to focus improvement. Marshall Smith and Jennifer O'Day had written, in an influential article, that systemic reform would set standards and require tests and accountability but leave schools and school systems free to devise their responses. Smith and O'Day cautioned that some schools would need help with professional development but argued that if schools had guidance, incentives, and autonomy, they could do the job. From this perspective, it made educational sense to delegate responsibility for filling out the frame of the reform to the states and responsibility for implementation to the schools.[10]

The second matter was political: any policy that was made in Washington had to operate in the federal system. States had primary authority in education, by virtue of the federal constitution and historical precedent, and local districts had primary operating responsibility, by historical precedent. Federal "control" of education was the Death Valley of American politics, a place that no politician wanted to visit. The delegation of authority to states and localities was a political necessity. That was fundamental, for it meant that IASA was designed to act directly on governments, not classrooms. Smith and O'Day's view that schools had the capability to change helped a scheme for educational improvement to fit with political necessity. That made good political sense as a guide to central policy in a decentralized system, for central influence and capability were quite limited, and Washington was not in a strong position to tell states how to respond.

Whether it made sense as a guide to educational change is another matter entirely. One problem was the policies' guiding ideas, for their regulatory regime was plausible only if two assumptions held. One was that the regime would offer sufficient guidance for instruction and strong incentives to follow it. Instruments vary in strength—their influence in practice—and salience—how closely they connect with what must happen in practice to achieve policy aims. The key question here is whether the instruments that IASA required the states to deploy would be salient for instruction and strong. The other assumption was that schools would respond constructively to guidance and incentives and improve. The key question here is whether schools, states, and districts had the capability to do just that.

The assumptions seem to have held only in part, in a few unusual cases. With respect to the first assumption, in 1994 there were few state standards that expressed the educational aims that Goals 2000 and IASA envisioned, and there were few state tests that aligned with the mostly nonexistent standards. Very few elements of the education system had any experience with academic standards, with improving instruction, or with the sorts of assessments that Goals 2000 and IASA contemplated. There was only a little experience with the "alignment" of such elements of guidance. There was no basis in experience to suppose either that the instructionally weak school systems could invent and operate an aligned regulatory regime of high academic standards, demanding assessments, and accountability or that these instruments could fruitfully connect with teaching and learning.

The authors of Goals 2000 understood that the key instruments did not exist, for the bill sought to create them. But then IASA would use these instruments to regulate schooling, by delegating most key decisions to the states. IASA thus presented a vivid and acute version of the dilemma of policy and practice: though policymakers define problems and devise remedies, they depend on the people and organizations that have the problem to solve them. That meant that the very people and organizations that incarnated the system's weakness—state and local school systems, and local schools—would devise the new instruments and then use them to regulate their own behavior. Analysts often deride such proposals for self-regulation when they are offered by hedge funds and other firms. Yet there were no agencies outside public education with any experience or expertise in such matters. One legacy of the scanty educational system that America had built was very modest capability to deal with the issues that IASA posed, and since there was little capability, another legacy was a weak understanding of the problems' nature and depth and of the likely limits of federal policy.

No one can tell whether the assessments and standards that Goals 2000 envisioned would have been salient for instruction, for in 1995 the new Republican House gutted the bill. Federal oversight of and support for standards and test development vaporized with repeal of the title that created NESIC; amazingly, the administration seems not to have opposed that, for, in Senate testimony, Education Secretary Richard Riley said that the repeal of NESIC would have no serious effect on Goals 2000.[11] But it did have a very serious effect, for, to begin with, the absence of NESIC left the development of standards and tests to IASA. Quite predictably, that would not yield strong standards and assessments, for states were to select tests, set standards, and decide the criteria for students' success, even though the states had little capability for standards and test development—thus the need for NESIC—and ran the schools and school systems that were the problem. There also were no compelling incentives for states to comply: their near-entitlement to funds remained in the Title I formula grant, and there were modest penalties for noncompliance. States could implement the requirements superficially and still get Title I funds. Most did. Many even missed deadlines set out in the legislation and regulations.[12]

Even if we put aside these features of IASA, the second assumption that animated the reforms (that, given guidance and incentives, schools would respond and improve) was implausible. The key reason is that the school system was pervasively weak. In part, this was attributable to the lack of government capability. Capability is essential to implementation because it consists of the resources that implementers and others bring to policy. Yet capability is relative: what is sufficient for a policy that departs only a bit from conventional practice will not be sufficient for a policy that departs much more dramatically. Capability varies with policy aims, instruments, and extant practice.

Though the governors had pressed for education reform, most state governments had only nominal influence on instruction or its instruments and little capability to do much with what influence they had. Instruction had long been a local prerogative, and states subsisted in a political system in which they had been weak; strong government was seen as an enemy of liberty and opportunity. Thomas Jefferson and Andrew Jackson, two liberal heroes, argued strenuously for limited government, and few states built much capability in education or social policy. Several key elements of educational infrastructure were delegated to private sector agencies; for instance, states outsourced testing and textbooks to private firms. Other elements of educational infrastructure were retained in government but overseen with a faint touch; for example, most teachers were educated in public universities and colleges with little state oversight. There also was nothing more than cursory supervision of teaching, by state or local authorities, at best. Guidance for instruction was mostly decentralized; until very recently, teachers received little guidance about the content or quality of their work from higher-level authorities, and in most cases they could teach pretty much as they liked, as long as they kept order. A series of close studies of teaching in the 1970s, for example, found that there was extensive variation in elementary school mathematics teaching, even within the same state, among teachers who used the same textbooks.[13] There was little basis in research or experience for the idea that state and local school systems had, or could soon develop, the capability to devise and implement the very demanding regulatory regime that IASA and Goals 2000 proposed.

Another reason that it was implausible to suppose that schools would respond and dramatically improve is that public education had never had the capability to offer excellent education to all students. It was a mass system that had been built to deliver education of modest quality to most students, while offering more ambitious fare to the few who were thought to be more talented or deserving. One structural feature of the system was routine instruction for most students, organized as batch processing; teaching and curricula were pitched at a low-level in most classrooms, and in every study that we have found that was done in the nineteenth and twentieth centuries, classrooms were reported to be routine and boring.[14]

Another feature of the system was very weak education for most teachers; there were few capable professional educators who could teach teachers how to do academically demanding work or help practicing teachers to improve, let alone to do so for those who worked in high-poverty schools. Still another feature of the system was assignment of the weakest teachers to the most needy students and schools. Another still was the lack of school leaders who understood instruction and its improvement; few school heads had been accomplished teachers. Another was norms of professional conduct that isolated teachers, kept practice private, and inhibited common work. By design and default, few schools had much of the capability that would be required to offer excellent education on a large scale. IASA assumed that schools could offer high-quality instruction to all, but nearly all research on public education showed that this was quite unlikely.

Still another reason to doubt schools' capability to improve was that the most important target of the policies—schools with many children from poor families—were even weaker than the surrounding systems. That already had shown up in Title I. There was extensive evidence that instruction in the program was persistently basic. There was clear evidence that Title I built on very unequal state and local programs, owing to pervasive inequality in state and local educational resources. Title I remained a near entitlement that modestly supplemented very unequal schools; the formula grant, Title I's central instrument, was well designed to keep central authority weak. Neither Goals 2000 nor IASA dealt with inequality in the educational resources on which Title I built; race and class equality in school outcomes was to be produced despite great race and class inequality in educational resources. The Clinton administration tried to increase funds for Title I, and it tried to send more money to high-poverty schools. The first proposal failed, and though the second was authorized, Congress did not fund it. Title I was hardly the basis for an aggressive effort to remake practice in the nation's schools, but it was the only federal program that offered reformers any national purchase on schools.

A final reason that the capability to respond was weak was that even if Goals 2000 had remained intact and even if suitable standards and tests had been devised, the most important work remained to be done—that is, to devise instruments that would bridge the gulf between standards and assessments, on the one hand, and teaching and learning, on the other. Those bridging instruments—key elements of an educational infrastructure—did not exist. Even if we assume that new standards would validly express the aims of instruction and new tests would validly measure those aims, neither standards nor tests are particularly salient to teaching and learning; standards can specify the topics to be covered, but curricula set out the material and academic tasks that make coverage possible in practice. In a reasonable world, such curricula would both represent the academic content for which standards call and be usable for teaching and learning.[15] Yet few states and localities had any capability for curriculum development, and IASA made no provision to build it.

Even if the capability had been built, a curriculum is not self-implementing: teachers would have to know how to use it effectively with students before teaching and learning could reflect standards in practice. Since the curricula were to embody ambitious academic work and enable teachers to greatly improve learning for disadvantaged students, they would represent very different work than most teachers could do. Few teachers would be able to use new curricula effectively and would need extended opportunities to learn. Hence, a second instrument to link standards and tests to teaching and learning would be teacher education—much of it on the job—that was tailored to the new curricula.

Here we enter the realm of the hypothetical, for no such instruments existed. U.S. schools never had created the infrastructure of which common curricula and teacher education would be parts. If, however, they did, and if teachers began to use the new curricula, they would need opportunities to try out what they had begun to learn, to make mistakes without being penalized, and to revise. That would require some neutral educational territory in which to rehearse new practices, to be supervised by practitioners who already knew how to teach the new curricula effectively and who knew how to guide teachers' learning and improved practice. It would require opportunities for school leaders to learn how to support teachers' effective use of new curricula and incentives to do so. And it would require opportunities for teachers to work together, to build coherent programs of instruction and common professional knowledge and skill. These opportunities could be encouraged by policy, but they would have to be created by school systems and other agencies in the environment.

These elements would be part of an educational infrastructure that could connect standards and tests to classroom practice. If such an infrastructure had existed, it would have operated well inside the regulatory frame that IASA and Goals 2000 proposed to build around schools, bridging between that frame and classroom practice. Had it existed, it could have enabled educators to develop a common language concerning teaching, learning, and academic content, for it would have provided a framework to define valid evidence of students' work and a common vocabulary with which to identify, investigate, discuss, and solve problems of teaching and learning. These things would have made it possible to develop common professional knowledge and skill, but none of them existed; without curricula, professional education, and other instruments that were salient to teaching and learning, IASA's regulatory frame could not have the intended effects, for however strong it might be, it was not salient to instruction. Neither standards nor tests could offer much useful guidance about how to do in class what the policies proposed, how to learn it, or how to judge whether one or one's students were performing appropriately.

This discussion of the missing and thus entirely hypothetical infrastructure is useful because, by helping to clarify what was missing in public education, it highlights the extraordinary challenge that the new policies faced. For IASA said little about instructional instruments; federal involvement in classroom work was still taboo. Goals

2000 offered support for improved instruments, but it focused on tests and standards. Tests and standards were made the key agents of change, and dealing with instruction was thought to be either unnecessary or impossible. The absence of educational infrastructure meant that IASA and NCLB faced an extraordinary challenge: improve instruction for children from poor families in a school system that lacked common instruments that were salient and strong enough to exert much influence on instruction. That lack was no oversight but a central feature in the design of public education: the new policies were to improve instruction in a system that had been carefully designed to impede central political and educational influence on instruction. The two bills sought to use policy to overcome politics, governance, and their educational effects.

Considered historically, IASA and Goals 2000 were unusually aggressive assertions of federal priorities. Yet their viability in practice depended not on historical comparisons but on whether the policies' instruments and capability in practice and its environments could enable the changes that the policies envisioned. Advocates of reform saw standards, tests, and accountability as instruments that would endow educators with new capability because they offered clear goals, tests to aim at, and incentives to teach effectively. But those instruments were neither salient nor strong for the practices that they were to change. Neither standards nor tests could offer much useful guidance about how to do what the policies proposed, how to learn to do it, or how to judge the results.

As a result, implementation of IASA tended to follow the states' inclinations. That was a working premise of the Clinton policies and probably was an advantage for the few states that had devised standards-based reforms of their own and could use IASA and Goals 2000 to support their own work. But most states had not adopted the reform in 1995; the appeal of Title I funds led most states to adopt a version of the new regulatory frame, but implementation was weak. Two organizations regularly studied standards, which were the leading edge of the reform. The Thomas B. Fordham Foundation reported in 2000:

The average grade has risen to "C-Minus." States are writing stronger standards with more detail and content and fewer digressions into pedagogical matters. We've identified eight states (and the District of Columbia) that now have solid enough standards to earn an "honors grade" when averaged across the subjects. (That compares with just three states in the previous [1998] round.) Of course, this means that 42 states still hold mediocre or inferior expectations for their K–12 students, at least in most subjects. Hence it must be said, 17 years after *A Nation at Risk*, 11 years after the Charlottesville Summit, and in the same year that our "National Education Goals" were to be met: most states still have not successfully completed the *first step* of standards-based reform.[16]

The AFT report began with a slightly more positive view just a year later: "29 states and the District of Columbia, up from just 13 states six years ago, have clear and specific standards in the core subject areas of English, mathematics, social studies, and science at three educational levels—elementary, middle, and high school."[17] But the report had little good to say thereafter:

Progress on standards-based reform falls short. Unaligned tests are driving the reform:

- Almost a third of the states' tests are based on weak standards;
- Forty-four percent of those tests are not aligned to the standards;
- Fewer than one-third of the tests are supported by adequate curriculum.[18]

Both Fordham and the AFT strongly supported standards-based reform, so these reports do not reflect hostility to the policies. They do reflect the effects of Washington's very weak influence on practice; weak capability in states, school districts, and schools; and most states' disinclination to use tests and standards that would yield reports of widespread educational failure.

Some of these problems could have been addressed in part by more aggressive enforcement, but, perhaps fearing trouble with House Republicans, the Clinton administration did not try that until near the end of its second term. The problems also could have been addressed in part by substantial efforts to build state and local capability, but the legislation made little provision for that. The federal Education Department had earlier tried to contract out the development of content standards, but the results were so troubled that it abandoned the effort. Goals 2000 was to have helped states evaluate and improve standards and tests, but that had been swept away by the Republican House in 1995–96. The states and the Department of Education then treated Goals 2000 grants as funds that the states could use at their discretion.

The problems that we have sketched also might have been addressed in part by systematic efforts to learn from state and local experience with implementation; this could have identified implementation problems before they became serious, but there was little of that in the legislation, save the short-lived Goals 2000 provisions for analysis and improvement of state standards and tests. Since the reforms began with scanty evidence on their feasibility or likely effects, such learning would have been especially useful—among other things, to illuminate whether instruments were strong or salient for practice, and why. Systematic study might even have helped to explain why, despite most states' perfunctory response to IASA, students' scores in NAEP math tests, which had begun to rise early in the 1990s, before Goals 2000 and IASA, continued to rise after IASA's passage and why reading scores moved very little.

No Child Left Behind

By the late 1990s, some liberal Democrats in Congress and advocates of reform were put out with what they saw as the schools' failure to take IASA seriously. The rise in NAEP math scores did not diminish the idea that the schools had failed to respond to efforts to improve them. A window for action opened as the date for the reauthorization of Title I approached; though reauthorization was required every five years and 1999 was on the five-year mark, it was also an election year, so the reauthorization was put off. George W. Bush campaigned on education, and after his victory was settled by the U.S. Supreme Court, his administration moved to deliver on his promise. The combination of the congressionally required reconsideration of Title I, the perception that many states and school systems had not responded in good faith to IASA, and a president with a strong attachment to education policy created an opening for more vigorous federal action. There also was no significant opposition to such action: public opinion had shifted toward support of standards and accountability since the early 1980s;[19] the main education groups—especially the NEA, NCTM, and AASA—had lost favor and access in Congress because of the bipartisan view that they had ignored IASA; and the main hesitation in Congress came from a few Democrats on that party's most liberal wing and from some conservative Republicans—the former of whom were out-maneuvered by Senator Ted Kennedy and Representative George Miller, the ranking Democrats on the key committees, and the latter of whom were reluctant to oppose their new president.[20]

The only consideration that might have caused some hesitation was worry that it might be very difficult for an aggressive federal intervention to succeed, but such concerns seem to have troubled no one in Congress or the administration. Elizabeth Debray wrote that "there was a notable absence of discussion on Capitol Hill, whether in hearings or in the committee, about what the new bill would actually mean *inside* high poverty schools. For instance, . . . none of the major players in the 107th, from the Bush administration to the Progressive Policy Institute, discussed what had been learned from . . . [the school-wide] initiative, how widespread its adoption had been, or how a new testing regime would affect it. . . . With the exception of the blanket observation of politicians of both parties alleging that Title I had failed to meet its original goals, the policy discourse was not focused on the condition of instruction in high-poverty schools so much as on accountability and getting kids out of schools that had 'failed.'"[21] Christopher Cross wrote that the "capability of institutions at all levels of education was never really a major factor in the discussions."[22]

After extensive negotiation with members of Congress, liberals and conservatives made common cause, and Bush signed No Child Left Behind into law in January 2002. One of the most conservative Republican presidents since Herbert Hoover, Bush championed a substantial expansion of federal authority in education. The bill retained the

central features of IASA: a reliance on standards, tests, and accountability as the key framework and the combination of aggressive assertion of federal priorities and delegation of essential decisions to states
and localities. But though NCLB accepted the policy framework that
IASA had set, it went well beyond that in several crucial respects. Following the Texas reform, it tightened the regulatory regime and required schedules of compliance; extensive tests that had to be phased
in on a tight schedule; test scores reported by race, class, gender, and
disability status; and the elimination of average race and class achievement inequality in twelve years. Yet, in a trade-off familiar from IASA,
states retained a good deal of discretion to choose standards and tests,
set criteria of proficiency, and other matters. States were required to
phase in testing of all students in grades three to eleven during several
years and to set criteria for students' "proficiency" on the tests, but
states would choose the tests and set criteria. If a school's student sub-
group scored at less than "proficient" for two years, by the state's definition of proficiency, the school must be identified as in need of
improvement. The LEA then had to devise a plan and a schedule to
improve students' scores; failing that, the state must improve the
school. If it continued to perform badly for five years, it must be "re-
constituted" or closed. States that participated but did not comply
would lose part of their Title I administrative allocation; no other
Title I funds would be lost unless states dropped the program. A few
threatened, but none did.

NCLB bolstered the instruments that IASA had deployed and
added some new ones. Yet the strength and salience of those instruments depended in part on capability in practice, which remained
weak. The bill did contain several provisions that sought to improve
state and local capability, yet the gaps between aims, instruments, and
capability that plagued IASA persisted or grew more profound with
NCLB. We discuss this in several of the bill's central initiatives.

Money.   In fiscal year (FY) 2001, before NCLB passed, Title I was
funded at $8.7 billion, but after it passed, in FY 2002, it was funded
at $10.35 billion.[23] That included two hitherto unfunded Clinton-era
formulas that were designed to send more money to high-poverty

schools and to states that had less interdistrict inequality and made more effort to support schools.[24] These two formulas comprised $2.81 billion of the total Title I appropriation.

One way to consider these changes is in terms of their local effect; they were large from the perspective of Washington, but NCLB boosted the federal share of total local revenues from 7.3 percent in 2000 to 9.2 percent in 2004–2005.[25] That meant that Title I funds for high-poverty schools could be quite substantial, but it was not a major change in schools' funds or the federal contribution. A recent study placed the average per-student Title I outlay in high-poverty elementary schools in 2004–2005 at $558 or roughly 5 percent of total revenues in those schools, which was a slight decrease from pre-NCLB funds.[26]

Another way to consider NCLB funding is to ask whether, as intended, it got more money to high-poverty districts and schools. There are several ways to answer this question. One concerns the allocation of Title I funds according to the incidence of poverty in school districts.[27] Title I Part A grants operate under several different formulas. In NCLB's first year, basic grants were 69 percent of the total Title I Part A appropriation, and they were fairly equally distributed across districts, irrespective of the incidence of poverty. The quintile of districts with the highest incidence of poverty (more than 38.24 percent) received 20.9 percent of the total basic grant allocation, while the quintile of districts with the lowest incidence of poverty (0–15.58 percent) received 19 percent of the total. For a program that was intended to combat the educational effects of poverty, this is hardly what one might expect; affluent districts received very nearly as large a share of basic grants as the districts with the greatest incidence of poverty. But the wide distribution of funds was key to the political design of the program, even though this practice ran across the grain of its educational intentions.

Another way to investigate whether NCLB got more money to high-poverty districts and schools concerns the effects of concentration grants. They were first effectively funded by Hawkins-Stafford, and they were 13 percent of total Title I grants in FY 2002. Though they were intended to concentrate funds in the poorest and most needy school systems, they did not. The most affluent quintile of districts did receive only 7.6 percent of total concentration grants in 2002, but the other four quintiles received roughly equal shares of the total, as with the basic grants. In fact, the second most affluent quintile of districts actually received a slightly greater share of these grants than the poorest quintile of districts.

Then there are two formulas (targeted grants and education finance incentive grants) that were designed to get more money to districts with the greatest incidence of poverty; they were devised during the Clinton administration but only funded by NCLB, and together they were 18 percent of total Title I Part A grants in FY 2002. They did succeed, modestly: the two poorest quintiles of districts received about 25 percent of each of these grants, while the two quintiles with the least incidence of poverty received about 15 percent of the total of each. That was remarkable progress, given Title I's political design, but it still was modest: the most affluent quintiles of districts still received substantial shares of the total, and the lion's share of Title I was in the basic and concentration grants, which sent as much money to affluent districts as to poor districts.

We also can ask how effective Title I was in getting funds to the poorest schools rather than to the poorest districts. The answers are presented in the accompanying figure. The per-student allocations in the highest-poverty schools in 2004–2005 were modestly lower than in schools in the middle quartiles and much lower than in the lowest-poverty schools. One reason for this is simply that there are many more disadvantaged students in high-poverty schools, so the nonequalizing Part A basic and concentration grants must be spread over many more students than in low-poverty schools. Another reason, not evident from the figure, is that the population of poor children in these schools grew at a rate that kept pace with the relatively large increase in Title I funds that the schools received from NCLB. Jay Chambers and his colleagues wrote that "The highest poverty schools did see a 25 percent increase in their total Title I funds during this period, but the growth in funding basically kept pace with the growth in the number of low-income students served in these schools (27 percent)."[28]

The chief moral of this story is that the political design of Title I sends a great deal of money to many schools with few poor children, which

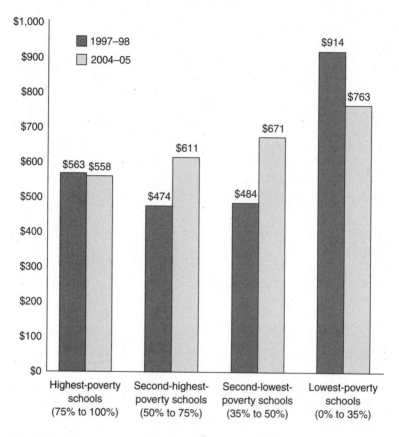

Title I funding per low-income student, by school poverty level, 1997–98 and 2004–2005, in constant 2004–2005 dollars. Source: Jay Chambers et al., p. 39; data from *Study of Education Resources and Federal Funding,* 1997–98 (*n* = 4,563 Title I schools); NLS-NCLB, school allocations, 2004–2005 (*n* = 8,564 Title I schools).

limits the strength of its main instrument; this fact of its political design seriously compromises its educational aims, despite NCLB's efforts to focus the program more intensely on high-poverty schools and districts. Part of the explanation is that the program's educational aims shifted between 1965 and 2002. At its creation, Title I was as much an effort to get federal aid to schools, somehow, as it was to fight poverty;

but more evidence on unequal school outcomes, more advocacy to focus the program on school outcomes, and changing ideas about education all pushed the program to concentrate on the schools with the greatest poverty and largest problems. But the formula grant that helped to win support for the ESEA in 1965 did so by spreading funds to more than 90 percent of school districts and every House district. This broad distribution of funds remained roughly intact, so Title I's political and fiscal design changed much less than its educational design. The political design that distributed funds so broadly impeded the program's educational aims throughout Title I's life, but the impediment became more pronounced as the program's ambitions soared.

The Quality of Teaching. The monies that NCLB added did offer the potential for more local capability in a modestly equalizing manner. But added money does not help unless it is used effectively, and to that end NCLB sought to improve teaching. Most famously, it required all schools to have "highly qualified teachers" in core academic subjects. That initiative broke new ground for Title I by attempting to improve teacher quality, which was an important step in principle. But the legislation was drawn in such a way that it broke only a bit of new ground in practice. One reason, as several analysts have observed, is that NCLB required qualifications for new teachers that were little different than existing certification requirements—i.e., an academic major and scores on entrance tests for teaching. States were permitted to set their own scores for passing the test, and many set them quite low. These qualifications are not strongly related to students' performance, a point that was known at the time.

For those teachers who already were at work, NCLB offered states an alternative: instead of academic majors and teacher tests, they could create a "High Objective Uniform State Standard of Evaluation" (HOUSSE), in which teachers' years of experience could count toward being highly qualified. Many studies have shown that teaching quality and students' learning do improve with teachers' experience, but only for the first three to five years. The teacher quality provisions of NCLB seem to have helped some states and localities to fire or reassign some of their most egregiously unqualified teachers, but there is no reason to think that these provisions seriously improved instructional capability. The Center on Education Policy (CEP) study of teacher quality in NCLB offered this assessment by Wayne Riddle, of the Congressional Research Service: ·

> The NCLBA's HQT [highly qualified teacher] requirements are closely linked to state teacher certification requirements and, in the case of secondary school teachers, attainment of baccalaureate or higher degrees with a major in the subject(s) taught. While widely accepted as minimum qualifications, these are not the only attributes closely associated with teacher effectiveness in improving student achievement, nor do they address issues of instructional methods used by teachers in the classroom. Further, there is evidence that a very large majority of teachers already met the HQT requirements when the NCLBA was enacted.[29]

As with other key decisions, each state sets its own criteria for "highly qualified" teachers.

Given that arrangement, and the conventional criteria, it is no surprise that within a few years, most states reported that most teachers were "highly qualified." A few set more demanding standards, but most did not. Even with very modest standards, high-poverty and high-minority schools had three times as many unqualified teachers as other schools.[30] The CEP reported that "our surveys and case studies asked states and school districts about the impact of the NCLB highly qualified teacher requirements on teacher effectiveness. Their responses suggested that the impact has not been major. More than one-third (38%) of state survey respondents and almost three-quarters (74%) of district survey respondents said that these requirements have had minimal or no impact on the effectiveness of the teacher workforce."[31]

These points are supported by research in classrooms; a detailed study of elementary schools concluded: "Classroom dynamics were not related to teachers' degree status or experience. Teachers met credentialing standards, but their classrooms, even if emotionally positive, were mediocre in terms of quality of instructional support. . . . These results are consistent with arguments that a focus on standards-based reform and teacher credentialing may lead to instruction that is overly broad and thin."[32] Absent educational infrastructure—including the curriculum to be taught and learned and teacher education oriented to that curriculum—NCLB's efforts to improve teaching were extraordinarily challenging.

NCLB also tried to encourage additional means to improve teaching. It required that school districts spend at least 5 percent of Part A funds on professional development for teachers, and the Act's Title II offered state grants to improve teacher education, to devise qualifications for teaching that would bypass conventional teacher education in favor of academic subject matter majors or test scores, and to offer "high quality" professional development. The most extensive study of this matter offered two conclusions of particular importance:

> Professional development activities that engage teachers in the learning process by having them apply knowledge to real-world classroom tasks . . . are more likely to facilitate instructional change. . . . Less than one-quarter of teachers reported that they participated in professional development that often provided opportunities to practice what they learned.[33]

> If high-quality professional development is defined minimally as at least one experience that is longer than a one-day workshop, most teachers were receiving high-quality professional development. However, if high-quality professional development means content-focused, sustained learning experiences, most teachers were not receiving high-quality professional development.[34]

Here again, NCLB's ambitions for demanding instruction were incommensurate with the capability contained in its instruments, in practice, and in the environment. Federal enforcement of the teacher quality requirements was not stringent, in part because one underlying problem was the lack of a large pool of qualified teachers who wished to work in difficult schools, and another problem was the absence of infrastructure that could support common criteria of quality. One leading analyst recently wrote:

> The teacher qualification gap is one of the most established in educational research. Students from lower-income families are much

more likely than students from higher-income families to have teachers who have little experience, graduated from less-selective colleges, and possess fewer credentials. There is a considerable amount of rhetoric on the need to address this inequity. Yet the pattern has persisted for decades across all policy levels: there are inequities among districts, inequities among schools within districts, and even inequities among classrooms within schools.[35]

These were not problems that NCLB caused, but as it sought to intervene in teaching and learning, these were the problems that shaped its design and implementation. Jack Jennings, director of the Washington-based CEP, a former House subcommittee staff director, and an expert on Title I, said, "The provisions dealing with teacher quality in No Child Left Behind have done a wonderful job of focusing attention on the issue of teacher quality in the United States. . . . The spotlight is wonderful; but what the spotlight has shown is a whole mess of problems that we're not seriously addressing in a systemic and sustained way."[36]

Accountability.   The heart of NCLB, however, was accountability not capability. Hawkins-Stafford implied that state and local governments were responsible for students' learning. IASA asserted it as a principle but set no schedule for compliance or stiff penalties for nonperformance. Some who devised that legislation appreciated the extraordinary changes that it required, and for that reason as well as political necessity, the bill was open-ended with respect to compliance.

NCLB tried to make compliance a reality, which was a sharp break with the Clinton policies. The mandate that state and local governments must either improve weak schools or suffer the consequences broke new ground by expanding government responsibility for schooling. Before NCLB, if children did poorly, the pain was theirs and perhaps also their parents' and teachers'; with NCLB, if students did poorly, school staff and government officials also would feel pain. Like several state policies, NCLB created a new calculus of political risk: it raised the educational and political stakes for governments and schools by making students' poor performance a problem for governments and schools.

The new calculus of risk had constructive potential, for it could strengthen the incentives to improve schools. It also could increase support for better education for poor children, if it led educators and others interested in schools to identify their interests with those of poor children.[37] This element of its design is important beyond school improvement, for antipoverty programs can work politically only if they gain broad support for action that directly benefits a politically weak minority. Widely distributed funds had done that for Title I in the past, but that made the formula grant, a near entitlement for states and localities, Title I's chief instrument. This meant that the agencies that had failed, and were to be improved, were Title I's chief constituents; the schools that were the problem had a firm grip on the money that was to reform them. That rather limited federal influence.

The accountability provisions of NCLB and other standards-based reforms worked in certain respects. They intensified educators' interest in improved student learning and expanded the constituency for improvement. Accountability was aimed at educators, but IASA and NCLB created a policy frame in which school failure could be contagious, infecting not only schools and districts but also municipalities and states. That is one reason why several big city mayors, governors, and state education officials took a growing interest in schools, and pressed educators for better work.

Those developments were positive, but professional accountability, like other policy instruments, depends on capability in practice and the environment, in addition to reconfigured political arrangements. Accountability could encourage academically demanding work only if there were valid measures of the outcomes in question, if schools and governments had or could soon develop the capability to improve and create those outcomes, and if the accountability regime was fair. Absent the first, teachers and students would have neither valid academic targets at which to direct their work, nor the curricula, assessments, and other instruments to use as they did that work; lacking those, the regime would likely be ineffective. Even if these conditions were satisfied, absent capability in schools and the environment, practice would not improve as the policies envisioned, and that could affect policy and politics. Absent fairness, accountability could lose legitimacy.

NCLB encountered problems on each of these counts. The question of what constitutes an educationally valid measure of the outcomes of state accountability schemes became more vexed in the wake of NCLB. The most common answer, consistent with the new policy frame, is tests that are "aligned" with state standards. In principle, that seems sensible, but in practice there are problems. One is whether alignment, in fact, exists. Another is that alignment itself is insufficient: it could reinforce weak education if there is no independent validation of the quality of standards and tests. Poor tests can be tightly aligned with poor standards. Two independent organizations recently evaluated the quality of state standards, and they agreed that academic demands, clarity, and quality have somewhat improved. In its 2008 report, the AFT considered standards for all of the twelve grades in all four "core" subjects: English, math, science, and social studies. It reported that the percentages of "clear, specific, content-rich" standards for the elementary grades were 47 percent for English, 78 percent for math, 53 percent for science, and 6 percent for social studies.[38] The Thomas B. Fordham Foundation offered a more dismal assessment in its 2006 report: "The modest good news is that most states have indeed *revised* or *replaced* their standards in many subjects [since the earlier Fordham report]. Thirty-seven states have updated at least one subject's standards since 2000, and 27 have revised all of their standards. The much more significant bad news, however, is that taken as a whole, state academic standards are no better in 2006 than they were six years earlier. And far too many of them are completely unsatisfactory."[39] The report concluded: "Two-thirds of U.S. children attend schools in states with mediocre standards or worse."[40]

The news is not all bad: these studies report improvements that might not have occurred in the absence of the federal policies: Chester E. Finn, Jr. and his colleagues at the Fordham Foundation found, for instance, that California, Massachusetts, and Indiana had outstanding standards in all the subjects they examined. They also reported that standards had become more specific since their pre-NCLB report and that perhaps a dozen states had good standards in two subjects.[41] But both reports reveal that state standards have a long way to go before they represent clear, specific, academically demanding content. That is no surprise, since standards of the sort for which federal policies call were unknown in the United States prior to the recent federal policies.

One next step could be to investigate whether state tests are educationally valid measures of the outcomes that standards were supposed to represent. These reports did not ask that question, perhaps because it would be difficult to answer. For in order to decide whether a state has educationally valid tests of the outcomes that standards depict, analysts would have to compare tests with standards that were judged to be sound and determine whether the tests did require the same knowledge and skills for which the standards called. We found one such independent investigation, which dealt with a few states; we discuss it later (pp. 167–170) in this chapter.

Since most standards are weak, it might be have been sensible to defer scrutiny of tests, and their consistency with standards, until strong standards had been devised, but states did not have that luxury. NCLB requires that they have tests that are aligned with standards, and most states report that they do. It appears, however, that many tests now in use are off-the-shelf standardized instruments, which test publishers sometimes modify somewhat to "align" them with state standards. Though we do not doubt that there has been more convergence between state tests and standards since IASA, it is not clear what that means, for there seems to be only one independent study of what such alignment, in fact, is. Other studies of this issue rely on teachers' reports, in surveys, of their view of consistency between standards and tests.[42] Until there is independent analysis of what academic knowledge and skills standards call for, and how consistent they are with the knowledge and skills for which tests call, it will be impossible to know how well tests actually measure the academic content for which standards call, or how well educators understand alignment. Absent such independent work, it also will be impossible to know whether teachers' reports of alignment represent a growing tendency to focus on the rather modest knowledge and skills for which many tests call or increasing consistency between demanding standards and demanding tests. Without such independent work, we also cannot know whether tests validly measure the growth in students' knowledge and skills over time, something that sound standards would represent. These problems arise from the inconsistency between NCLB's requirements and weak technical capability for assessment and academic standards; the law required technical and professional capability that barely existed. In this respect as in many others, accountability added to the incommensurate relationship between the new policy and capability in schools and the environment.

A less obvious but equally fundamental problem is whether schools had the curricula and other instruments that students and teachers could use to satisfy academically demanding standards and assessments, had such things existed. Curriculum also is a matter on which the AFT and Fordham reports are silent and on which we can find no other studies. That is no surprise—federal influence on curriculum was and still seems to be a political taboo. But it was implausible to suppose that local schools and school districts could develop curricula in the core academic subjects, given their long-running lack of capability for such work. The result often seems to be that tests become a protocurriculum, but we could find no evidence on the frequency of this practice.

No state appears to have developed curricula, though a few moved in that direction, as have a few cities. Hence, few of the tests now used are strongly linked to specific curricula; there has, as a result, not been the close alignment that advocates of standards-based reform expected among demanding standards, ambitious curricula, what teachers taught, and what tests measured. That reflects several fundamental weaknesses in the design of public education in the United States. As Paul Barton of the Educational Testing Service wrote, "Testing, with its theories of 'mental measurement,' grew up largely as a separate enterprise from instruction. . . . [These tests are] joined with instruction in the classrooms in a shotgun marriage."[43]

Another problem of technical capability arose because standardized tests were not designed to be valid measures of academic growth; the forms of the tests vary from grade to grade since they are designed to profile achievement at one moment, not to measure change over time.[44] In addition, the measure of progress—the percentage of students proficient—that NCLB required states to use was prone to extensive error. One source of error is student mobility: especially in high-poverty schools, where mobility is often very high, many who are tested in the third grade have left by the fourth grade, replaced by others who were in the school only briefly before testing. Hence, test gains or losses may not reflect what happened in the school; percent proficient could rise or fall for reasons unrelated to what teachers and students did.

In response to these and other problems, the federal Department of Education permitted ten states to modify the measurement of "proficiency" by testing the same students' learning over time, rather than the original plan to compare test results for different cohorts of students at different points in time. It makes intuitive sense to assess students' learning on the basis of change in time since learning is dynamic, and it seems reasonable to expect better evidence on change in school performance from such measures. At the same time, there are deep problems with value-added assessment. Dale Ballou summed up a growing body of expert views when he wrote that "our instruments of assessment are not precise or dependable enough for this purpose . . . 1) current methods of testing don't measure gains very accurately; 2) some of the gains may be attributable to factors other than the quality of a given school or teacher; and 3) we lack a firm basis for comparing gains of students of different levels of ability."[45] In addition, when tests are not deeply grounded in curricula, the chances grow that students will be tested on things that they did not study and that their scores will not be a valid measure of their academic accomplishment. This problem, like the others associated with standards and testing, results from the imposition of rigid policy requirements and ambitious aims on school systems that were instructionally weak and lacked the technical capability for tests and standards that the policy required. The lack of valid measures of students' learning is a fundamental problem for standards-based reform.[46] Absent such measures, NCLB's legitimacy will be open to serious question, as will decisions about teachers, students, and schools that are made with existing measures.[47] NCLB seems to have specific aims when it requires that test scores be the criterion of schools' success, but the specificity is more apparent than real because the validity of the tests that the act requires is compromised.[48]

There also are several problems of fairness, the third difficulty mentioned above. One is that accountability focuses on professionals in an enterprise in which students do the work of learning. To make educators alone responsible for students' work, when learning is jointly produced, is difficult to justify ethically or educationally. In addition, such unbalanced accountability creates incentives for teachers to focus their work on students whose work can most easily be improved, rather than on those who have the most difficulty and who need much more help to improve. There is evidence that this is happening. A recent RAND study of the classroom effects of NCLB quoted an elementary school teacher in California:

> [T]he high-basic child that's almost proficient . . . that's what we call our target group. . . . Every teacher got a printout of their target group. Every teacher has about four to five kids in their class. We went over strategies on how to make sure you involve them and you get them involved. We talked about seating. These children should be closer up to you. Whenever another child answers a question, refer back to that student and make sure, "Can you tell me what the answer was?" or, "What did Johnny say?" and always keep those four to five kids questioning and making sure they're their target. They're the kids that we need to push up to proficient.[49]

A very different problem of fairness arises in comparisons among states. NCLB followed IASA by delegating to states the responsibility to decide on tests and to set criteria for "proficiency." The percentage of students who are proficient is NCLB's working definition of competent academic work and thus one potential measure of the policy's success. Delegation of these decisions to the states was politically expedient, but it meant that states could make those decisions to suit their political and educational preferences. The result has been great variability among states in the fraction of students who are "proficient." A few years ago, Texas reported that more than 80 percent of its students were proficient in fourth- and eighth-grade reading, while California, which also has many disadvantaged students, had proficiency rates in the 30 percent range for the same grades and subjects. The differences may be easy to understand as a political matter, but they are difficult to justify as fair, especially when damaging consequences for schools and teachers follow on low proficiency rates. Analysts increasingly see the state-to-state variation as a fundamental flaw in NCLB.[50]

School Improvement.   If students' work fails to satisfy state proficiency criteria, remedial action is required. NCLB creates a three-stage process to improve schools in which some or all groups of students do not achieve proficiency. All of these steps were previously set out in IASA, state reform policies, or both; the difference is that NCLB enclosed them in a rigid schedule of compliance. There is an odd contrast between the lack of knowledge about how to improve schools and the rigidity and specificity of NCLB's requirements. If a school fails to meet some or all proficiency targets for two consecutive years, it must be "identified" for improvement by the state. That requires the creation of a school improvement plan by school and district officials; the act specifies that all plans conform to a list of nine elements, which officials in the Department of Education seem to have treated as requirements.[51] Local and state staff also must improve the school's capacity by teaching teachers and school managers how to use students' work to improve instruction, how to identify and use strategies for better instruction, and how to align the school's budget with the school improvement plan.

If students' work does not improve and satisfy state proficiency criteria during these two years, the state must then place the school in "corrective action." State and local central office officials are expected to act more aggressively, and NCLB sets out a list of actions, and the school must choose from the menu, which includes selecting new curricula, reorganizing the school's operations, or allocating more time to instruction. If the school fails to meet state proficiency standards during the two years of corrective action (during which the state proficiency criteria have very likely been increasing), the school enters a two-year period of "restructuring." During this phase, the act requires that the state select one action from a new menu: close and reopen the school as a charter, take over direct operation of the school, replace the entire school staff, or turn management of the school over to a private agency.

School improvement plays a key role in NCLB's effectiveness: if most weak schools can be improved, the policy can deliver on its promise to create much better education in America's worst schools; if large numbers of schools cannot be improved, the policy will not have delivered on its promise. Yet the central role that school improvement plays in NCLB has not been matched either by the instruments that the act offers to support improvement or by the state and local response. The act envisions a division of labor in which the failing schools and districts carry out improvement, while expert planning, educational guidance, and funding come from the states. Thus, NCLB required each state to set aside 4 percent of its Title I Part A grant in a School Improvement Fund (SIF), to support improvement of identified schools between FY 2004 and 2007. Ninety-five percent of the fund must be allocated to local districts and schools for their use in improvement; schools and districts must apply for these grants, with the lowest-achieving and/or most needy schools having priority. The state retains 5 percent for use in managing the SIF, planning, and assisting and monitoring local improvement efforts.[52]

The act sets out detailed advice about how states should organize and administer their assistance: it requires each state to "establish a statewide system of intensive and sustained support and improvement for local educational agencies and schools receiving [Title I] funds, in order to increase the opportunity for all students . . . to meet the state's academic . . . achievement standards." Phyllis McClure, in a study of this aspect of NCLB, writes that "The architects of NCLB envisioned that this statewide system should consist of: (1) school support teams; (2) distinguished principals and teachers; and (3) collaboration with federally-funded regional technical assistance centers, higher education institutions, private providers of scientifically-based technical assistance, and other sources of expertise. The statute expresses a clear preference for school support teams."[53] These teams consist of "distinguished educators," parents, experts from higher education, and others; their tasks include everything from a detailed review of each school's operations and proposals for improvement to working with schools as they design and implement a plan, monitoring schools' implementation of the plan, and offering comments and advice at least twice a year. The federal Department of Education has treated these teams as a requirement under the law.[54]

These federal requirements are paradoxical in two respects: they are very prescriptive, despite the lack of much knowledge about how to improve schools, and the central importance of school improvement is not matched by the assistance that NCLB offers. The act presumes that most of the costs of school improvement will be paid from local and perhaps state funds, and that local grants from the state fund will cover expenses at the margin. "The grants supported by school improvement funds are short-term, uncertain, and modest, ranging from $15,000 to $85,000 for one year."[55] Since the grant application process is annual, in part because state Title I appropriations often vary annually as the eligible population changes, states advise localities not to put recurring staff costs on these grants but to use the funds to pay for part-time advisors, intermittent professional development, and similar things.

Thus, it is no surprise that analysts see deficiencies in the design for improving schools. Phyllis McClure, a strong advocate for NCLB, writes that "The one-size-fits-all approach to school improvement does not fit all. States need a repertoire of approaches. They need to diagnose schools' problems and issues before recommending or prescribing possible remedies. To do this, states need to build capacity. They cannot continue to rely on the same cadre of 'distinguished principals and teachers' to work with other schools when they are needed back in their home districts." She continues: "The shortcomings in states' capacity are not just a question of money, although expecting to operate a statewide system of *intense* and *sustained* support on 5 percent of the school improvement money is unrealistic. It is also a matter of developing the knowledge and the people that could provide an effective system that replicates successes."[56] McClure concludes: "the whole approach to improving the performance of low-achieving schools, as embodied in NCLB, does not seem to be equal to the task."[57]

Another, more detailed, study of school improvement under NCLB turned up problems in every aspect of the process. Most states reported that they were unable to extensively monitor local implementation and provide technical assistance; roughly four-fifths of the states reported that they lacked the staff and funds to properly perform these tasks.[58] Depending on the strategies in question, between 19 and 39 percent of states reported that they did not know how effective the strategies to improve schools were; one state official said: "We do not have adequate data to determine most effective intervention strategies."[59] Though district officials often had positive reports on aspects of their school improvement work, more than one-third said they lacked the capability to do what NCLB required for corrective action and restructuring. Half of those districts reported that they lacked the money and staff to replace all or most school staff, and 40–50 percent reported that they lacked the money, staff, or expertise to reopen schools as charters or to use a private firm to manage a school.[60] Districts that reported success with restructuring often used other strategies than those urged by the act.[61] NCLB has had quite constructive effects in prompting much more state and local attention to school improvement, but these studies reveal pervasive weaknesses in the instruments that the act deploys and in the capability of schools, school systems, and state education agencies to improve low-achieving schools.

The Search for Proficiency.   A similar paradox marks efforts to discern NCLB's effect on students' learning: the act mobilizes unprecedented pressure to boost academic performance, but it is difficult to arrive at valid estimates of those effects, owing to the weakness of capability in the act's instruments, in practice, and in the environment. There is, for example, evidence that students' performance on state and local tests has improved; this makes sense, for those are the tests that count in state accountability schemes and thus are the tests that teachers attend to. But they also are the tests whose cut points for passing have been set quite low in many states, and they are the tests for which many teachers work hard to prep students. There is considerable evidence that schools and school systems have reduced the time and effort that teachers devote to subjects other than reading and math, and many teachers spend more time preparing students to take the tests.[62] These conditions alone would be sufficient to create serious doubt about whether state test results reflect the ambitious academic work that the policies promoted.

Several sorts of variation in proficiency reinforce these doubts. The one that has received the most attention concerns the criteria for proficiency that states set. Many states have either used less demanding tests, or set cut points for proficiency low, or both. That approach permits states to report very large proportions of students as "proficient" and to reduce the state's obligations in school improvement. In the fall of 2008, only 8 percent of Mississippi's schools were rated as "in need of improvement," as were only 10 percent of Alabama's; these are among the poorest states in the nation, with many of disadvantaged students and weak schools. In contrast, Massachusetts, with one of the strongest state systems and a much more prosperous population, rated 48.6 percent of its schools in need of improvement, and Connecticut, with a strong state system, a long history of improvement, and a prosperous population, rated 29 percent of its schools as requiring improvement. Both of the latter states have much more demanding standards and steeper criteria for proficiency than do Alabama and Mississippi.[63]

The approach that Alabama and other states took makes a certain sense, for weak instructional capability encourages officials in many states and localities to relax standards and penalties to create the appearance of success rather than to stiffen standards and penalties and expand failures in practice. To do otherwise is to produce growing numbers of failing schools and to increase the burden of school improvement for precisely those states and localities that are the weakest and whose schools need the most attention. But it hardly promotes the ambitious teaching and learning that NCLB announced as its aim. The less seriously states take NCLB's ambitious academic aims, the more they are rewarded with less imposing school improvement requirements. In this respect as in others, the design of the law undermines its professed aims.

NCLB's authors saw that such discrepancies were likely and required all states to administer the NAEP in grades four and eight and to report students' NAEP scores along with scores on state tests. The idea was that NAEP tests would provide an independent and demanding comparison for state scores, either encouraging the states to play it straight or at least informing the public about the possible weakness of state tests. There have been several studies of the relationship between scores on NAEP tests and scores on the tests that states use to measure students' performance. The Institute of Education Sciences (IES), the federal education research agency, concluded in a study of state tests and NAEP scores in 2005 that "there is a weak relationship between states' percent [of students] proficient and states' performance on NAEP."[64] The study also showed that many states in which most students were "proficient" or better on state tests—Texas and Mississippi are examples—scored well below "basic" on the relevant NAEP test. On the fourth-grade reading NAEP test, all but a half-dozen states had average scores below basic.[65] These often-stark differences between NAEP and state tests further erode confidence in estimates of NCLB's effect on learning.

Comparisons with the NAEP, however, are not necessarily the most suitable. One problem is that the NAEP tests are carefully designed to not align with particular state standards or curricula; hence, the NAEP very likely includes material that students did not study and were unlikely to learn. To use it as a standard against which to judge the difficulty of state tests or levels of student performance is therefore dubious—unless one takes the NAEP tests to be representative of what every student should learn. Though some Americans do see the NAEP that way, Robert Linn, one of the nation's most distinguished experts on testing, has shown that the NAEP standards for proficiency are so steep that they are not achieved by most students, even in school systems that regularly outperform the United States on cross-national studies of achievement.[66] Thus to compare state performance levels with those on the NAEP almost certainly overstates the weakness of student performance in most states.

Researchers at the Northwest Evaluation Association (NWEA) tried to solve this problem by creating proficiency levels that were aligned with state standards, but were independent of how states set proficiency on their own tests. Because the NWEA has a very large bank of test items, it was able to fashion criteria of proficiency that were aligned with state standards but as independent of state tests as the NAEP. The result is a more accurate view of the quality of state criteria of academic proficiency than NAEP.

The NWEA found several sorts of differences between proficiency on its own tests and those of the state tests. It found variation among states in the difficulty level at which they set proficiency standards in the same subject and grade; the NWEA asked whether proficiency levels were consistent and comparable among states:

> The answer is no.... In 3rd grade reading, for example, estimated minimum proficiency scores were calculated for 12 of the 14 states. These ranged from the 67th percentile (South Carolina...) to the 13th percentile (Colorado & Texas...).... In 8th grade reading, estimated cut scores were also available for 12 states. These showed greater range with the highest cut score set at the 74th percentile (Wyoming...) and the lowest at the 12th percentile (Colorado...). Six states set their 8th grade standard near the low end of the range with proficiency scores ranging from the 32nd to the 38th percentile.[67]

The NWEA also noted that "a pattern of greater consistency seems to be emerging. Prior studies have found large differences in state proficiency standards. We discovered similar differences in range, still we found that many state standards did cluster in a fairly narrow range of difficulty, particularly in reading."[68]

Still, the differences often create sharp interstate differences in proficiency:

> An 8th grade student who can correctly answer items like sample question 1 would achieve the highest performance level in Arizona, Oregon, and Montana. That same student would not be assured of achieving the minimum proficiency score in Wyoming, a state in which students must perform at the 89th percentile equivalent to receive that designation.... [I]t is clear that the differences among the standards reflect dramatically different visions of what it means to be proficient.[69]

Within states, the NWEA also found that proficiency was not consistent and comparable within subjects across grades. In such cases, proficiency for a lower elementary grade was set at levels that were inconsistent with those set for an upper elementary grade, such that students who were judged proficient in grade three would, even if they maintained the same position in percentile rankings relative to their age, be far from proficient in grade eight. Proficiency levels also were quite different across academic subjects: "In all states but Oregon, the proficiency standard set for mathematics was more difficult than the standard for reading. In a few states the difference was very large. In Arizona . . . the mathematics proficiency score would not be achieved by about 75% of our norm group, while only 47% would not achieve the minimum score in reading."[70]

The NWEA researchers conclude that NCLB "leaves it to states to determine the level of performance that reflects adequate preparation or proficiency. From the evidence we and others have collected so far, it is clear that there are very large differences in the difficulty of the various state proficiency standards." The report continues: "It is not rational to reconstitute some schools because all students didn't get to the 80th percentile [in the NWEA national sample] in mathematics and simultaneously reward schools in other states that are barely making Adequate Yearly Progress toward a standard set at the 20th percentile. We do not act purposefully if we set artificially low standards at third grade that prevent us from identifying students who need help to reach the standard at eighth. It does not seem prudent to expect students to achieve math performance that college students might find challenging while setting standards in reading that are not equivalent to the level of performance required to read a daily newspaper."[71]

The chief result of this situation is that it is impossible to get valid answers to the question that NCLB defines as the most important: what are its effects on students' learning? NAEP tests are the only available national criterion measures against which to weigh state results, but they are criteria of doubtful validity for the reasons sketched above. There have been some improvements in some state and local test results, but the gains are modest at best, and there are good reasons to doubt that they represent anything like the ambitious academic work that NCLB announced. Scores on the fourth-grade math NAEP tests have improved appreciably, but that improvement far predates NCLB, and the gains seem to have fallen off in the few years following the act's passage. NAEP fourth-grade reading scores also have improved, but only slightly, and the eighth-grade NAEP results have been close to flat.[72]

There is, however, nothing in these results that can confidently be traced to NCLB and much to suggest that influences on NAEP scores are older, broader, and more diffuse than NCLB. One possible explanation for improved math scores, for example, is that new math curricula helped classroom work to improve. Another is that mathematics is more sensitive to instruction in the United States than reading, because math skills depend less on family literacy than reading and thus are less vulnerable to the educational disadvantages that accompany poverty. Still another explanation is that continuing messages of concern about weak education and pressure for more demanding academic work encouraged many educators to respond. The governance of U.S. schools was carefully designed to make them vulnerable to public pressure at the same time that it protected them from central power, and that was no less true in the 1990s than in the 1890s. The concern about academic performance that the reform movement began to mobilize in the 1980s filtered into public education and probably influenced practice. Though the policies were weak, they helped to strengthen a climate of opinion that encouraged reform.[73]

Here again, NCLB is paradoxical. It played an important constructive role by calling attention to serious inequality in school performance, but neither the act nor most states and localities have the technical capability needed to produce either valid criteria of proficiency or accurate estimates of how many students achieved it. The paradox would be less troublesome if large amounts of teachers' and students' work, state and local money, and public perceptions of the schools were not strongly influenced by the flawed testing technology that NCLB brought to bear.

The collision among NCLB's rigid regulatory regime, weak technical capability in measurement, and weak school systems created a policy context marked by high risk and low capability. One result is that an act that championed demanding academic work has promoted something like the opposite in many states and localities; as we wrote earlier, the design of the statute is at odds with its announced aims. Another is that educators are spending enormous effort to achieve goals and correct problems that, in many cases, are likely to be incorrectly defined; NCLB requires action for which adequate technical instruments do not exist.

Public schools were long a focus of hope in American life, but standards-based reform added a dose of something potentially poisonous: government responsibility for student failure on tests of achievement. If the poison provoked the improvement that policies promise, the reassignment of risk will have been a sort of educational digitalis, a stimulant that is constructive in judicious doses. As IASA and NCLB required states, localities, and schools to take responsibility for students' learning, they moved policy much closer to the heart of public education. That was a dramatic and in some respects a progressive move, for it brought the problems that teachers and students face nearer to front and center in policy, politics, and public life. Weak teaching, school leadership, reading curricula, and many related matters became front-page news and grist for federal and state policy and politics.

Yet NCLB prescribed doses that were too large for states and LEAs to handle; the reasons include weakness in the policy's instruments, an inappropriate testing technology, weak capability in schools and school systems, and a regulatory regime that made the operating agencies the regulators of their own behavior. These things led to real and apparent practice failure, eroded the schools' legitimacy, and damaged policy and its sponsors. Tough regulation might have been appropriate if there had been substantial evidence that schools and school systems had, or could quickly develop, the capability to respond to regulation. But the evidence, before and since NCLB's passage, points to a systemic lack of capability. As a result, the legislation has had a cascade of perverse effects. In many schools and classrooms, tests have become a protocurriculum, and teachers spend weeks drilling students on test questions. The less seriously states take the law's academic ambitions, and the weaker they make their tests and criteria of proficiency, the less effort they must make to improve schools. There are incentives for teachers to focus on the students whose work can most easily be improved, ignoring those who need the most help. The success of standards-based reform depends not just on reassigning the risk of failure but on building the capability to teach and learn; thus far the policies have not done that on anything like the required scale.

Build Educational Infrastructure

There are a few examples of how the creation of educational infrastructure has helped to improve schools. One concerns a few of the Comprehensive School Reform Designs. Like standards-based reform, America's Choice and Success for All sought much improved achievement and much less unequal school outcomes. But unlike standards-based reform, AC and SFA intervened directly to change what went on inside schools: they offered improved curricula, teacher education, changed school organization, expanded leadership for instruction and leadership education, tutoring for especially weak students, and more. Advocates of standards-based reform assumed that schools would respond constructively as long as the exoskeleton of standards, tests, and accountability was properly designed and implemented. If so, there would be no need to meddle with what happened inside schools; that could be left to educators. In contrast, AC and SFA were premised on the view that the educational problems in high-poverty schools were so profound that they could be solved only by direct, sustained, and comprehensive intervention in schools and classrooms; these two CSRDs created infrastructure to support improved teaching and learning. If standards-based reform assumed that schools' problems could be solved by vigorous external regulation, the CSRDs assumed that those problems could be solved only by directly changing teaching, learning, school organization, and other elements of schools' educational programs.[74]

SFA and AC produced impressive changes in instruction; for example, Brian Rowan and his colleagues found that "across grades 3–5 in our study, students in SFA schools experienced about 28% more reading comprehension instruction (341 days versus 265) than did students in comparison schools. Similarly, students in AC schools experienced about 36% more writing instruction (264 days versus 194) than students in the comparison schools."[75] These changes were reflected in gains in students' performance. "An average student beginning our study at the 30th percentile in a comparison school, for example, finished the end of 2nd grade at about the 40th percentile. The SFA effect moved a comparable student in the average SFA school from the 30th percentile to the 50th percentile. Similar effects were observed for students in AC schools. In addition, the longer students were enrolled, and the better schools' implementation of these two models were, the stronger were students' achievement gains."[76] The other CSRD model that Rowan and his colleagues studied did not build comparable educational infrastructure, and did not produce gains of this sort.[77]

The two CSRD models and standards-based reform could reinforce each other, and for a time they did. It is very unlikely that SFA and AC could have found such a large market without the pressure for school improvement that the standards movement helped to create, and the two CSRDs helped schools to deliver on the aims of the reform policies. But the Obey-Porter amendment aside, those policies did not systematically provide for the creation and sustenance of the educational capability that several of the CSRDs helped to build, and they had much more difficulty in the wake of NCLB and then the economic collapse of 2008–2009.

Another example of infrastructure that helped to improve schools is the action that a few states took. Minnesota presents a well documented case, in which the state and non-governmental partners undertook a major effort to improve the teaching and learning of mathematics. In the mid-1990s the mathematics performance of students in the state was at about the U.S. average on the Third International Assessment of Mathematics and Science (TIMMS), but the U.S. average was quite low in comparison with other developed nations. Educators, political, and business leaders in the state undertook a major effort to improve math teaching and learning. The standards for math teaching were focused much more clearly on deeper work in a limited set of key mathematical topics; that was a major change from the much larger and more diffuse set of topics, which was conventional for mathematics in Minnesota and the rest of the United States. The standards were built so that the mathematics that they represented was intellectually coherent, within and across grades. State and local leaders and math educators used the standards to focus the mathematics curriculum, and teacher education was used to help teachers learn how to use the curriculum. Assessments were focused on the topics that fit with the standards and curriculum, and the results were made available to educators and the public.[78]

The effort produced more focused instruction and improved student performance. Teachers covered fewer topics in more depth, and students' achievement improved. In 1996, before the reform got going, 24 percent of the state's fourth grade students' math performance on the NAEP was "below basic," and 26 percent were "proficient"; in 2007 13 percent of the state's students were below basic, and 41 percent were proficient. 3 percent were "advanced" in 1996, as against 9 percent in 2007. In addition, the black-white achievement gap was slightly reduced for fourth graders: "In 2007, Black students had an average score that was lower than that of White students by 31 points. In 1992, the average score for Black students was lower than that of White students by 38 points."[79] But the results for grade eight math performance were less encouraging. The distribution of eighth grade average scores in 1996 was only a little different than those in the fourth grade that year, but by 2007 more eighth graders were below basic than fourth graders (19 percent), and fewer were proficient (32 percent).[80]

Unlike most states, Minnesota not only significantly raised standards for math instruction, but also created some elements of infrastructure—including curriculum, teacher education, and assessment—that enabled those at work in the schools to make constructive use of the standards. Yet the effort was far from unblemished. The black-white achievement gap widened in the eighth grade, rather than narrowing as it had in the fourth. In addition, in both the fourth and eighth grades, the average achievement differences between students at the 25th and 75th percentiles grew between 1996 and 2007; the reforms boosted average math performance, but at the expense of increased inequality in math performance.[81] And in the spring of 2009 the state legislature and the governor significantly weakened the state's reform agenda, by removing the requirement that high school students pass a series of demanding, high-stakes math tests in order to graduate. Now they can either pass the tests or fail them three times in order to graduate. This new standard will do a good deal to avoid embarrassing failures, but it is a sign that the schools have far to go to build the capability required to carry the reforms forward.[82]

A third, even more mixed case of the creation of educational infrastructure, is Reading First. NCLB created this program to strengthen reading in the lower elementary grades in high-poverty schools. It is the most directive federal education program in U.S. history: not only did it come close to requiring a curriculum for schools that sought and were awarded grants, but it also required the use of common assessments, common diagnostic tools for teaching and learning reading, and extensive support for reading teachers.[83] Reading First had some success in early reading, where, in addition to these elements of educational infrastructure, there also was a substantial body of knowledge and skill concerning the teaching and learning of phonemic awareness, word recognition, and related matters. In contrast, the program had no discernable success in improving students' reading comprehension, where knowledge, skill, and other elements of infrastructure were less well developed.[84]

There is more than one way to build infrastructure that can help schools to improve, but the examples have several common features. In each case, new instruments that significantly improved instructional capability were deployed, including curriculum, teacher education, and assessment. In each case, the design of intervention was significantly different than conventional education policy. The CSRDs not only designed comprehensive programs of instructional change and made them available to schools, but they also built organizations that offered those schools extensive and sustained help in learning to use the designs effectively. Minnesota used public and private agencies not only to devise new mathematics standards, but they also built coherent and focused standards, and benchmarked them to the curricula of the highest performing school systems in the world. This alone was very different than most other states. In addition, the state and its allies urged and assisted the translation of standards into curriculum, and organized sustained programs of teacher education and assessment to support the effective use of the curriculum. And Reading First combined a very prescriptive federal program with curriculum, assessments, supervision, evaluation, and well developed knowledge of how to teach early reading to affect practice in districts and schools that chose to participate. In all three cases, instruments were deployed and capability was built in ways that made it possible to connect ambitious policy with classroom practice.

At the same time, all three initiatives operated in an environment that is marked by pervasive inequality in public education, and that weakened the implementation not only of these three unusual initiatives, but also of IASA, NCLB, and many state standards-based reforms. The inequality arises in part from the educational resources that schools offer: money, teacher qualifications, and other things are quite unequal among districts in at least half of the states; they are quite unequal among schools, especially within urban districts; and they are very unequal among states.[85] High-poverty elementary schools, for instance, typically have fewer capable teachers, among many other educational resources.[86] Inequality arises in another part from the educational resources that students bring to school: on average, students from poor families are much less likely to have parents who read to them and help with homework, to have space at home in which to work quietly, and to have decent health care and nutrition. The schools and districts that have access to the most educational resources are likely to have the fewest students who are eligible for Title I, while the schools and districts with the most students who are eligible for Title I are likely to have access to fewer educational resources. Title I is no more than a supplement to these unequal local school programs. The quality of education that Title I can support depends on the schools that it supplements, and the education on which it builds is significantly weaker in less advantaged schools and districts. As a result, the schools' capability to make effective use of the instruments that IASA and NCLB deployed is quite unequal; the states, districts, and schools that IASA and NCLB press for the greatest improvement have fewer of the resources that could support a constructive response. Those schools, districts, and states also are likely to have more students who are less able on their own to make effective use of whatever educational resources their schools offer. IASA and NCLB made schools the chief agent for dealing with the educational effects of enormous social and economic inequalities that arose outside schools. The three cases that we just discussed show that when very aggressive efforts are made to build educational infrastructure, it is possible to overcome some effects of these inequalities. But in every case, the improvements were less than what had been intended, and the academic performance of children from poor, black and Hispanic families remained far below the average performance of advantaged white students.

Hawkins-Stafford, IASA, and NCLB brought sweeping change in education policy: they drew federal and state governments closer to the schools' operating core and focused more attention on problems there. That was progress for a program that aimed to improve teaching and learning, but the deepest problems in public education reside in that core; if those problems cannot be solved, it is unlikely that NCLB can succeed. High-poverty schools can improve, but in most cases improvement seems to require intensive, continuing assistance from capable outside agents that work closely with schools for years, offering detailed guidance and assistance in curriculum planning, the creation of new roles, improved and expanded leadership, and professional education. IASA offered a little assistance, and NCLB offered more help with building capability, but not a great deal more. Because the legislation used regulation of governments to try to shape practice in classrooms, it focused its strongest instruments on the state and local governments whose manifold weaknesses had been an essential source of poor education for generations, and focused its weakest instruments on building the capability to improve work in classrooms.

We found much that is constructive in the recent reformulations of Title I but also much that is not. Our aim, however, has not been to evaluate Title I or the new policies, let alone to judge how much NCLB contributed to improved student learning. Rather, we used the analytic framework that we set out in Chapter 2 to clarify the challenges NCLB and other standards-based policies faced in managing the dilemma of policy and practice. Examining these policies in terms of the aims, instruments, and capability that they mobilized led us to highlight what the new policies lack, especially an educational infrastructure that includes curricula, assessments, and teacher education.

Regulation is not an inherently defective strategy for educational improvement, but it is likely to be viable only if the regulatory instruments are appropriate to the aims, if the system to be regulated and agencies in the environment have or can soon develop the capability to respond constructively, and if regulatory agencies are independent of operating agencies. NCLB, like other standards-based reforms, does not do these things: its instruments are not nearly adequate to the policies' aims, the regulatory regime is incommensurate with most schools' and school systems' capability to respond, and the operating agencies also are the regulatory agencies. These elements of the design of these policies are at cross-purposes with the greatly improved teaching and learning that the policies seek.

CHAPTER 7

Title I: Past and Present

We promised to discuss how the weak Title I program of 1965 became today's aggressive program and why it is beset with such difficulty, has had such perverse effects, and has been so controversial. Here we pull together and develop the answers that we offered, bit by bit, in the preceding chapters. This discussion reaches beyond the issues that previously occupied students of Title I, for the program has been absorbed into larger ambitions; we can no longer understand Title I apart from the broader efforts to revise public education that Goals 2000, IASA, and NCLB undertook.

Our answer to the first question—how the weak program of 1965 became today's aggressive program—begins with Title I's vulnerability to developments in politics and society. Our account of how Title I changed has been chiefly a tale of how other ideas and claims shaped a program that lacked the means to shape itself educationally. One source of the program's vulnerability was also the source of Title I: it is a creature of government and thus open to the political influences that operate there. These influences included the movement from divided to unified government, changes in executive and legislative branch leadership, new political coalitions that included more conservatives and greater diversity among liberals, and shifts in ideology, especially about the role of government.

These things were important, and other scholars have appropriately drawn attention to them,[1] but there are other government programs, including some in education, that have been less vulnerable and have changed much less; Head Start and Impact Aid—neither of which are in the Education Department—are two such examples. This fact suggests limits on purely political explanations for Title I's vulnerability.

In addition, Title I was quite vulnerable to changing ideas—which include everything from beliefs about political principles to empirical evidence—about education. Political studies of Title I have attended to the role of ideas but primarily to ideas about the appropriate role of government. Ideas of this sort are manifested through ideological shifts and often find expression in policies like those that promote school choice and accountability standards. Such ideas are important, but other important ideas are specific to policy; for Title I, this includes ideas about teaching, learning, the effects of prior program implementation, how schools work, and what would make them work better.[2] Politics matters for such ideas, for policymakers, political groups, and policies themselves provide pathways for the expression of ideas and the transmission of knowledge.[3] Yet, without the particular ideas about education that played such an important role for Title I, the political arrangements and ideas about politics probably would have led elsewhere. The influence of education-specific knowledge and ideas suffuses the entire educational enterprise, including top policymakers' views of policy options.[4]

Either knowledge or its absence can be influential, and the lack of knowledge was one source of Title I's vulnerability: the program had no independent source of guidance for improving education and no authoritative basis to judge the quality of its educational work. The program lacked the means to systematically learn how to improve schools and thereby to change or confirm its actions. Title I's design as a federally funded but locally operated formula-grant program frustrated such learning, and federal legislators and executives failed to see how important systematic learning could be, educationally and politically, to add to the program's capability to learn from experience and validate program improvement.

No one can know what might have happened if Title I had systematically learned how to improve schools and validate its actions, but we do know that the program began with little knowledge about how to improve education for poor children and that few provisions were made to build that knowledge. The program created no agenda for learning, and few steps were taken to build knowledge about school improvement. Since systematic knowledge about how to improve education for disadvantaged students did not develop in the program, there was very little basis for either self-correction or authoritative claims about its effects in the national program and local operations. That left the program exceptionally vulnerable both to political changes and to others' ideas about how to improve education as well as to others' claims about its effectiveness.[5]

The earliest example of that vulnerability came in the form of challenges to the program's guiding ideas soon after Title I became law. One study reported that program funds were being misused, and an evaluation reported that Title I did not have the expected effects on students' test scores. In retrospect, we can say that these findings should have been no surprise, for there was little capability to improve education for poor children; educators and governments had long neglected that work. Title I tasked the people and organizations that had the problem with solving it, but most knew little about how to do so, and many cared less. It would have been amazing if broad change had been quickly made, but the program lacked the means even to make these elementary points. One result was early reports of practice failure, and another was changes in politics and policy. The reports of practice failure threatened Title I's political support, as advocates worried that the program was in trouble and opponents attacked it or called for more inquiries.

In the view of those who managed and championed Title I at the outset, educational capability was not the problem. Educators and politicians assumed that books, teachers, and other resources were potent independent influences on learning and that the money that bought these things would be a strong instrument; sending federal dollars seemed a plain way to help schools to turn themselves around. Confidence in these ideas was one reason the negative early evaluation evidence was such a shock. Another reason, and another shock, was research that seemed to show that the evaluation reports were well founded. In separate studies, James Coleman, Christopher Jencks, and their colleagues showed that differences in schools' educational resources were weakly related to differences in their average student performance. That seemed to mean that Title I's effort to improve schools by sending money was misguided. The combination of these studies put the program on the defensive. Liberal supporters were surprised and outraged; many attacked social research, and some Democrats in Congress who supported Title I became skeptics about research. Some conservatives took comfort in the results, used them to buttress their doubts about Title I, and became fans of research.

Two studies that were done in the 1970s, in response to these developments, found that Title I did have modest positive effects on students' scores. Though they revealed limitations in the earlier research that provoked doubts about Title I, the later studies also were limited. They were one-shot efforts, not part of an ongoing program to build knowledge about improving education for disadvantaged students and using that knowledge to inform the program. Title I had been presented as the answer to a pressing question—how to improve education for the children of poor families?—but in operation it provoked many more questions than it answered. Since the program made no continuing effort to answer the questions and had no way to validate the effectiveness of approaches to improving education, it was regularly on the defensive.

Another influence to which the program was vulnerable was change in the policy environment. In the 1970s, for example, state governments began to require students to acquire minimum competencies or basic skills. States tried to regulate learning and teaching by requiring outcomes and offering students disincentives for failure. The policies expressed a mixture of impatience with conventional resource allocation, concern about weak achievement in schools that served poor students, and hostility to educational practices of the 1960s that were seen as permissive. The policies were not a great success, but they set a new direction: state governments would shape educational practice by direct regulation of outcomes.

Still another influence was new knowledge about how schools worked. In response to Coleman's and Jencks's studies, several academics undertook to figure out how schools did affect learning. They showed that resources mattered but that the effects depended on their use: different schools and teachers did different things with the same resources, with different effects on learning. To discern those effects, researchers had to identify educational practices and link them to resources on one side and outcomes on the other. One implication was that if one wished to influence educational outcomes, intervention in practice was more likely to pay off than just sending money. Another was that if the effects of resources depended on their use, then practice would influence how policies turned out. And if that was so, then the classic instruments of education policy—funding and regulation—were not as potent as had been thought, because their effects would depend on their use in practice. That was not good news for Title I.

The new knowledge shook inherited views about the power of conventional policies, but it fit nicely with state policymakers' efforts to regulate learning. Most important for our purposes, the new policies and research took a very different direction than the one that was built into Title I's formula grant and federal dependence on state and local use of federal money: if Title I was to work, it would have to find ways to intervene in practice. The Title I program did not produce these ideas, but such ideas held great importance for the program.

A particularly important influence on Title I was a dramatic change in ideas about the problem that it was to solve. Several studies had revealed large differences in average achievement between black and white students and between advantaged and disadvantaged students. Those differences had been known by school officials and some researchers but had not been public knowledge before the passage of Title I and the publication of Coleman's 1966 report. They pointed to a large problem: schools were supposed to be the guarantor of equal opportunity in the United States, but opportunity seemed far from equal when class and race were so closely associated with school outcomes. If Title I could not solve that problem, what good was it? Cross-national studies in the late 1970s and early 1980s showed that students in the United States performed less well, on average, than those in Japan and other nations. That made the poor performance of Title I students seem to be only part of a larger problem—that is, a school system that did poorly for most Americans.

These ideas might not have had much political traction by themselves, but they gained some from the belief that the United States faced serious economic problems that were related to education. The economy did poorly in the late 1970s, with very high interest rates, inflation, and economic stagnation. Business leaders and researchers began to argue, in the late 1970s and early 1980s, that if the economy was to improve, it had to move into the "information age," in which workers would need more brains than brawn. That was thought to mean that a school system that had been oriented chiefly to the basics would have to reorient itself to much more ambitious and demanding work.

These ideas also did not stem from Title I, but they had a large impact on public education and on the program. They were taken to mean that both economic and educational problems might be solved by fundamental change in schools: if schools offered the demanding academic work for which *A Nation at Risk* argued, students would be much better educated and could do the more demanding jobs that would move America into the information age and make it more competitive in the world. Change in schools could change the economy. If so, that might be just the thing for the achievement gap. Hence, even though research in the 1970s reported the good news that Title I had modest positive effects, that was also bad news, since the gains were so modest compared with the gap. In that light, more demanding standards, tests, and accountability seemed promising; Title I students might benefit more from measures that would fundamentally change education than from the program's own modest resources.

The new ideas had broad appeal. They linked the educational problems of poor children to problems that most American students were said to have. If their problems were the same, special-purpose programs for the minority of students who were poor or black should seek the same ends, and use the same methods, as programs for all American students. That was an enormous change both for Title I and for education policy in general. Quality and equality, excellence and equity, could be partners rather than opponents.

These developments set the stage for dramatic change in Title I, even though their sources lay far outside the program. By the middle and late 1980s, business and civic leaders were gaining recognition and public approval for criticism of school problems—they claimed that the nation suffered from fundamental deficiencies of school quality—and for proposed changes. Politicians began to find a payoff in such work. Texas, California, and Kentucky adopted standards-based reforms in the mid- and late 1980s; for the first time in the nation's history, schools would be shaped by academic standards, the schools' quality would be judged by students' performance on tests that would embody the standards, and schools would be accountable for students' performance. The education of disadvantaged students was increasingly portrayed as part of that larger problem; in a paper that first circulated in the late 1980s, Marshall Smith and Jennifer O'Day argued that "systemic reform" could solve both the larger problems of low quality in many U.S. schools and the particular problems of students from poor families.

In 1988, the Hawkins-Stafford amendments to Title I responded in part to these influences: federal oversight would focus on students' learning, and schools would be held accountable for improving that learning. That was a fundamental change in Title I, and it was due both to political developments outside the program and to the lack of independent and systematic evidence on the program's operation and effects. It was only the beginning. After the 1989 Charlottesville Summit, the National Panel on Educational Goals further developed and publicized the reform ideas. Several states adopted the new policies. IASA and Goals 2000 followed in 1994 and NCLB in 2002. These federal statutes changed Title I profoundly: improved education for disadvantaged students would henceforth depend on states' use of standards, tests, and accountability to improve schools. The effects of Title I would turn on how well a new and untried policy framework worked in practice. That rested a great deal on the strength and salience of three regulatory instruments: tests, standards, and accountability.

That was a problem, for little in the new policy instruments could connect with practice, and little in Title I could help. The program was still a formula grant and a near entitlement, and it had very modest leverage because it was still a modest supplement to very unequally distributed state and local educational resources. Neither the instruments of standards-based reform nor those of Title I had strong or salient connections with practice. The new policies had revolutionary ambitions for schools, but the instruments that they deployed were far from commensurate with those ambitions.

That problem seems not to have been clear to those who urged and made policy in the 1980s and 1990s. One reason may have been that the changes were so sweeping that those involved did not understand very well what they would entail. Reformers and policymakers could not draw on the experience of nations outside the United States, for no school systems had the relationships that these reforms proposed. Many systems had examinations that determined students' access to secondary school, and they had high school leaving examinations that determined their access to further education and occupations. But none of those systems had standards of the sort that American reformers proposed, though all of them had some version of an educational infrastructure. None had the sorts of tests that U.S. schools used, and none had anything remotely like the accountability schemes that the reformers proposed. Moreover, most of the other systems, like those in Singapore, France, or Germany, were very selective: examinations at the end of elementary school determined students' secondary education, and examinations at the end of secondary school determined what further education, if any, students would have. None of these three systems, or others like them, offered equal access to a great range of students from a great range of economic and social backgrounds, as U.S. reformers proposed. There were no school systems that resembled those that policy sought to create, from which advocates and policymakers in the United States might have learned.

Those advocates and policymakers also could not draw on personal experience, because, like most Americans, they were products of the schools that were to be reformed; few had been students in the sorts of ambitious schools for which these policies called, because there were few such schools. Few could have much idea of what would be entailed for students, and even fewer had worked in systems in which such education was offered. They could have had little idea of what would be involved for teachers and school managers.

Finally, advocates and policymakers could not learn from previous efforts to make the sort of changes that they were proposing. There never had been a nation that even remotely resembled the United

States that had attempted to graft anything that remotely resembled the proposed system onto its fragmented and decentralized school system. There simply was no evidence about whether such a system transplant could work or what might be required to make it work.

These were extraordinary deficiencies of knowledge, yet they seemed to encourage credulity rather than caution. Instead of inspiring doubt in the minds of advocates and policymakers or provoking efforts to try the changes on a modest scale and learn from what happened, ignorance seems to have encouraged advocates and policymakers to think that once a new framework of standards, tests, and accountability was built, educators and students would do as they were told. A few advocates saw that teacher education and curricula would have to be invented to bridge the gap between the framework and practice, but they did not present that as a serious problem. There were no signs that advocates and policymakers suspected that major problems were certain to arise.[6]

The new policies were a faith-based initiative: they rested on neither strong evidence nor extensive experience but rather on an extraordinary belief in the power of particular policies. More precisely, Title I owed its new form to a potent combination of despair, hope, and ignorance: despair about schools and the modest gains that they had produced with Title I; hope for better education for all American students, but especially those from poor families, and for an entirely new sort of policy; and ignorance about the problems that policy was certain to encounter. Policymakers and educators now struggle with the consequences.

The second question that we have tried to answer is why the new Title I has been so difficult to implement and so controversial. Our answer is best framed in three paradoxes. One concerns government. IASA and NCLB were to bring coherence to education by creating rational relationships among academic standards, educational processes, and outcomes: academic standards would express educational content and outcomes; owing to their accountability, educators would orient schools to those outcomes; and tests would check on performance and provide targets for improvement. Yet this system was to be put into practice in many thousands of state and local jurisdictions and individual schools, which had long been fragmented and weak and in which schools, teachers, and districts had great autonomy. IASA and NCLB were to turn an extraordinarily fragmented educational nonsystem into fifty coherent systems in which teaching and learning followed standards and tests. Yet they would do this by changing policy alone, with no change in the fragmented governance. Changed political arrangements contributed to the passage of IASA and NCLB and created a much more assertive role for the federal government, but those changes in policy were not matched with parallel changes to correct the effects of government fragmentation, such as the development of common curricula; substantial improvement in state and local capability to manage teaching, curricula, and the design and oversight of teacher education; and consistency among these things. All of these and other matters related to classrooms were, of course, thought to be off limits to the central government. The political system that caused the incoherence was to implement IASA and NCLB. This returns us to the dilemma: the fragmented governments that caused the incoherence that policy sought to correct would be the chief agents for implementing policies that sought to create coherence.

Governments alone could not deliver on that assignment. The collision of ambitious policy with government incoherence and weak capability led to considerable inconsistency among the states' standards and tests. In most cases, there also is considerable inconsistency between the standards and tests that each state requires. There also is considerable inconsistency between each state's standards and tests, on the one hand, and curricula, on the other. And there are similar inconsistencies among districts, within states, in curricula. These inconsistencies have been the basis for continuing controversy about the extent of the policies' implementation, and they are among the main sources of implementation problems. These things should have been no surprise, for the policies dealt not with the structural basis of incoherence in government and the private sector, but with its manifestation in tests and standards. The fragmented organization of U.S. public education suffused implementation of IASA and NCLB with symptoms of the disease that they were meant to cure.

A second paradox concerns capability. Successful implementation of the new policies would require extensive knowledge, skill, and determination to improve teaching and learning, new technologies of assessment, and much more, if they were to have the intended effects; but it was precisely the absence of that capability that explained why the schools had not previously improved. Advocates argued that this was because schools had not been held accountable for student learning, with appropriate penalties and rewards, and had no common standards for what should be taught and learned. If they had such standards, and were accountable, educators would know what to teach, they would have incentives to teach as standards and tests proposed, and students would learn more.

Yet if educators were to make effective use of the new policies, a great deal would have to change. New standards would have to be devised. New assessments, consistent with the standards, would have to be created. Curricula that were consistent with the standards and assessments would have to be created. These things would only be the beginning, for educators would have to learn how to use the new standards, assessments, and curricula effectively. That would be a huge assignment, for no states and very few local school systems had the know-how to help teachers learn how to help their students to do much better work, and very few school managers knew how to oversee such work. Very few faculty members in education schools and departments knew much about how to improve teaching or leadership in high-poverty schools. Staffers in state departments, local school systems, and research agencies had little knowledge or know-how about how to sharply improve high-poverty schools.

Fundamental changes would be required. An infrastructure of curriculum, professional education, and assessment would have to be built; practitioners at all levels of the education system would have to acquire a great deal of new knowledge and know-how concerning teaching, management, and school improvement; and to do these things they would have to unlearn many familiar practices. Accomplishing all this would require extensive learning for organizations and individuals, and that could not occur without systematic efforts to enable such learning, in professional education and research on implementation.

As an historical matter, Title I had helped to build the capability to solve problems of poverty in public education. If we compare the situation in 1965 with that when NCLB became law, by 2002 many more educators had experience trying to improve teaching in high-poverty schools, and many more school managers had experience managing such efforts. There were many problems, but there had been gains in capability. The most convincing evidence comes from studies that show that, despite being a modest supplement for schools with many weaknesses, Title I modestly improved students' learning.[7]

Yet, practitioners' capability is always relative to the task at hand, not to that of the past, and IASA and NCLB dramatically expanded those tasks and increased their difficulty. The new policies opened a great distance between policy aims and practice, without creating the capability that would enable effective implementation; hence, great incompetence was created in practice, and the risks of practice failure and contagion to policy and politics grew. IASA created this unprecedented distance between policy and practice, but because compliance was left open, the risks of practice failure, and the threats to policy, were not acute. NCLB changed that by rigidly specifying tight compliance schedules and targets, greatly increasing incompetence in practice and the risks of failure in practice and policy. The new policies required much more practical, professional, and scientific knowledge than did their predecessors; otherwise, schools, states, and districts could not deliver on the outcomes for which they were now accountable. How could systems that lacked so much capability, and had failed millions of children, quickly acquire the capability to make them succeed?

A third paradox concerns excellence and equality. IASA and NCLB required states to set high standards for academic performance and to use tests and accountability to guide and encourage that performance. Yet, academic excellence was quite unfamiliar, even in most schools that were relatively untouched by poverty: most local school systems offered a modest basic education for most students while sometimes offering more substantial fare to a few students who showed special talent or to a few families that demanded more. Schools in the U.S. mainstream never aspired to offer ambitious work on a large scale, so the capability for mass educational excellence did not exist.

Yet at the same time that school outcomes were to improve for all, states were required to make average school outcomes equal among races and social classes. If academic excellence was largely unfamiliar in the educational mainstream, it was even less familiar in the high-poverty schools that Title I served. School funding is unequal among districts within at least half of the states, and it is quite unequal among the states. The schools that poor students attend are much more likely to have less adequate resources than the schools that children from affluent families attend. Money alone cannot cure weak schools, but a chief source of academic weakness in these schools is the badly educated teachers and poor working conditions that inadequate revenues and local teacher assignment practices underwrite.

Families and communities also provide educational resources, including help with reading and writing, encouragement for academic success, and time and space in which to work. Many Title I students suffer from poor health and nutrition, inadequate housing, and absent or distracted parents, among other things. These effects of poverty reflect enormous income inequality, a long history of discrimination, and policies in employment, housing, and health care that do little to remedy the problems. Decades of research have shown that social and economic inequality is a major source of race and class inequality in student achievement. Could schools eliminate average race and class achievement differences while at the same time holding all students to high standards, when the schools, students, communities, and families in question suffer from large, and sometimes huge, class and racial inequality in educational resources, and the capability for mass educational excellence did not exist?

IASA's and NCLB's press for equality of excellence in academic outcomes is profoundly at odds with the unequal conditions of education in the United States. Neither policy was paired with policies that supported improved employment, better health care, and early education, nor did either make a substantial effort to reduce unequal educational resources among schools within districts, among districts within states, or among states. The two bills addressed public education as though schools could dramatically change their operations quite in isolation from the political, social, and economic sources of educational problems.

In fact, in the 1980s and 1990s, as policymakers pressed schools to eliminate unequal outcomes, Republican and Democratic politicians held the line or cut back on social policies that redressed poverty and inequality, including school desegregation, support for health care and child care, public assistance, education and employment programs, and early education. Politicians reduced social and economic support for academic learning as they increased demands on schools for academic learning. Could standards, accountability, and tests reverse the educational effects of the economic, social, and educational disadvantages that burden students and schools and create learning that is, on average, equal to that for students who have many economic, social, and educational advantages?

The answer to our second question—why has the new Title I been so difficult to implement, had such perverse effects, and been so controversial?—is that the new policy aims of equality and excellence collided with weak capability, limited policy instruments, and very unequal access to educational resources, to create unprecedented incompetence in educational practice. That led to many unexpected effects, to intense controversy, and to a large-scale exercise in defining excellence down. As state and federal agencies pressed schools to set demanding criteria for "proficiency" and to meet them, most responded by setting modest or low standards on tests.

It is one of the great curiosities of the age that Title I, a modest supplement to a very unequal system of schooling, was used as the lever to remedy the educational effects of an extraordinarily fragmented system of education, which lacked the educational infrastructure that could connect policy and practice. That is a chief source of the difficulty and controversy that bedevil Title I and a chief cause of its very mixed effects. It is not a reason to abandon efforts to improve education, either for children from poor families or for everyone else. It is a reason to recognize that the problems that have plagued Title I are unlikely to be dealt with satisfactorily unless the solutions are paired with efforts to address the paradoxes much more directly. That implies the creation of much more adequate infrastructure and the reduction of inequality. We take up these matters in the next chapter.

CHAPTER 8

Epilogue: What Is to Be Done?

Title I faces many problems. Some have been with the program from the outset, most prominently including its difficult role as a modest supplement to very unequal schools, and the absence of the educational infrastructure that might have permitted more effective influence on teaching and learning. Others have been the result of recent policies that used Title I to try to make fundamental change in education without the instruments and capability that such change would require.

In this chapter we consider possible solutions, both to the problems at which Title I has aimed from the outset, and the problems that resulted from the collision among ambitious policies, unsuitable instruments, and weak capability. To do this we consider other leading approaches to solving those problems. How might other reform initiatives help solve the problems that Title I has run into, and which seem most promising?

This is no small task. We do not set out a reform program, but sketch how our earlier analysis can shed light on current efforts to make the improvements in public education that Title I sought. We offer no new evidence, but review existing scholarship in light of our analysis of the relations between policy and practice.

We discuss several leading reform initiatives. Some aim to improve human capital in school systems; others aim to fundamentally change the political control and management of urban school systems; still others seek radical change in failing schools; and others focus on the creation of new schools and school systems. Finally, there is standards-based reform, which began with a few states in the 1980s, moved to the federal level with IASA and NCLB, and now seems to be moving back to the states with the recent initiative of the National Governors Association (NGA) and the Council of Chief State School Officers (CCSSO). These are not the only current efforts to improve schools, but they are the most important. They also are not independent of each other: Title I/NCLB is overdue to be reauthorized, and the form that takes is likely to influence everything else. These five initiatives include government and non-government interventions, but we view them all in roughly the same terms as we discussed education policy in the preceding chapters. Each intervention has aims; each deploys instruments to shape public education; and practitioners' response to each depends on the capability that they, and agencies in the environment, bring to the work.

But before we consider these, we probe how the current political and economic situation is likely to shape both Title I and related efforts to improve education. The political and economic environment has had an enormous influence on Title I in the past, including deep political divisions over federal and state authority, the political requirement of broad and thin distribution of Title I funds, and the vastly unequal educational foundations on which Title I has to build. Such things are likely to influence the more recent reform initiatives as well.

The Political and Economic Context of Reform

We write in May and June 2009, at an extraordinary time. Though public schools are under the greatest pressure to improve, from the greatest variety of sources than ever before, those pressures bear on schools at a time of deep economic and political stress. Some state and local systems have been hit very hard by the budget cuts that followed the economic collapse of late 2008 and early 2009. Jobs are being lost and poverty grows. These developments increase uncertainty and constrain capability.

Under the American Recovery and Reinvestment Act (ARRA), also known as "the stimulus package," states are receiving, among other funds, $10 billion of additional Title I aid, and $44 billion of state funding and stabilization funds (SFSF).[1] These represent "a historic infusion of funds that is expected to be temporary. Depending on the program, these funds are available for only two to three years."[2] The money is intended to save jobs in education, and will help to protect students and teachers in the Title I program. The ARRA forbids states from reducing educational expenditures below 2006 levels for the two years of the Act's duration. Despite that, many teachers and central office staff are being laid off, and many school systems are downsizing, slashing payrolls, and closing schools. The cuts and layoffs will help school systems survive the current crisis, but they are unlikely to enhance their capability to improve. In addition to the sheer effects of lost people, the situation has increased uncertainty.

One reason is that the ARRA funds are limited to two years. Will there be more federal money after that? The Department of Education expects the money to be "temporary." Will school systems use either the additional Title I funds or other stimulus money to develop improvement programs that would end in two years, and hire people who would be let go in two years? Or, as has sometimes been done in the past, are they more likely to spend it on paying for existing staff, or for non-recurring expenses, like books and equipment, to avoid hiring and then firing new staff? It is unlikely that many systems will begin significant improvement efforts with money that will soon vanish, at a time when they can see more cuts in local and state funds ahead; when the ARRA expires, its restriction on state and local budget cuts also expires.[3] A recent report notes, "Even in states where the fiscal outlook is brighter, districts are reluctant to create new programs or hire new staff members because most of the stimulus funding is for one time only."[4]

Another limit on the capability for improvement is that many school systems will not use the billions to press reform as urgently as the Obama administration wishes. The Education Department urges two very different aims for the stimulus package: "We must advance ARRA's short-term economic goals by investing quickly, and we must support ARRA's long-term economic goals by investing wisely, using these funds to strengthen education, drive reforms, and improve results for students."[5] The state applications require governors and state education officials to specify how they will use the money to support education reform in four key areas, but there is increasing evidence of tension between the ARRA's two aims. In "a number of states, including several with ambitious school reform plans on the shelf, massive deficits threaten to swallow a hefty portion of the stimulus aid, leaving less money for sweeping improvement efforts."[6] The first analysis of how thirty-one states with completed applications are spending the State Fiscal Stimulus money revealed that 87 percent was to be used "to fill in K-12 and higher education cuts they already made in fiscal 2009, or cuts they would have had to make in 2010. One official commented, 'We're all disappointed.... How are we supposed to make systemic change if the dollars are just buying the same thing we've been buying in the past?'"[7]

Yet many states and local school systems are under terrific financial pressure. That led Rep. David R. Obey, D-Wisc., to tell Secretary of Education Arne Duncan that schools "face a devastating storm just in terms of economic conditions," and that "it's legitimate to question whether it's realistic to ask them to also implement dramatic new reforms. I don't want to set them up for failure in the public eye because they can't do two things at once."[8] Obey was a key author of the ARRA, and is very influential in congressional appropriations; the Obama administration could not ignore his concerns.

There are two chief federal initiatives that are specifically targeted for reform. One is a proposal for the 2010 budget, to shift about $1 billion from Title I Part A grants to the part of NCLB that supports school improvement. This proposal has not made its way through the House or Senate, and several influential legislators—Rep. David Obey and Sen. Tom Harkin, D-Iowa, among them—have challenged the secretary of education about the proposal.[9] The other initiative, part of the ARRA that is hopefully titled "Race to the Top," is a $4.4 billion program that is intended to help some states and localities foot the cost of reform. This program does offer the administration some leverage with states and localities, but it is not yet clear whether the funds will be used to build educational capability or for more initiatives of the sort that are familiar from the Bush and Clinton years. We return to this initiative below.

Improvement efforts are likely to play out very differently among the states, because some are in a relatively strong financial position and seem at this point able to ride out the recession, while others— California and Michigan top the list—are in a perilous condition.[10] Some local districts that are in weak or desperate financial shape, especially those in states that are similarly afflicted, may want to use Title I funds to supplant local and state funds in Title I schools, so the supplanted local monies can be used elsewhere. In the past, federal officials held the line on such things, but will they continue to do so if states and localities slide toward an abyss? That is another unknown, but the appetite for ambitious reform and the capability to pursue it are likely to shrink in many places.

Any funding shrinkage is important because Title I builds on uneven fiscal and educational foundations among states, localities, and schools; hence developing differences in state and local fiscal health could easily create even more educational inequality within and among states.[11] The foundations on which the program builds will become even more unequal, with strengthening in some states and weakening in others. How this plays out will depend at least as much on whether the recession extends and deepens, and how state and local economies grow or shrink, as on what Congress and the president do.

It is an obvious but fundamental point that, because the United States has fifty state school systems and more than 14,000 local systems, each with its own fiscal structure, there is no established national policy framework within which the federal government can frame a coherent response to the educational effects of economic problems, let alone a response that takes account of state and local differences in fiscal and educational capability. The ARRA stimulus package is an emergency measure, and a sequel seems unlikely. Another reason, in addition to the economic stress just discussed, is the enormous and growing federal budget deficit, and the economic and political threats it poses. How the federal government deals with its deficit remains to be seen. President Barack Obama has vowed to begin to cut federal spending soon, to move toward a more balanced budget.

Another reason that a sequel to ARRA seems unlikely is competition for federal and state funds from other policies, prominently health care and health care reform. It seems likely that education policy and practice will have to work within the limits of existing budgets. This could be the best-case alternative. If the economy fails to gain significant strength, federal and state budgets will shrink further, and there could be even less money for schools.

As job losses increase, more people need a social safety net. This net is smaller, due in part to the Clinton welfare reforms and in part to state cuts in Medicaid and the reconfiguration of other social services. During this recession the number of poor families is growing, thus more children are eligible for Title I assistance. The Title I program never covered all the students who were eligible, and it covered many thinly. Now the job and social safety net losses are producing even more eligible students.

Title I is therefore likely to face conflicting pressures: cover more students versus reform. The stimulus package may defer at least some of this conflict for a year or so, but beyond ARRA's two-year limit, what will happen? Will districts use the additional $10 billion allocated to Title I to include more eligible students, or will districts expand the program briefly and then contract it? Will they intensify services for those already covered in order to press improvement, or will they simply use the funds to hold existing staff and programs that otherwise might be lost to budget cuts? Will Title I's politically winning broad distribution formula be stretched to cover more students or will reform be the priority? The answers are likely to differ depending on each state's finances. States and localities that are hard-pressed will almost certainly lose capability to respond to federal and other pressures for deeper reform. One small example is the New York City school system's recent decision to fill teaching vacancies from the "reserve pool" of experienced teachers who had been let go from their previous positions, rather than to hire new teachers from Teach for America or similar sources.[12]

If our analysis is roughly correct, despite the ARRA, little in the economic or political environment, aside from the Race to the Top program, is likely to strengthen the capability for reform. Several things seem likely to weaken it. There are, however, other approaches to re-form, many in the private sector, which could help to solve the prob-lems of weak instruments and capability that Title I has faced. We discuss them now, asking in each case about the extent to which they bring strong and salient instruments to bear on practice that are likely to help solve problems.

Build Human Capital

Some initiatives that focus on human capital seek in various ways to get more qualified teachers into schools and school systems. Other initiatives seek to distinguish more qualified teachers from less qualified teachers, in order to reward the former (merit pay), reduce the latter, or both. The best known of the first sort are Teach for America (TFA) and the New Teacher Project (NTP), with its Teach-ing Fellows (TF) programs. The chief instrument is the recruitment of bright and engaged people to teach in high-poverty schools. Viewed in terms of the dilemma of policy and practice, both TFA and the NTP seek to re-staff damaged organizations, rather than to re-shape those who work there through policy changes. They raise private funds to support their operations; they recruit well-educated, engaged, bright young people who want to teach in high-poverty schools, at least for a few years; they offer education and supervision that is intended to help the teachers succeed. These programs have succeeded in the sense that they have recruited many thousands of teachers. The NTP estimates that it has "trained or hired" ap-proximately 33,000 high-quality teachers for disadvantaged schools, and has pioneered the development of alternative programs of teacher certification.[13] Teach for America has placed thousands of academically high-achieving college graduates in high-poverty schools since it began twenty years ago. It reports, "In the 2009–10 school year, over 7,300 first- and second-year Teach For America corps members will teach in more than 100 school districts in 27 states and the District of Columbia."[14] The pool of recruits to these programs is growing, which also can be counted as a success. The influx of new teachers is encouraging, and represents an important change, especially given the thirty-year drop in the average SAT scores of entering teachers.

Yet the educational effectiveness of the TFA/NTP approach depends on three things: a ready supply of very bright, highly educated people; the sponsors' capability to educate their recruits to do good work under difficult conditions; and the schools' and school systems' capability to use the new recruits effectively. The evidence on their effects on student performance is mixed. One study of high schools in North Carolina reported that the students of TFA teachers do as well as or better than the students of conventional teachers, but a national study of TFA teachers in elementary schools reported that their students did no worse but no better than conventional teachers in the same schools.[15] That they do no worse, despite their lack of much professional education and experience, is probably the real news. Though it is not a ringing endorsement of the education or qualifications of the regular teachers to whom the new recruits' work is compared, neither does it suggest that the new recruits are, on average, a dramatic improvement. But the programs are changing as their staffs learn from experience, and much remains to be learned about their operation and effects.

The key point, given our earlier analysis, concerns schools' and school systems' capability to use the new recruits effectively. It is only in the last few years that a few school systems have made serious efforts to build the capability to use new recruits effectively. One issue is whether schools are managed in ways that are well designed to improve teaching and learning, which typically requires concerted work on curriculum, teaching, teacher education, and inspection of students' work, among other things. The absence of concerted work is one hallmark of weak schools, and a chief reason that they are weak. A related issue is whether the new recruits are part of a strategy to improve particular schools, or are simply used to plug vacancies that come up in the system. They are much less likely to have a sustained effect in the latter situation, which is typically how TFA teachers have been used. As with any other educational resource, the new recruits' impact depends at least as much on the schools' ability to use them effectively as on the recruits' talent and energy. That, of course, applies with equal force to the teachers already at work in the schools.

The local action that is likely to make the new recruits more effective also would be likely to make the existing teachers more effective. Such action depends a great deal on state and local school systems, and somewhat less on the new recruits and their sponsors. Local capability is indispensable, whatever the initiative and however appealing it seems.

Assess Teaching Quality

The initiatives that seek to distinguish more versus less qualified teachers center on using longitudinal measures of student achievement, called value-added measures (VAMs), to estimate the teachers' contribution to students' learning. The aim is either to reward the more qualified, which is commonly referred to as merit pay, or to reduce the less qualified, or both. The ideas have considerable political appeal—both President Obama and Education Secretary Duncan have declared themselves to favor merit pay, and several states and localities are attempting to implement such schemes—but research suggests that the knowledge lags well behind enthusiasm. The ideas' appeal arises from the promise of large improvement in schools and student performance, without fundamental re-design of the system or a huge investment. But there is little evidence that the assessment technology can support such approaches to the assessment of teaching.

One problem is disagreement among sources of evidence on teacher quality. In most studies there are significant differences between expert observers' evaluation of teaching and test results. There are only modest correlations between the value that teachers add to students' scores and how observers rank teaching quality. In the largest and most systematic study of these issues in elementary schools, Robert Pianta and his colleagues report that, based on the work of expert raters, "observed classroom experiences . . . matter somewhat when it comes to producing gains in children's performance."[16] In a careful review of the evidence, Heather Hill concluded, "the weight of the evidence . . . suggests that observational and value-added indicators of teacher effectiveness do converge, but the extent of convergence is unknown. . . . More research in this arena is certainly needed; in the meantime, caution seems wise."[17]

Another problem is inconsistency among different tests of what is thought to be the same academic material. Hill notes that there are only two studies of how closely related different tests are in value-added analyses of student gains.[18] They report very large differences in the test results, hence there would be large differences in how teachers would be rated in value-added accountability schemes, depending on the test used. Hill writes, "If this district had been using a pay-for-performance plan similar to the one in place in Houston, Texas, swapping outcome measures would affect the performance bonuses of nearly half of all teachers."[19]

If teacher evaluation were done at the state level, and if states required that only the same statewide test be used for student and teacher evaluation, the problem of variation among tests could be obviated within states. It would not be obviated among states that use different tests. Teachers in some states might be rated as ineffective, but they might be rated as effective in another state that used a different test. It could be politically and perhaps legally difficult for states to sustain their teacher rating schemes in the face of such irrationality.

But hold that problem aside for a moment. Forget variation of tests among states. Assume the political and legal primacy of state decisions, and ask: Would using the same test in value-added formats yield usable and defensible scores within a state? The answer depends on several things. One is the tests' validity: How "truthful" are the reports of teachers' effects on students' learning? Several economists and measurement experts roughly agree that the VAMs are at least somewhat invalid measures of teachers' contribution to students' learning because students are not randomly assigned to teachers. Some teachers systematically get more able or less able students. Merit pay schemes that used such VAMs would reward some teachers for being assigned to or having recruited more able students, and penalize those who work with less able students.[20]

Another part of the answer depends on the tests' reliability, that is, how much error there is in measurement of gains in students' achievement. One can think about this as the consistency between scores on the same test, given to the same students, at two closely related times. Researchers persistently find test re-test reliability to be low. Hill says there would be "an inability to accurately distinguish between two teachers unless they are very far apart in effectiveness. This renders accountability systems with specific cut-points—for instance, to pay or not pay a bonus—problematic. Two individuals on either side of the cut-point may be indistinguishable in score, from a statistical perspective, because each score lies within the confidence interval of the other. Yet these teachers would have very different outcomes."[21]

There are several other considerations that would tend to weaken the strength and salience of VAMs as policy instruments. First, resources are unequal. Students in high-poverty schools and poorer districts often have fewer educational resources than their peers in more advantaged schools and districts. Second, high-poverty schools typically have larger classes, weaker leadership, more student and teacher mobility, as well as other socioeconomic factors. Such inequality could reduce the value that teachers in poorly resourced schools add to students' scores. Teachers would be penalized for conditions beyond their control, thus erroneously reducing the "quality" scores and eroding the schemes' legitimacy and political and legal standing. As has often been the case with Title I, the schools' environment can have a potent impact on the effects that policy instruments have.

Another problem is the effect that accountability often has on behavior. Existing tests are vulnerable to invalidity because, with NCLB and related state policies, they have been designed to focus on basic work to make scores seem strong. There also is a frequent lack of alignment between tests and curriculum, or between tests and standards. In such situations tests tend to become a protocurriculum, especially when high or moderate stakes for educators are attached to them: Teachers teach to the tests, which helps students to do well, thus altering scores. Though this might be a less serious problem in low-stakes merit pay schemes, it would be much more serious for high-stakes schemes. The high stakes teachers attach to students' test scores in both schemes would create incentives for teachers to cheat, to teach to the tests, and to work with students whose scores were just below the class average and could relatively easily be improved, rather than weaker students whose improvement would require more work, skill, time, and determination. The problem here is not that an instrument is weak or not salient, but that it encourages a very different sort of behavior than what Title I intended.

Still another problem is the misdirected use of a policy instrument. Teachers are the chief target of accountability in state and federal standards-based reforms, but teachers cannot produce learning without the learners' active engagement. Teaching is a practice of human improvement, in which the people to be improved play a central role. Contrary to nineteenth-century usage, teachers cannot "learn" students; only students can do the learning, with teachers' assistance. If students are not accountable for their learning, and if many of them resist or have difficulty, teachers would have strong incentives to work with students whose scores can most easily be boosted rather than with weaker students. NCLB's accountability provisions create such effects. A recent RAND study of the classroom effects of NCLB, to which we referred in Chapter 6, presented vivid examples of teachers targeting their attention toward children who were almost "proficient," which meant that students who were in more academic trouble would get less help because their problems were more difficult to solve.[22]

There are two morals of this story. One is that the validity of value-added measures of teaching quality is very sensitive to the tests used, and to how teachers and students are assigned to work together, among other things. Given the existing tests and related knowledge, it seems likely that these schemes would incorrectly identify many teachers as effective or ineffective. The current assessment technology cannot support what its advocates propose. This is another version of the capability deficit that surfaced in our analysis of the testing regime that states have developed to comply with NCLB. The education system lacks the instruments and knowledge that this approach to human capital improvement requires.

The other moral is that value-added approaches to judging the quality of teaching are an effort to short-circuit the underlying problem of teaching quality in U.S. schools. Public education systems in the United States never developed the common instruments that are found in many national school systems and in a few U.S. subsystems, including common curricula or curriculum frameworks, common examinations that are tied to the curricula, teacher education that is grounded in learning to teach the curricula that students are to learn, and a teaching force whose members succeeded in those curricula and exams as students. Such infrastructure can inform assessment of quality in teaching. For given common curricula and teacher education grounded in the curricula, it would be possible to devise standards of teaching quality that are referenced to teaching those curricula. It would be possible to devise standards that specify which elements of the subject should be taught, and even how they can be effectively taught. It also would be possible to create standards for students' performance that are grounded in the curriculum. It is precisely this sort of common educational frame that could offer an educationally valid way to judge the quality of teaching and learning. Efforts to short-circuit such a frame could be used more quickly, but it is unlikely that they would yield technically valid and educationally usable means to judge and decide on quality in teaching.

Improve Leadership

The intention to improve capability by reshaping human capital also lies behind another important but less well known initiative: recruit and educate new leadership for urban schools. The Broad Center created by The Foundations is a key player in this effort. Begun in 1999, it promotes "the development of school system leadership as a means of improving the education of students in large, urban public school districts."[23] The foundation states its aims include "focusing on the most important dimensions of an urban superintendency—instructional alignment, operational excellence and stakeholder engagement," "recruiting participants who have superb leadership skills," and expecting their graduates "to quickly and significantly raise student achievement."[24] Here again, the chief instrument is the recruitment and education of more engaged and qualified educators, though in this case they are to be system leaders rather than teachers.

The new leaders' education is concentrated in the Broad Residency,

> a management development program that places talented early career executives from the private or civic sectors into two-year,

full-time, paid positions at the top levels of urban school systems across the country. Broad Residents work to improve management practices of urban education systems so that critical resources can be pushed down to the classroom. During their two-year "residency," participants receive intensive professional development and access to a nationwide network of education leaders. Broad Residents in [a recent] . . . class all have M.B.A.s or other advanced degrees. Most come from leading business, public policy and law schools such as Harvard, Kellogg or Columbia and have a minimum of four years of distinguished work experience. Participants in this [2008] class will be working in 17 school districts and four charter management organizations across the country.[25]

The Broad Foundation has begun to recruit and educate a new cadre of leaders. The foundation claims that it has placed members of a "very different breed of manager in dozens of school systems," and that "current and former Broad Residents today are working in 29 urban school systems nationwide. Nine out of ten graduates today still work in urban education."[26] This initial success is due in part to the lack of competition from higher education; only a handful of universities make a serious effort to recruit and educate urban school leaders. Universities and their education schools have focused little effort on the nation's deepest educational problems, a point we noted repeatedly in earlier chapters in connection with the weakness of most teacher education. The foundation brings considerable money to the enterprise—it also has given many millions of dollars to charter schools—and has attracted prominent reformers and corporate leaders to its cause, including Chancellor Joe Klein of the New York City Department of Education, U.S. Secretary of Education Arne Duncan, and Chancellor Michelle Rhee of the District of Columbia Public Schools System.

We could find no independent analysis on the educational effects of this initiative, nor of its effects on the management of education. There is, however, evidence of controversy. One review depicts the foundation as part of a corporate effort to override locally elected officials and teachers' unions, to install school system leaders who fit a corporate mold.[27] We could find no independent evidence for these claims, but the foundation's initiative is a striking example of an entirely unaccountable private agency trying to make fundamental change in a politically accountable public enterprise. Taken together with the large investments that the Gates Foundation has made in educational reform, this raises questions that are as puzzling as they are troubling. Both the Broad Foundation and the Gates Foundation are responding to serious failures in the education professions and higher education. Neither the education professions nor higher education have made much effort to improve either the management of or teaching in urban schools. There also have been few energetic local efforts to use democratic channels to improve school system management. Yet there is not even any sign of an independent evaluation of either foundation's work, a striking contrast to Teach for America opening itself to several independent studies. The lack of independent inquiry is often tied to a lack of systematic learning from experience that has long troubled Title I. Given the lack of independent evaluation, it is especially worrisome to contemplate the influence that such entirely politically unaccountable agencies may exert on public schools that are supposed to be governed democratically.

Mayoral Control

One can get a very rough sense of the influence of mayoral control on human capital improvement efforts in a few cases in which they were linked in larger efforts to fundamentally change the political control and management of urban school systems (the second initiative that we mentioned earlier). Three major cities—Chicago, New York, and Washington—have instituted mayoral control of the schools, and used that political change to improve human capital management among many other things. When Michelle Rhee took the leadership of the Washington, DC, schools, in the most recent of the three makeovers, she positioned herself in the nation's weakest urban school system. She took on the problems with unprecedented aggressiveness: she fired teachers whom she found to be weak and replaced them with young, well educated and engaged teachers; she closed or reorganized failing schools; she is trying to end teacher tenure and to reward teachers who boost students' learning with higher salaries; and she is rebuilding the central administration by cutting many positions and filling others with managers who will help her focus the system on better work in the schools.

As all of this is just beginning, it is much too early for any solid evidence on the effects of the Washington reforms on teaching and learning. But two years into her tenure, some evidence is emerging. Chancellor Rhee has deployed an impressive array of instruments, using them aggressively, perhaps more so than any other big-city superintendent. There can be little doubt that she has pushed harder, on more fronts, more quickly, than any of her predecessors. Yet there also is evidence that her efforts have alienated many supporters and potential supporters, and created obstacles to the success of her reforms.[28]

The more fundamental questions parallel those that came up in our earlier analysis. One concerns the schools' political environment. Chancellor Rhee's aggressive intervention is enabled in part by Mayor Adrian Fenty's support, and in part by Washington's unique political situation. It is not located in a state, and thus Fenty and Rhee do not have to contend with a state legislature in which teacher unions and other interested parties have influence. But Fenty will not be mayor forever. There is a City Council, and the city also is accountable to the U.S. House of Representatives. Urban politics are notoriously fickle. It is conceivable but far from certain that, if the reforms continue to stand alone, they will survive.

That is in part because there is a question about the depth of the educational capability that these reforms bring. It is one thing to replace ineffective veteran teachers with younger people from Teach for America and similar programs, but few of the new breed are career teachers, and most leave the schools just when their few years of experience begin to pay off for students' learning. The higher salaries that Chancellor Rhee is trying to arrange for those who are more effective will doubtless hold some, at least for a few more years, but that is unlikely to build a stable force of capable teachers who can solidly anchor the schools' work and help to guide others. Building such a teaching force will require several of the other elements of an educational infrastructure that we discussed earlier, including much improved curriculum, assessment, and teacher education, in addition to recruitment and salaries. In this respect as in several others, though Chancellor Rhee's work is impressive, it may be less difficult than what will be required to build a stable and capable local system, in which quality work will last well beyond her leadership.

The same issues are presented by the mayoral reforms in Chicago and New York. In both cities, the new mayoral regimes focused on rebuilding the central administrations, using tests to evaluate schools' performance, changing principals in weak schools, hiring new teachers, and creating new approaches to the education of school leaders. In both cities private philanthropy has been key to support for some of these and other initiatives, something to which the previous managers had little access. There also has been continuing political conflict over the new regimes, though it has been more acute in Mayor Michael Bloomberg's New York than in Mayor Richard Daley's Chicago. Mayoral control in both cities also requires action by the state legislature, and that affords doubters and opponents some leverage. In New York State, the legislature is now considering whether to renew or modify the arrangement for New York City.

Both Chicago and New York also focused much more aggressively on improved teaching and learning than their predecessors, a clear result of mayoral control. The new regimes also brought more human and fiscal resources to the enterprise than their predecessors had done. The New York City schools have begun to build infrastructure, including elements of common curricula, a system to rate schools' quality that goes beyond test scores, and the beginning of an inspectorate system. Higher education and philanthropies in Chicago created a remarkably effective independent source of high-quality research on the city schools and efforts to reform them. The Consortium on Chicago School Research has not been replicated in any other city. Partly because the new regimes have been primarily managerial, the central question is whether they will build the educational infrastructure that might create capability that would endure. Management and leadership are essential, whether for schools or entire systems, and they have been important for efforts to set a new course for public education in these cities. The systems' quality is tied to the extraordinary work by those at the top. Such consistency in quality is unlikely to be sustained in rough and changeable urban politics. The reconstruction of these systems will require an infrastructure that can enable capable people at all levels of the system to regularly do good work. In these matters as in others, heroism is not enough.

The relatively modest investment thus far in infrastructure may help to explain the quite modest academic effects of the reforms. The evidence is contested, and, given the political stakes, the system leaders and their mayoral sponsors have been at pains to see signs of progress. Yet, though students' scores in both cities have improved modestly on the state and local tests that count for accountability, scores on the NAEP urban assessments are less impressive. That reflects, among other things, differences between tests for which students were likely to prepare and tests for which they did not prepare, and differences in the difficulty of the two sorts of tests.[29]

One way to interpret these very modest score changes is to note that in neither New York City nor Chicago was there a central focus on the creation of educational infrastructure; instead there was intense attention to testing, accountability, and management. New York seems to have done more to build some elements of infrastructure than Chicago, and that may be one reason for the somewhat better scores in New York. Another way to view the modest score changes, however, is that there was no regression, which is no small thing in cities that continue to undergo demographic change during a period in which incomes for working class and poor Americans continued to contract while the cost of living rose. In addition, no one knows what the correct time horizon is to judge the success of such extraordinary undertakings. The reforms aim to make fundamental change in large organizations that have been burdened with difficult problems that accumulated for more than a century. Our subjective estimate is that the changes are the work of at least a generation—twenty-five to thirty years—a time span that amounts to several light-years in the hurtling world of big-city politics. Will it be possible to mobilize continuing political support for improvement while insulating schools from the political conflict and pressures to which they have been so vulnerable? We hope so, but it would require an unprecedented set of constructive developments in local and state politics, education, and finance. The difficulty of that work is appreciably increased if, as has been the case thus far, each city must continue to invent and sustain solutions on its own.

School "Turnaround"

One assumption that underlay standards-based reform was that failing schools would find ways to succeed if there were clear standards, aligned assessments, and professional accountability. That did not happen: neither experience with standards-based reform nor evidence from research supports that idea. Massachusetts, for instance, is widely acknowledged as the state with the most demanding academic standards, the toughest assessments, and the most serious accountability. A recent article notes, "When the Massachusetts Education Reform Act was passed 15 years ago, it ushered in a new era in which high standards were set for all students, with an expectation that the huge infusion of new state funding to poorer districts, combined with strict accountability measurements, would lift achievement there to the levels seen in more affluent districts."[30] Yet Paul Reville, the state's current secretary of education, and one of the designers of the Massachusetts reform, recently declared failure. He said that reformers had intended to "eradicate the correlation between socioeconomic status and educational attainment. . . . Fifteen years into education reform, we'd have to say we've failed on that."[31] Most of the poorly performing schools in the state enroll students from low-income families, and the state reforms did not make them successful. In this respect as in others, the new policies have been much more effective in calling attention to educational problems than in solving them.

The solution to the problem of failing schools, in Massachusetts and elsewhere, is thought to be school restructuring, called "turnaround." If the central elements of NCLB persist, it will be no small endeavor. In the 2007–2008 school year nearly 30,000 U.S. schools failed to make adequate yearly progress (AYP) under NCLB, and more than 3,500 of those schools were several years into the school improvement process without showing signs of sufficient improvement.[32] In California, there are more than 1,000 schools that failed to make AYP. As requirements for AYP rise, as states come closer to the 2014 deadline under NCLB, the number of failing schools also will rise.

The numbers explain why interest in turnaround is growing. States are trying to expand their capability to improve weak schools,[33] and the federal government intends to offer major support. President Obama and Secretary Duncan recently announced plans to spend $5 billion to turn around 5,000 failing schools in five years.[34] When asked what might be done to turn such schools around Secretary Duncan said that it "might mean firing an entire staff and bringing in a new one, replacing a principal or turning a school over to a charter school operator. The point, he said, is to take bold action in persistently low-achieving schools."[35]

The proposal is paradoxical. The news story that we just quoted noted that Secretary Duncan was the just-former school superintendent in Chicago, and that he "has plenty of experience with school turnarounds. Chicago targeted several public schools for turnaround, eight of them last year, while Duncan was still in charge." But the same story continued, "It's too soon to know how the eight fared."[36] That is consistent with the evidence on turnaround. There are few studies of such efforts in education because, until recently, few districts seriously attempted it. There also are a few accounts of heroic and apparently successful efforts to turn weak schools into strong ones, but these are few and far between.[37] More to the point, the studies that seriously scrutinized research and practice on the subject produced daunting results. They agree that the work is very difficult and that the success rate is low. Whether researchers consider efforts to turn around schools or private sector firms, they estimate that one in five or one in four turnaround efforts succeed; that is not an impressive success rate.[38] When studies focus only on schools, they find that though many enter the restructuring process, few exit successfully, even after many years.[39] The political costs for the state or local leaders who undertake such efforts are reported to be quite high, in part because of resistance to school closings and in part because success is so rare. Even when significant changes are made, researchers report that the improvements are difficult to sustain. The Center on Education Policy, which closely studied such efforts in five states, concluded in its report on California that the process worked poorly: "federal restructuring strategies have very rarely helped schools improve student achievement."[40] Most of the studies also noted that school turnaround is complicated by the difficult economic and social conditions of students in high-poverty schools.

The studies of school turnaround also share two curious features. One is that the schools in question are treated as individual cases, each of which is to be solved individually. The schools are seen as individual failures, not as manifestations of system failure; turnaround efforts do not include treating them as part of educational systems. The other is that the research on turnaround almost completely ignores the educational content of schooling. The common elements of success are said to include strong new leadership, dismissal of all teachers and hiring new staff, the use of coaches or "distinguished educators" to advise principals and teachers, and tight student discipline that includes dismissing students who reject the regime. One study managed to discuss the subject of school turnaround for more than thirty pages, without ever mentioning curriculum, teaching, or teacher education.[41]

Improving weak schools is an essential part of efforts to solve the problems that Title I has encountered, and a good bit of the work must be done in each school. Yet, as with efforts to improve districts with mayoral control, if each school turnaround must be accomplished on its own, apart from a common instructional frame, success would require the repeated reinvention of the educational wheel. Maintaining that success would require continuing heroic efforts to sustain each unique effort. When school improvement is understood and dealt with in such an individualistic manner, rather than as one manifestation of a systemic problem, the barriers to success increase, in large part because the capability to offer quality education is more difficult to either build or sustain in stand-alone schools.

New Schools and School Systems

One way to deal with the systemic elements of school turnaround in particular, and school improvement more generally, has been to create new schools and school systems. For the most part, this has meant charter schools and charter school networks. There now are roughly 4,500 charter schools, enrolling more than a million students. Contrary to early worries about these schools, independent researchers report that

> overall . . . it does not appear that charter schools are systematically skimming high-achieving students or dramatically affecting the racial mix of schools for transferring students. Students transferring to charter schools had prior achievement levels that were generally similar to or lower than those of their TPS [traditional public schools] peers. And transfers had surprisingly little effect on racial distributions across the sites: Typically, students transferring to charter schools moved to schools with racial distributions similar to those of the TPSs from which they came. There is some evidence, however, that African American students transferring to charters are more likely to end up in schools with higher percentages of students of their own race, a finding that is consistent with prior results in North Carolina.[42]

But also contrary to earlier expectations, on average these new schools did not deliver the better education that their sponsors had expected. Several independent research reports, including one that was sponsored by foundations that vigorously backed charter schools, have reached essentially the same conclusion: on average, student achievement in charter schools does not outperform achievement in conventional public schools.[43]

How can that be explained? Steven F. Wilson, an advocate for and operator of charter schools, wrote,

> Advocates had expected that the structural advantages of charters—the new bargain extended to founders of authority and autonomy in exchange for accountability for results; the shared purpose that would result from faculty and students who had chosen the school,

rather than been assigned to it; and the freedom from tenure and union contracts—would prove decisive. These privileges alone did not unleash a new generation of dramatically superior schools, as many charter proponents had hoped . . . the charter school movement as a whole has disappointed.[44]

But Wilson pointed out that "a small number of the new schools have posted arresting results, with their low-income students, primarily African-American and Hispanic, outperforming students statewide—and in some cases, their white peers from affluent suburban districts."[45] He argues that at best there were 200 such schools, nationwide, and asks what explains their success. His answer is familiar from other recent accounts: they are schools of choice, not zoned neighborhood schools. They hire very selectively, taking only "highly educated, driven, and generally young" teachers; they are small; staff work long hours; conventional, whole-class teaching is typical; the schools embrace state standards and tests and teach to them aggressively; there is tight discipline and very clear standards of conduct; and interim tests to judge progress are common.[46]

Wilson has no quarrel with this view of what he and others term "no excuses" schools. His question is whether such schools can reach a scale that would serve the many thousands of children from poor families who have not been well served by many public schools. The key barrier to large-scale use of the model is also the schools' great strength: their unusual staff.

> The Boston No Excuses schools draw their teachers primarily from the most selective colleges and universities. Many have been trained and acculturated by Teach For America, not by education schools, as most career educators. The result is a labor pool with not only fundamentally different academic preparation for the classroom but also attitudes and beliefs different from (if not opposing) those of the traditional teacher labor pool. The qualities No Excuses schools seek in teacher candidates mirror these differences.[47]

Even if the pool of teachers who fit this pattern were greatly expanded, such that half of the entire graduating cohort from very selective institutions of higher education spent two years teaching in the most needy schools, "only one-third of urban students would benefit at any time from such a teacher."[48] In Wilson's view, even on the most optimistic assumptions about both the supply of such candidates and their professional education, the effort "would fall well short of the needs of the No Excuses model at scale."[49] They would not be a systemic solution to the educational problems of high-poverty schools.

That returns us to the dilemma that we posed near the beginning of this book: Can the weak schools be helped to become strong? Wilson's version of this question is: "Could the engine of No Excuses schooling be modified so that it could be fueled by more broadly available human capital?"[50] More precisely, could "career educators who, though they may not have attended elite colleges and universities, are nonetheless committed to rigorous academic standards, the continuous improvement of their craft, and a path to college for every child . . . be equipped with a powerful set of tools—provided the intellectual property—that permitted them, too, to produce gap-closing results? And enjoy a sustainable work schedule and pay scale that permits them to remain in teaching and raise a family?"[51]

Wilson argues that it could be done, if schools treated instructional improvement as a problem of building educational systems.[52] In his view that means the use of coherent, academically focused designs for instruction and management, including curricula, assessments, and teacher development to help capable people to do good work, even if they had families, worked a regular work week, and did not graduate from Princeton or Amherst. Without using the term, he argues for what we have called educational infrastructure within and among networks of charter schools. One example that he offers concerns SABIS,[53] which is

> an international operator of college preparatory schools. SABIS's schooling model has much in common with that of the No Excuses schools: a college preparatory focus; teacher led, whole-class instruction; explicit lesson objectives aligned with state standards; frequent testing; large class sizes; tight discipline; clear staff ac-

countabilities; schools structured as charters free of district collective bargaining contracts; and empowered school leaders. SABIS differs from the No Excuses schools in its deployment of its proprietary instructional materials according to specific protocols (600 short books, spanning all grades and academic subjects, through advanced placement classes in high school), electronic weekly assessments that provide teachers prompt feedback on students' mastery of the material (so that concepts may be re-taught as necessary and gaps in knowledge do not form), pacing charts, and school management software that links the system's components. A schoolwide system of peer tutoring and school culture-building tools encourages students to take responsibility for their own learning and that of their peers.[54]

Wilson's paper is a reminder that few of the human capital initiatives that we discussed earlier deal with the content of instruction, let alone with instructional systems; instead they deal with the quality of membership in the teaching force and the quality of managers. In the terms of our analysis, these human capital initiatives do not bring to bear the strong and salient instruments that would be required to substantially improve schooling, especially in high-poverty schools. Wilson's argument is consistent with the evidence on Core Knowledge, America's Choice, and Success for All, three comprehensive school reform designs (discussed in Chapters 2 and 6) that treat instruction and instructional improvement as a systems problem. These CSRDs significantly improved teaching and learning in thousands of high-poverty elementary schools, and did it with detailed, coherent designs for teaching and learning and extensive support for quality implementation of the designs.

Standards-Based Reform, Redux

One important feature of these charter systems and CSRDs is that they take on the problem of improved teaching and learning at the level of practice. The work is premised on the idea that, though other resources can help, the improvement of practice is most effectively

accomplished in and with practice. In contrast, standards-based reform, whether in its initial versions in the California and Kentucky
reforms of the 1980s, the Clinton policies of the mid-1990s, or NCLB,
appeared to assume that schools can be made to improve by requiring
them to use a new framework of standards, tests, and accountability.
These things helped: they drew unprecedented attention to the problems that Title I was originally intended to solve; they turned those
problems into the nation's top educational priority; they prompted
extraordinary action to improve public education by many states and
localities; they helped to modestly improve math scores for minority
group students on the NAEP; they helped to bring many people and
other resources to educational improvement; and they prompted extensive research on schools and school improvement.

These policies can only help to more substantially improve teaching
and learning if the people and schools that are performing poorly can
make effective use of the policies and the resources that they offer.
That requires the very capability that those schools often lack. Early in
this book we pointed out that the relations between policy and practice embody a dilemma: policies identify problems and offer solutions,
yet the key problem solvers often are the offending, needy, or damaged
people and organizations that policies aim to correct. Governments
can devise instruments to encourage implementation, yet they only
help if they are used well by those who are said to be the problem,
whose capability therefore is likely to be modest. If those organizations and people lack capability, they are unlikely to respond effectively to policy without substantial improvement in that capability.

Yet the traditions and structure of U.S. education and government
meant that instructional capability was not a matter that state and
federal agencies either were inclined to attend to, or with which they
could readily offer much help. State and federal agencies thus tended
to over-invest in the instruments that were familiar and relatively easy
for them to deploy, such as tests, and to under-invest in measures,
such as curricula and professional education, that could help to build
schools' capability to improve education. The result was a collision between policy pressure for more ambitious work at the state and federal
level, and weak capability in practice, in local schools and school

systems. In addition to the constructive effects, therefore, these policies led many states to set modest standards and cut-points on tests in
order to increase the number of schools that seemed to do well, and
thus protect against practice failure and its contagion to policy. The
required state tests often became a proto-curriculum, on which students were drilled. Many weak schools improved little or not at all.
Policies that announced the need for much more demanding academic work turned out, in many states and localities, to encourage an
intense focus on much less ambitious work. As constructive as the
policies were in some respects, they did not invest nearly as heavily in
improving practice as in changing the policy framework within which
practice occurred.

This issue is likely to come up in connection with three developing
initiatives: the Obama administration's use of the Race to the Top
funds, the reauthorization of Title I/NCLB, and a recent state initiative. We focus chiefly on the state initiative because it has considerable
appeal and momentum, it seems likely to play an important part in
the Title I/NCLB reauthorization, and the issues it raises are crucial
for any conceivable reauthorization of Title I/NCLB.

The National Governors Association, the Council of Chief State
School Officers, and Achieve began their recent *Benchmarking for Success* report, "Governors recognize that new economic realities mean
it no longer matters how one U.S. state compares to another on a national test; what matters is how a state's students compare to those in
countries around the globe. America must seize this moment to ensure that we have workers whose knowledge, skills, and talents are
competitive with the best in the world."[55]

The report sets out what it terms a "roadmap" for educational and
economic success. It proposes five key steps for states to take.

> *Action 1:* Upgrade state standards by adopting a common core of
> internationally benchmarked standards in math and language arts
> for grades K–12 to ensure that students are equipped with the nec-
> essary knowledge and skills to be globally competitive.
>
> *Action 2:* Leverage states' collective influence to ensure that text-
> books, digital media, curricula, and assessments are aligned to

internationally benchmarked standards and draw on lessons from high-performing nations and states.

Action 3: Revise state policies for recruiting, preparing, developing, and supporting teachers and school leaders to reflect the human capital practices of top-performing nations and states around the world.

Action 4: Hold schools and systems accountable through monitoring, interventions, and support to ensure consistently high performance, drawing upon international best practices.

Action 5: Measure state-level education performance globally by examining student achievement and attainment in an international context to ensure that, over time, students are receiving the education they need to compete in the 21st century economy.[56]

These few sentences offer an extraordinary prescription for change in U.S. education policy. The report assigns states and their partners the central role in setting voluntary common national academic standards and in using those standards to regulate schools. It assigns the federal government

an enabling role as states engage in the critical but challenging work of international benchmarking. First, federal policymakers should offer funds to help underwrite the cost for states to take the five action steps described above. At the same time, policymakers should boost federal research and development (R&D) investments to provide state leaders with more and better information about international best practices, and should help states develop streamlined assessment strategies that facilitate cost-effective international comparisons of student performance.[57]

This is a rather different role than the more familiar IASA and NCLB mandates.

In the late winter and early spring of 2009, the NGA, CCSSO, and Achieve took the next step, announcing a project to develop common core state standards for the nation's schools, an initiative built on the work sketched above. A CCSSO press release enthused:

These common standards will bring about real and meaningful transformation of our education system to benefit all students. . . . The purpose of this effort is to raise the bar for all students and states . . . to increase the rigor and relevance of state standards across all participating states; therefore, no state will see a decrease in the level of student expectations that exist in their current state standards. . . . The first standards being addressed are English-language arts and mathematics in grades K–12. [The] goal is to release the core of high school standards late this summer, and then, in the fall [of 2009], develop K–12 grade-by-grade standards.[58]

The proposal might be read politically as an effort by the states to take more of the initiative in education policy that has accumulated in Washington, by seizing the reins and setting tasks for themselves that trump anything that the federal government might attempt. Though that seems plausible, federal officials welcomed the state initiative. Rep. George Miller, D-Calif., the influential chair of the House Education and Labor Committee, and a strong advocate of NCLB, heaped praise on the initiative during hearings in April 2009. "With standards varying vastly from state to state, a high school diploma no longer guarantees that students are proficient enough to succeed in college or a career or to compete with their international peers, it's become increasingly clear that a rigorous, common core of standards is essential to help teachers teach and students learn. It's critical to our goal of building world class schools that prepare all Americans to compete in 21st century jobs and our global economy." Miller's counterpart on the panel, Rep. Howard P. McKeon, R-Calif., averred, "We know that rigorous academic standards are necessary to prepare today's students to succeed in tomorrow's competitive world. And we also know that the federal government is ill-equipped—and ill-suited—to make decisions about what and how our children should learn."[59]

Education Secretary Duncan joined the chorus a few weeks later when he announced that the Education Department would offer the project as much as $350 million to help develop tests that aligned with the yet-to-be-developed standards. One likely reason that federal officials support the initiative is that the states can press for common state standards, something that would be nearly impossible for the central government to do. As Washington heads into the reauthorization of Title I and NCLB in 2009, it could be helpful that the states had promised to do most of the heavy political and educational lifting. Federal policymakers could support common standards, leave most of the most difficult work to the states, and adopt a role that includes assistance and some oversight.

Nearly everything remains to be seen. If the initiative develops well, it could be an historic step, bringing greater educational coherence and quality, and perhaps even less inequality. How it develops will depend in good measure on how the states and the supporting organizations deal with five key issues. One is whether the common core standards project will actually set standards that, to paraphrase its own language, raise the bar for all students, are rigorous, and become the common core of state education systems. Will states devise a set of policy instruments that are both salient for instruction, and strong? Given the enormous variation in capability within and among states, and the potentially devastating consequences for state policy and politics of persistent failure or weak performance in practice (the contagion discussed in Chapter 2), it will not be easy for some states to adopt and hold to demanding standards. Thus far, only a few states—Massachusetts and Minnesota among them—have aggressively taken on such work. Though both improved test scores for many students, there are major problems with the education of children from poor families in both states.[60] We did not find any suggestions of how states will enforce the commitment to aggressive work; the standards are described as voluntary. The CCSSO acknowledged the states' primacy: "States will adopt the Common Core State Standards Initiative through a process that will respect unique state contexts and states' right to set standards. . . . Once the standards have been developed, states will then have the opportunity to adopt the standards or align them into their current content standards. . . . States will have the opportunity to review the standards during and throughout the entire development process."[61] This could lead to the variety in state standards that currently troubles so many former advocates for NCLB.

One way to reduce the political risk, of course, is to improve performance in practice. That leads to the second issue: Will states follow through on the *Benchmarking for Success* report's proposal that states act together, and use common standards to shape the content of texts, tests, teacher education, and curriculum? Will they be able to make the firms that produce tests and texts produce what the states want, and to align tests and texts with each other? In other words, will the states build the capability to support more focused, coherent, and improved instruction? That would require not only agreement on academic standards, but also on the content and quality of instruction and teacher education. The latter would require quite forceful intervention in higher education, something that states have rarely done. To follow through on actions two and three in the *Benchmarking* report (see above) thus would have states working together to shape markets and build educational infrastructure, in ways that are quite unprecedented. Such clear and detailed guidance for instruction and teacher education, and the assistance to make the changes, is more than any state has offered. The report wades into historically chilly educational waters, into which few states have dipped more than a toe. Kati Haycock, president of the Education Trust, a leading advocacy and research agency for disadvantaged children, said, "Who is going to do the work? And if college readiness is going to mean anything, then the colleges need to be pretty heavily involved. . . . Having new standards does us exactly no good until we have curriculum and assessments that go with it. . . . The big risk is: So we have standards. Now what?"[62]

Capability extends well beyond the standards, curricula, and assessments that can be printed on paper. It includes the people who would use the instruments and the organizations in which they work. To use common standards to guide instruction would take more skilled people in and around state education agencies, and in intermediate agencies within many states. Agencies would have to re-define their missions and operations to focus much more intensively on instruction. Changes would be quite expensive. It would shift the balance of influence in education in many states. And success would require that most people in education learn a great deal, at the same time as they unlearn much of what they thought they knew. Some state agencies have moved a bit in this direction in response to IASA and NCLB, but only a bit.[63] The "turnaround" of most state agencies, teacher education programs, intermediate agencies, and school districts would be the same sort of change as what is expected of failing schools.

A third issue concerns Americans' deep disagreement about what should be taught and learned, and how. Officials leading the effort were reported to have said "there will be no prescription for how teachers get there, avoiding nettlesome discussions about whether phonics or whole language is a better method of teaching reading; whether students should be drilled in math facts; or whether eighth-graders should read *The Great Gatsby* or *To Kill a Mockingbird*."[64] But one way to avoid that is to do as many standards have done already: write them generally to paper over such disagreements with vague language that offers little guidance. Another way to avoid conflict is to include nearly everything, which also offers little guidance. But those leading the effort insist that standards will be more focused, more coherent, and more rigorous. The mission is not impossible. For example, Minnesota pared down its mathematics standards, and used them to guide teaching, teacher education, and students' learning. But it is difficult. Michael J. Petrilli, vice president for national programs and policy at the Thomas B. Fordham Institution, and a strong advocate for stiff common standards, said, "All the groups, the math educators and the English professors and the liberals and the conservatives will want to weigh in." He continued, "There are fundamental disagreements in our society about what kids should learn."[65]

If the state initiative follows the *Benchmarking for Success* report's proposal to use standards to shape instruction and teacher education, such disagreements would probably multiply as states attempted to shape several key elements of educational infrastructure, in more detail than has been the norm. In addition to parents and political interest groups, there are professional agencies, such as the National Council of Teachers of Mathematics and the International Reading Association, that would expect to have a significant role in the development of standards and texts, as well as teacher education and other matters. When asked about this, one official insisted that these organizations and others will be involved, but the problem is less one of participation than decision. Each professional organization, similar to many parents and political interest groups, sees teaching and learning differently. One source of the difficulty is, as Petrilli said, deep disagreements about education, but another is that part of the environment which we call history. Most of the points at issue are old, many dating to the origins of public education. Americans have little experience with setting differences aside, or finding agreement, in order to advance some larger, common educational interest. Moreover, we live in a political system that offers a great variety of openings to exert influence. Equally important, the disagreements do not occur only at the periphery of the education system, in legislatures, advisory groups, and state boards of education. If that were the case, then the issues could be settled there; teachers and school managers would follow suit. Disagreements, however, permeate the instructional enterprise. Teachers hold different views and deploy very different practices concerning what should be taught, and how. Moreover, they work in organizations that, until recently, left most instructional decisions to teachers, who made them behind classroom doors. The governors are well situated politically to address these problems, but it would be a difficult and quite unfamiliar role. Even if they can settle on strong common standards, that would only be the beginning.

The fourth issue concerns assessment. As Secretary Duncan said in a recent speech, even if we assume the existence of excellent common standards, developing assessments that reflect and represent those standards would be a large assignment, unprecedented in educational research and development.[66] Differences among state standards are quite likely, and they will complicate any effort to frame common assessments. Many of the same disagreements that are likely to surface around standards—including how difficult to make them—would very likely re-surface concerning assessment. If the governors and their allies hold to their aim of internationally benchmarked standards, the assessments would require a much greater range of difficulty than most state tests, which tilt strongly toward basic skills. And the assessments will have to form a system that is linked among the grades, which is another feature that is uncommon in U.S. tests. These considerations signal another quite substantial problem of capability.

There also is a potential problem concerning accountability. Though the common state standards announcements state that there must be tests that are linked to the standards, little has been said about the tests' relation to accountability, as it has been understood in standards-based reform. The *Benchmarking for Success* report sketches an approach to what it terms accountability (action four, see above) that is quite different than what became typical in standards-based reform. The central elements include direct inspection of the quality of work in schools by external professional agencies such as inspectorates, whole school self-reviews, close monitoring of students' performance in order to prevent anyone from falling far behind, and professional norms and expectations consistent within schools and across systems.[67] If the states' work follows this sketch, it would be a remarkable departure from the approach associated with IASA, NCLB, and related state policies, because it would focus on various ways to collect information that would inform and improve practice, and presumably would separate that from any sort of external test-based accountability. If one aim of such separation would be to invest more in building the capability to improve practice, another would be to avoid the unfortunate experience with NCLB-required tests, which confound external accountability with practice improvement. But the *Benchmarking* report's approach would require very substantial additional capability, for most of the elements that it sketches are quite unfamiliar in U.S. education systems.

The last issue, and the most fundamental, is that the states' initiative is a version of standards-based reform, in which state policymakers and their allies seek to drive change in practice from the outside. Our analysis strongly suggests that this would be unlikely to work well, absent parallel efforts to build capability in practice from the inside.

What might it take to build that capability?

There is no easy answer, in part because the question has only recently been asked. The most promising initial answers are contained in Comprehensive School Reform Designs such as Success for All, America's Choice, and Core Knowledge (discussed in Chapters 2 and

6), and in several charter networks. In these cases educational entre-
preneurs carefully worked out designs for instruction—they built educational infrastructure. They devised organizations to sponsor the
work. They recruited staff and cultivated expertise to help high-poverty
schools to use the designs. They linked those schools in networks—
school systems, really—to create coherent communities of practice, to
support the schools' work. They did all this with the aim of using high-
poverty schools' Title I funds to pay for a large share of the work.[68]
They raised other monies and in many other ways managed the environment so as to sustain the schools' work.[69] There is anecdotal evidence that several charter school networks are trying roughly similar
strategies. The common threads in the work include building coherent
and detailed educational infrastructure, organizing schools and school
leadership to support coherent curriculum and instruction, and investing in teacher education that is tied to the curriculum. The evidence shows that the CSRDs discussed in this book have strong positive effects on students' performance.[70]

These are the best cases of successful efforts to build capability in
practice; the CSRDs strike us as a useful beginning for building more
ambitious and coherent systems of education, in response to a reauthorized NCLB or the common core standards, or both. However, little is likely to happen spontaneously, and there are a few strategies
that would encourage the growth of similar systems. One is for states
to devise programs to support charter networks that used coherent
curricula that were consistent with the developing standards. Similar
state programs to support CSRDs that have a proven record of effectiveness, and are willing to build additional networks of schools, also
would help. It is worth noting that Core Knowledge, America's Choice,
and Success for All already have most of the human resources and
educational instruments in place to do such work. It would be especially helpful if these CSRDs were able to replicate themselves in
state or regional networks. Given the problems of teacher supply and
the weakness of university teacher education, it also would help if
states enabled CSRD and charter networks that have a solid record
of improved teaching and learning to build the capability to offer pre-
service as well as continuing teacher education.

These points assume that schools are more likely to improve and sustain improvement if their work is situated in joint efforts to build inward to practice from state policy and management, while building outward from practice at the same time. They also assume that the capability of practice cannot be built entirely from the outside. It can be informed, guided, and supported by state and federal action, but if practice is to improve, practitioners must make and understand the improvements. That requires much more than following directions. Teachers who can only follow directions are unlikely to be able to teach demanding academic material. Just as teachers cannot "learn" students, though they can help a great deal, policy cannot "learn" practice. The people and organizations that constitute practice must do the most important work. That returns us to the dilemma with which we began. Policy can define problems, offer guidance, deploy instruments, and mobilize resources, but the ultimate problem solvers are the people and agencies at which policy is aimed. If they do not have the capability to make sense of what policy proposes, and to turn it into practice, policy is unlikely to succeed. Policy and the instruments that it deploys can help, but organizations in practice, whose mission and expertise is to build that capability, are no less important.

Additionally, policy will always be quite incomplete, even when it is detailed. However excellent the work of state policymakers and their allies, a great deal will remain open, unspecified, and unanticipated, hence a great deal will remain to be learned and revised in practice. Because the object of the effort is to improve practice, much can only be done by those in schools, and in agencies that work with schools, to improve practice. If the people and agencies in practice do not do these things, how could they be done?

In explaining why Title I/NCLB was so difficult to implement, and so controversial, we identified three paradoxes in the relations between the policy and educational practice. We return to them here, in conclusion, because they also will play a central role in the design and implementation of the reauthorized NCLB and the common core standards. The paradoxes describe three distinct elements of the collision between established political institutions, the social and economic environment, and educational arrangements, on the one hand, and policies that attempt fundamental change, on the other.

One paradox concerns government. Both the common core standards project and any conceivable reauthorization of Title I/NCLB aim to bring coherence to education by creating rational relationships among academic standards, assessments, educational processes, and student outcomes. Yet the policies will be put into practice in many thousands of state and local jurisdictions and individual schools that are a leading source of the incoherence. Long fragmented, there has been little strong and salient guidance for instruction; teachers, schools, and districts have had great autonomy. The political system that caused the incoherence will be the chief agent for implementing policies that seek to create coherence. This collision was at the root of much of the inconsistency in state, local, and classroom responses to IASA and NCLB, and it concisely describes sources of inconsistency in state, local, and classroom responses to new or revised policies.

The second paradox concerns capability. Successful implementation of the new policies will require extensive knowledge, skill, and determination to improve teaching and learning, new technologies of assessment, and much more, if they are to have the intended effects. But it is precisely the absence of that capability that explains why so many schools are weak and unable to improve. The very modestly capable organizations, which are the sources of the educational weakness that the new or revised policies seek to overcome, will be the key agents for implementing those new policies. The collision between ambitious policies and weakly capable educational systems is a key source of the generally weak responses to IASA and NCLB. It will be a central problem in state, local, and classroom responses to new or revised policies.

The third paradox concerns excellence and equality. IASA and NCLB required states to set high standards for academic performance, and to use tests and accountability to guide and encourage that performance. The common core project uses very similar language, as would any conceivable reauthorized version of NCLB. Yet at the same time that school outcomes were to improve for all, states were required to make average school outcomes equal among races and social classes. Academic excellence always has been challenging, even in schools relatively untouched by poverty; it is even more challenging in the high-poverty schools that Title I serves. The press for equality of excellence in group academic outcomes is profoundly at odds with the unequal conditions of education in the United States. None of the recent or new education policies are paired with policies that support improved employment, better health care, and early education, nor do they make a substantial effort to reduce unequal educational resources among schools within districts, among districts within states, or among states. Educational, social, and economic inequality are potent sources of unequal educational quality and outcomes, yet all recent policies address public education as though schools could dramatically change their operations apart from the political, social, and economic sources of educational problems. Unequal schools, which operate in one of the most unequal societies in human history, have been selected to be the chief or even sole agent that corrects the educational effects of those inequalities.

There is no way that a reauthorized NCLB or the common core project can avoid the collisions that these paradoxes describe. The question is whether policymakers, practitioners, and interested parties can find relatively effective ways to manage them, in order to improve education. One key point is to understand that the conditions the paradoxes describe are among the most important problems that practitioners and policymakers must solve, if they are to succeed; it will not help to ignore them. Another key aspect is to see that, as the paradoxes imply, these policies aim to fundamentally change education, and to do so root and branch; such attempts are never easy or quick. Endurance is as essential as intelligence. Still another key point is to recognize that such change will require rebuilding education both from policy inward and from practice outward; arrangements that enable both also will be essential. Change of this scope and depth is, among other things, a matter of learning and unlearning. It includes acquiring new capability while relinquishing the old, and it will depend on devising ways for individuals, organizations, and systems to learn systematically from experience. Only then will policymakers and practitioners be able to capitalize on what seems to work and revise what does not. Arrangements that support such learning in practice, policy, and independent inquiry could be very useful. Finally, it would help to acknowledge that, though educators must do their very best to overcome the educational effects of social, economic, and educational inequality, schools, children, and teachers do not live and work in a social and economic vacuum. Reducing the inequalities that frame their work is as important an educational intervention as reducing inequalities in the classroom.

Notes

1. The Transformation of Title I?

1. Joseph J. Ellis, *Founding Brothers: The Revolutionary Generation* (New York: Vintage, 2000), offers a lively account of these worries. See, for example, pp. 7–8, as well as his discussions of Hamilton, Jefferson, and John Adams. See also James Roger Sharp, *American Politics in the Early Republic* (New Haven, CT: Yale University Press, 1993), 53–113.

2. These divisions shaped the development of American state capacity across policy domains. See Stephen Skowronek, *Building a New American State: The Expansion of National Administrative Capacities, 1877–1920* (New York: Cambridge University Press, 1982), for thoughtful analysis of this tension in the context of the U.S. military, civil service, and market regulation.

3. F. J. Munger and R. F. Fenno, *National Politics and Federal Aid to Education* (Syracuse, NY: Syracuse University Press, 1962). See also Hugh Davis Graham, *The Uncertain Triumph: Federal Education Policy in the Kennedy and Johnson Years* (Chapel Hill: University of North Carolina Press, 1984).

4. For detailed accounts of Title I's passage and early administration, see Stephen Bailey and Edith Mosher, *ESEA: The Office of Education Administers a Law* (Syracuse, NY: Syracuse University Press, 1968); Eugene Eidenberg and Roy Morey, *An Act of Congress: The Legislative Process and the Making of Education Policy* (New York: W. W. Norton, 1969); Julie Roy Jeffrey, *Education for Children of the Poor: A Study of the Origins and Implementation of the Elementary and Secondary Education Act of 1965* (Columbus: Ohio State University Press, 1978); and Graham, *The Uncertain Triumph.*

5. Horace Mann, Annual Reports of the Secretary of the Massachusetts Board of Education for the years 1845–1848, *Life and Works of Horace Mann. Twelfth Report,* vol. 4 (Boston: Lee and Shepard Publishers, 1891), 251.

6. Christopher Cross notes "Title I formula takes into account the states average per pupil expenditure, so that the unequal resources available to states based on their tax base is magnified by this factor." Personal Communication, March 2009.

7. John F. Jennings, "The Elementary and Secondary Education Act: The 1960s and 1970s," in *A Compilation of Papers on the Twentieth Anniversary of the Elementary and Secondary Education Act of 1965,* compiled by the Subcommittee on Elementary and Secondary and Vocational Education, House of Representatives (Washington, DC: Government Printing Office, 1985), 55–60.

8. However, in many states, including California and Texas, localities choose texts from state adoption lists.

9. The Regents exams implied a curriculum, and students who sought a Regents degree to prepare for the exams. Similarly, students who participated in the countrywide AP program studied common curricula in mathematics, history, and other subjects. The curricula were referenced to AP examinations that were used to determine whether participants could be exempted from university courses. Teachers who taught AP courses, along with college professors who taught the same subjects, judged and graded students' exams each year and devised the next year's exams.

10. William J. Reese, *America's Public Schools* (Baltimore: Johns Hopkins University Press, 2005).

11. One early documentation of poor conditions in Northern schools attended by African American students concerned the Smith School in the *Boston Grammar School Visiting Committee Report.* This report appears in Alexander Young, Aurelius D. Parker, Winslow Lewis, Samuel G. Howe, and Ezra Palmer, *Reports of the Annual Visiting Committees of the Public Schools of the City of Boston* (Boston: J. H. Eastburn, City Printer, 1845). A more recent analysis is Marguerite Roza and Paul Hill, "How Within-District Inequalities Help Some Schools to Fail," in *Brookings Papers on Education, 2004,* ed. Diane Ravitch (Washington, DC: Brookings Institution Press, 2004).

12. At the time, federal data collections were limited to descriptive tallies of school enrollment, attendance, graduation rates, basic school expenditures, and other palpable resources. See W. Vance Grant, "Statistics in the U.S. Department of Education: Highlights from the Past 120 Years," in *120 Years of American Education: A Statistical Portrait,* ed. Thomas D. Snyder (Washington, DC: National Center for Education Statistics, 1993). These collections relied on state and local self-reporting, resulting, at times, in inconsistent and unreliable data. NAEP was created, at least in former USOE Commissioner Francis Keppel's view, as a way to gather data that might one day enable some comparisons.

13. J. Murphy, *Grease the Squeaky Wheel* (Lexington, MA: Lexington Books, 1974).

14. Federal Impact Aid compensated communities for reductions in their tax bases resulting from federal installations. It was a federal funding stream, since it imposed no substantive educational requirements.

15. Brenda Turnbull noted (Personal Communication, May 2009), Title I's five-year studies typically examined issues that appeared salient to Congress at the time, and were not a cumulative effort to build usable knowledge about the program.

16. See Theda Skocpol, *Social Policy in the United States: Future Possibilities in Historical Perspective* (Princeton, NJ: Princeton University Press, 1997), 252–253, for discussion of the relationship between poverty and social influence.

17. Sidney Verba, Kay Lehman Schlozman, and Henry E. Brady, *Voice and Equality: Civic Voluntarism and American Politics* (Cambridge, MA: Harvard University Press, 1995); Steven Rosenstone and John Mark Hansen, *Mobilization, Participation, and Democracy in America* (New York: Macmillan, 1993); Raymond Wolfinger and Steven Rosenstone, *Who Votes?* (New Haven, CT: Yale University Press, 1980).

18. Verba, Lehman Schlozman, and Brady, *Voice and Equality,* 195.

19. Andrea Louise Campbell, "Universalism, Targeting and Participation," in *Remaking America: Democracy and Public Policy in an Age of Inequality,* ed. Joe Soss, Jacob S. Hacker, and Suzanne Mettler (New York: Russell Sage Foundation, 2007), 123.

20. Margaret Weir, Ann Shola Orloff, and Theda Skocpol, *The Politics of Social Policy in the United States* (Princeton, NJ: Princeton University Press, 1988), 429–441.

21. Skocpol, *Social Policy in the United States,* 253.

22. By spreading benefits broadly and mobilizing broad support, Title I has shaped politics. Paul Pierson, "When Effect Becomes Cause: Policy Feedback and Political Change," *World Politics* 45 (July 1993): 595–628; Andrea Louise Campbell, *How Policies Make Citizens: Senior Political Activism and the American Welfare State* (Princeton, NJ: Princeton University Press, 2003); Suzanne Mettler, *Soldiers to Citizens: The G.I. Bill and the Making of the Greatest Generation* (New York: Oxford University Press, 2005).

23. P. L. Donahue, *NAEP 2008 Trends in Academic Progress* (NCES 2009–479) (Washington, DC: National Center for Education Statistics, Institute of Education Sciences, U.S. Department of Education, 2009), Figure 7, p. 29.

24. Ibid., 9, 14.

25. G. Gage Kingsbury, Allan Olson, John Cronin, Carl Hauser, and Ron Houser, *The State of State Standards: Research Investigating Proficiency Levels in*

Fourteen States (Portland, OR: Northwest Evaluation Association, 2004), 11–18; B. Fuller, K. Gesicki, E. Kang, and J. Wright, *Is the No Child Left Behind Act Working? The Reliability of How States Track Achievement* (Berkeley, CA: PACE, 2006), 1–21. As Kingsbury et al. note, there is considerable controversy over proficiency levels on the NAEP tests, with several experts asserting that they are more demanding than tests in most other nations.

26. Diane Ravitch, "Every State Left Behind," *New York Times,* November 7, 2005.

27. Douglas B. Downey, Paul T. von Hippel, and Beckett A. Broh, "Are Schools the Great Equalizer? Cognitive Inequality during the Summer Months and the School Year," *American Sociological Review* 79, no. 5 (October 2004): 613–635. See also Richard Rothstein, *Class and Schools—Using Social, Economic, and Educational Reform to Close the Black-White Achievement Gap* (Washington, DC: Economic Policy Institute, 2004).

28. See Table 3, "Student membership and current expenditures per pupil for public elementary and secondary education, by function, subfunction, and state or jurisdiction: Fiscal year 2006," in National Center for Education Statistics, *Revenues and Expenditures for Public Elementary and Secondary Education: School Year 2005–06 (Fiscal Year 2006),* http://www.eric.ed.gov/ERICDocs/data/ ericdocs2sql/content_storage_01/0000019b/80/3d/60/b1.pdf.

2. Policy and Practice

Portions of this chapter were published as David K. Cohen, Susan L. Moffitt, and Simona Goldin, "Policy and Practice: The Dilemma," *American Journal of Education* 134, no. 4 (September 2007): 515–548.

1. Top-down theorists often consider policymakers to be those at higher levels of government, i.e., federal and state officials. See Eugene Bardach, *The Implementation Game* (Cambridge, MA: MIT Press, 1977); Daniel A. Mazmanian and Paul A. Sabatier, *Implementation and Public Policy* (Lanham, MD: University Press of America, 1989).

2. The literature on implementation is extensive. Among the most useful accounts are Richard F. Elmore, "Organizational Models of Social Program Implementation," *Public Policy* 23, no. 2 (1978): 185–228; Richard F. Elmore, "Backward Mapping: Implementation Research and Policy Decisions," *Political Science Quarterly* 94, no. 4 (1979–1980): 601–616; Charles Lindblom, "The Science of 'Muddling Through,'" *Public Administration Review* 19, no. 2 (Spring 1959): 79–88; Michael Lipsky, *Street-Level Bureaucracy: Dilemmas of the Individual in Public Service*

(New York: Russell Sage, 1980); Mazmanian and Sabatier, *Implementation and Public Policy;* Milbrey W. McLaughlin, "Learning from Experience: Lessons from Policy Implementation," in *Education Policy Implementation,* ed. Allan R. Odden (Albany: State University of New York Press, 1991), 185–196; Milbrey W. McLaughlin, "The RAND Change Agent Study: Ten Years Later," in *Education Policy Implementation,* ed. Allan R. Odden (Albany: State University of New York Press, 1991), 143–156; Jeffrey L. Pressman and Aaron B. Wildavsky, *Implementation,* 3rd ed. (Berkeley: University of California Press, 1984); and Donald S. Van Meter and Carl E. Van Horn, "The Policy Implementation Process: A Conceptual Framework," *Administration and Society* 6, no. 4 (1975): 445–488.

3. E. J. Mosbaek, F. R. Frola, K. F. Gordon, and J. W. Harrison, *Analysis of Compensatory Education in Five School Districts* (Washington, DC: TEMPO, 1969).

4. "The notion that policymakers exercise—or ought to exercise—some kind of direct and determinant control over policy implementation might be called the 'noble lie' of conventional public administration and policy analysis"; Elmore, "Backward Mapping," 603.

5. Paul Berman and Milbrey W. McLaughlin, *Federal Programs Supporting Educational Change* (Santa Monica, CA: RAND, 1979), 8:21.

6. McLaughlin, "Learning from Experience," 187. Ten years after the RAND Change Agent Study, McLaughlin ("The RAND Change Agent Study," 149) revised her view: "Belief or commitment can follow mandated or 'coerced' involvement at both the individual and the system level. . . . We did not see or did not recognize instances in which belief follows practice. Individuals required [by policy] to change routines or take up new practices can [thereby] become 'believers.' "

7. Berman and McLaughlin, *Federal Programs Supporting Educational Change;* Elmore, "Backward Mapping"; Ann Chih Lin, *Reform in the Making: The Implementation of Social Policy in Prison* (Princeton, NJ: Princeton University Press, 2000); Lipsky, *Street-Level Bureaucracy.*

8. McLaughlin, "Learning from Experience," 189.

9. Lipsky, *Street-Level Bureaucracy.*

10. David K. Cohen, Steven Raudenbush, and Deborah L. Ball, "Resources, Instruction and Research," *Educational Evaluation and Policy Analysis* 25, no. 2 (2003): 119–142.

11. Eric Hanushek has argued that the effects of resources depend on their use, a point that has been overlooked in disputes about his discussions of weak resource effects. Eric Hanushek, "School Resources and Student Performance," in *Does Money Matter? The Effect of School Resources on Student Achievement and Adult Success,* ed. Gary Burtless (Washington, DC: Brookings, 1996), 43–73.

12. Explaining intraorganizational issues through principal agent theory recognizes control and compliance problems at several points along an implementation path, which might imply that a "bottom" can also be a "top." See John Brehm and Scott Gates, *Working, Shirking, and Sabotage: Bureaucratic Response to a Democratic Public* (Ann Arbor: University of Michigan Press, 1997). But doing so treats these relations as layered, in isolation, even though individuals or agencies often play both roles.

13. For a helpful, somewhat parallel discussion, see Richard F. Elmore, "Agency, Reciprocity, and Accountability in Democratic Education," in *The Public Schools,* ed. Susan Fuhrman and Marvin Lazerson (Oxford: Oxford University Press, 2005), 277–301.

14. Eric M. Patashnik, *Reforms at Risk: What Happens after Major Policy Changes Are Enacted* (Princeton, NJ: Princeton University Press, 2008), 19. For an analysis of Title I that uses a regime change framework, see Patrick J. McGuinn, *No Child Left Behind and the Transformation of Federal Education Policy, 1965–2005* (Lawrence: University of Kansas Press, 2006), 19.

15. Stephen Skowronek, *Building a New American State: The Expansion of National Administrative Capacities, 1877–1920* (New York: Cambridge University Press, 1982), 15.

16. This builds on policy feedback frameworks. See Paul Pierson, "When Effect Becomes Cause: Policy Feedback and Political Change," *World Politics* 45 (July 1993): 595–628; Andrea Louise Campbell, *How Policies Make Citizens: Senior Political Activism and the American Welfare State* (Princeton, NJ: Princeton University Press, 2003); Suzanne Mettler, *Soldiers to Citizens: The G.I. Bill and the Making of the Greatest Generation* (New York: Oxford University Press, 2005).

17. See Patashnik, *Reforms at Risk,* 154. Enacting policies like airline deregulation and emission trading did not require the building of significant new technical and administrative capabilities. Almost by definition, such policies reduce the role of and demands on government. Yet, such policies have entailments for capability in practice; airline deregulation, for instance, placed new burdens on air traffic controllers to manage burgeoning workloads and on customers to manage the changed technical environment. The question is not whether policies have entailments for practice and politics but how different types of policy allocate the entailments.

18. Janet A. Weiss, "Ideas and Inducements in Mental Health Policy," *Journal of Policy Analysis and Management* 9, no. 2 (1990): 178–200.

19. David K. Cohen, "Revolution in One Classroom," *Educational Evaluation and Policy Analysis* 12, no. 3 (1990): 311–329.

20. David K. Cohen and Carol A. Barnes, "A New Pedagogy for Policy?" in *Teaching for Understanding: Challenges for Policy and Practice*, ed. David K. Cohen, Milbrey W. McLaughlin, and Joan E. Talbert (San Francisco, CA: Jossey-Bass, 1993), 240–275; David K. Cohen and Carol A. Barnes, "Pedagogy and Policy," in Cohen, McLaughlin, and Talbert, *Teaching for Understanding*, 207–239.

21. James P. Spillane and Charles L. Thompson, "Reconstructing Conceptions of Local Capacity: The Local Education Agency's Capacity for Ambitious Instructional Reform," *Educational Evaluation and Policy Analysis* 19, no. 2 (1997): 195–203; James P. Spillane and John S. Zeuli, "Reform and Mathematics Teaching: Exploring Patterns of Practice in the Context of National State Reforms," *Educational Evaluation and Policy Analysis* 21, no. 1 (1999): 1–27; David K. Cohen and Heather C. Hill, *Learning Policy: When State Education Reform Works* (New Haven, CT: Yale University Press, 2001).

22. Cynthia E. Coburn and Mary Kay Stein, "Communities of Practice Theory and the Role of Teacher Professional Community in Policy Implementation," in *New Directions in Education Policy Implementation: Confronting Complexity*, ed. Meredith I. Honig (Albany: State University of New York Press, 2006), 25–46.

23. Several of these studies were collected in a recent volume, Honig, *New Directions in Education Policy Implementation*. See, e.g., Heather C. Hill, "Language Matters: How Characteristics of Language Complicate Policy Implementation," in Honig, *New Directions in Education Policy Implementation*, 65–82.

24. Dvora Yanow, *How Does a Policy Mean?* (Washington, DC: Georgetown University Press, 1996).

25. James P. Spillane, Brian J. Reiser, and Louis M. Gomez, "Policy Implementation and Cognition: The Role of Human, Social, and Distributed Cognition in Framing Policy Implementation," in Honig, *New Directions in Education Policy Implementation*, 63.

26. Although this point has not been central to most analyses of implementation, several scholars have called attention to aspects of it. Richard Elmore ("Backward Mapping," 611) wrote that "unless the initiators of a policy can galvanize the energy, attention, and skills of those affected by it . . . the effects of policy are unlikely to be anything but weak and diffuse." Milbrey McLaughlin ("Learning from Experience," 189) wrote that policy implementation is a "problem of the smallest unit." Elmore and McLaughlin wrote that the fate of reforms ultimately depends on those who are the object of distrust (Richard F. Elmore and Milbrey W. McLaughlin, *Steady Work: Policy, Practice, and the Reform of American Education* [Santa Monica, CA: RAND, 1988]). Ann Chih Lin (*Reform*

in the Making, 14) writes that "every grand idea and good wish that policymakers have lies in the hands of others who implement them."

27. E. E. Schattschneider, *Politics, Pressures, and the Tariff* (New York: Prentice-Hall, 1935); Pierson, "When Effect Becomes Cause"; Campbell, *How Policies Make Citizens;* Mettler, *Soldiers to Citizens.*

28. Joe Soss, "Lessons from Welfare: Policy Design, Political Learning, and Political Action," *American Political Science Review* 93, no. 2 (1999): 363–380.

29. Bardach, *The Implementation Game.*

30. This does not mean that preexisting competencies that might have achieved new aims were obliterated; quite the contrary, it means that new aims in public endeavors created demands for competencies whose existence grows less likely as aims grow more ambitious.

31. Margaret Weir, "Ideas and the Politics of Bounded Innovation," in *Structuring Politics: Historical Institutionalism in Comparative Analysis,* ed. Sven Steinmo, Kathleen Thelen, and Frank Longstreth (New York: Cambridge University Press, 1992), 194–195.

32. On ideas as policy instruments, see Janet A. Weiss and Judith E. Gruber, "Using Knowledge for Control in Fragmented Policy Arenas," *Journal of Policy Analysis and Management* 3, no. 2 (1984): 225–247; Janet A. Weiss, "Ideas and Inducements in Mental Health Policy"; Janet A. Weiss and Mary Tschirhart, "Public Information Campaigns as Policy Instruments," *Journal of Policy Analysis and Management* 13, no. 1 (1994): 82–119; Cohen and Hill, *Learning Policy.*

33. We base our use of the term *instruments* on McDonnell and Elmore's explanation of the term: "the mechanisms that translate substantive policy goals (e.g., improved student achievement, higher quality entering teachers) into actions." Lorraine M. McDonnell and Richard F. Elmore, "Getting the Job Done: Alternative Policy Instruments," *Educational Evaluation and Policy Analysis* 9, no. 2 (1987): 134. They do not address either adaptability or instruments' salience for practice. For discussion of the former, see McLaughlin, "Learning from Experience"; for discussion of the latter, see Cohen and Hill, *Learning Policy,* 2–8, 148–151, 166–167, 180, 184.

34. We prefer "capability" since warehouses have capacity but people and organizations have capability. Studies of education policy implementation often mention capacity, but we found no analysis of the concept; typically it refers to knowledge and skill. There is a literature on capability in the philosophy of economics, due largely to Amartya Sen's use of the concept in his critiques of utilitarian views of the quality of life. Sen's view and several related discussions can be found in Martha C. Nussbaum and Amartya K. Sen, *The Quality of Life* (Oxford: Oxford University Press, 1993).

35. James P. Spillane, "Cognition and Policy Implementation: District Policy-Makers and the Reform of Mathematics Education," *Cognition and Instruction* 18, no. 2 (2000): 141–170.

36. Giandomenico Majone and Aaron Wildarsky, "Implementation as Evolution," in *Implementation,* by Jeffrey Pressman and Aaron Wildarsky (Berkeley: University of Califorinia Press, 1984), 177–194.

37. Ibid., 176.

38. Evelyn Z. Brodkin, "Implementation as Policy Politics," in *Implementation and the Policy Process: Opening up the Black Box,* ed. Dennis J. Palumbo and Donald J. Calista (New York: Greenwood, 1990), 107–118.

39. Michael Kirst, interview conducted by David K. Cohen and Susan L. Moffitt, September 1995.

40. This feature of Title I resembles weak state school finance policies that were nonetheless seen as powerful means to equalize educational opportunity.

41. Lynn Olson, "A 'Proficient' Score Depends on Geography," *Education Week,* February 20, 2002; Susan Saulny, "State to State: Varied Ideas of Proficient," *New York Times,* January 19, 2005, 8.

42. Doubts about the use of tests in Title I did surface intermittently, when every five-year reauthorization brought evaluations to estimate the effects of Title I.

43. Herbert A. Simon, Donald W. Smithburg, and Victor A. Thompson, *Public Administration* (New York: Knopf, 1950), 415.

44. Susan H. Fuhrman and Richard F. Elmore, "Takeover and Deregulation: Working Models of New State and Local Regulatory Relationships," CPRE Research Report no. RR-24 (New Brunswick, NJ: Consortium for Policy Research in Education, Rutgers University, 1992); Susan H. Fuhrman and Richard F. Elmore, "Ruling Out Rules: The Evolution of Deregulation in State Education Policy," *Teachers College Record* 97, no. 2 (1995): 279–309.

45. Peter Dow, *Schoolhouse Politics: Lessons from the Sputnik Era* (Cambridge, MA: Harvard University Press, 1993); Seymour Sarason, *The Culture of the School and the Problem of Change* (New York: Wiley, 1973).

46. Simon, Smithburg, and Thompson, *Public Administration,* 415.

47. Dow, *Schoolhouse Politics,* offers an account of these problems for one such curriculum.

48. Dan Koretz, *Measuring Up* (Cambridge, MA: Harvard University Press, 2008).

49. Lin, *Reform in the Making.*

50. Bardach, *The Implementation Game.*

51. Jay Chambers, Thomas Parrish, Margaret Goertz, Camille Marder, and Christine Padilla, *Translating Dollars into Services: Chapter 1 Resources in the*

Context of State and Local Resources for Education. Final Report (Washington, DC: United States Department of Education, Office of Policy and Planning, 1993).

52. Jay G. Chambers, Irene Lam, Kanya Mahitivanichcha, Phil Esra, Larisa Shambaugh, and Stephanie Stullich, *State and Local Implementation of the No Child Left Behind Act: Volume VI—Targeting and Uses of Federal Education Funds* (Washington, DC: U.S. Department of Education, 2009), Exhibit 1, p. 2. This estimate does not include funds distributed as part of the 2009 stimulus package, The American Recovery and Reinvestment Act of 2009.

53. David K. Cohen and James P. Spillane, "Policy and Practice: The Relations between Governance and Instruction," in *Review of Research in Education,* ed. Gerald Grant (Washington, DC: American Educational Research Association, 1992).

54. The Obey-Porter amendment (Public Law 105-78) to Title I was passed in 1997, and provided about $150 million annually to support comprehensive school reform designs like SFA and AC. We discuss these further in Chapter 6, pp. 172–173.

55. Bardach, *The Implementation Game,* 126.

56. Capability, in this view, is a crucial element in political coalitions and policy support.

57. Anthony S. Bryk and Barbara Schneider, *Trust in Schools: A Core Resource for Improvement* (New York: Russell Sage, 2002).

58. Ideas require political support for programs to persist and for program administrators to "'learn from their mistakes' and modify policy accordingly" (Weir, "Ideas and the Politics of Bounded Innovation," 193–194).

59. Ira Katznelson and Margaret Weir, *Schooling for All: Class, Race, and the Decline of the Democratic Ideal* (New York: Basic Books, 1985).

60. Ibid.; Margaret Weir, Ann Shola Orloff, and Theda Skocpol, *The Politics of Social Policy in the United States* (Princeton, NJ: Princeton University Press, 1988).

61. Chambers et al., *Translating Dollars,* 134.

62. Milbrey McLaughlin ("Learning from Experience," 188) wrote: "Experience shows that some balance of pressure and support is essential. Pressure is required in most settings to focus attention on a reform objective; support is needed to enable implementation."

3. Recovering from Practice Failure

1. Elizabeth Debray, *Politics, Ideology, and Education* (New York: Teachers College Press, 2006), 13.

2. On social science, see, e.g., Kenneth B. Clark, "Education of Minority Poor: The Key to the War on Poverty," in *Disadvantaged Poor: Education and Employment, Third Report of the Task Force on Economic Growth Opportunity* (Washington, DC: Chamber of Commerce of the United States, 1966), 175, cited in Paul Peterson, Barry Rabe, and Kenneth Wong, *When Federalism Works* (Washington, DC: Brookings Institution, 1986). On the administration's view, see comments from Commissioner Keppel and Secretary Celebrezze. U.S. House Committee on Education and Labor, *Aid to Elementary and Secondary Education,* 89th Cong., 1st sess., 1965, 65–83, cited in P. Meranto, *The Politics of Federal Aid to Education in 1965: A Study in Political Innovation* (Syracuse, NY: Syracuse University Press, 1967), 36–37.

3. U.S. Senate, Committee on Labor and Public Welfare, *Elementary and Secondary Education Act of 1965: Background Material with Related Presidential Recommendations,* 89th Cong., 1st sess., 1965, 5–7, cited in Meranto, *The Politics of Federal Aid to Education,* 34.

4. E. J. Mosbaek, *Analysis of Compensatory Education in Five School Districts* (Washington, DC: G. E. TEMPO, 1968).

5. The Washington Research Project co-sponsored the report.

6. Ruby Martin and Phyllis McClure, *Title I of ESEA: Is It Helping Poor Children?* (Washington, DC: Washington Research Project of the Southern Center for Studies in Public Policy and the NAACP Legal Defense and Education Fund, 1969).

7. Their report argued that language in Title I's authorizing legislation suggested Congress intended it to be an antipoverty program. See Martin and McClure, *Title I of ESEA,* 6–26. Phyllis McClure, interview conducted by Susan L. Moffitt, December 1994.

8. The Martin-McClure report illustrated ways in which local practice was incompliant with regulations and provisions on proper fund use, such as the supplement-not-supplant principle. See, e.g., C.F.R § 116.17 (h), cited in Martin and McClure, *Title I of ESEA,* 124.

9. Martin and McClure, *Title I of ESEA,* 16–17, 86–87.

10. Citing USOE documents, Jerome Murphy argued that 30 percent of students participating in Title I in 1968 were not disadvantaged, while millions of disadvantaged children received no aid. See J. Murphy, "Title I: Bureaucratic Politics and Poverty Politics," *Inequality in Education* 6 (November 1970): 9–15.

11. Eidenberg and Morey note that Republican opponents put a chart in the 1966 committee report showing that "the ten most wealthy counties in the nation received more aid during the first year than the ten poorest counties."

See E. Eidenberg and R. Morey, *An Act of Congress: The Legislative Process and the Making of Education Policy* (New York: W. W. Norton, 1969), 183–184.

12. How much Title I added per pupil at the time is unclear. M. Kirst and R. Jung cite $116 as the amount Title I added in 1966, in "The Utility of a Longitudinal Approach in Assessing Implementation: A Thirteen-Year View of Title I, ESEA," in *Educational Evaluation and Policy Analysis* 2, no. 5 (1980), 23. Martin and McClure cite 1965–1966 per pupil served amounts at $96, 1966–1967 at $99, and 1968–1969 at $108 (Martin and McClure, *Title I of ESEA*). The TEMPO study found that "There is a general tendency to allocate . . . 20 percent of Title I funds to a very small number of pupils and to allocate the other 80% over such a large number of pupils that in most cases the funds amount to less than $5 per pupil" (cited in Martin and McClure, *Title I of ESEA*, 18–19). J. Berke and M. Kirst argue that by 1970, Title I added, on average, $95 per pupil served; see *Federal Aid to Education—Who Benefits? Who Governs?* (New Britain, CT: Lexington Books, 1972). S. K. Bailey and E. K. Mosher write that variations around those averages were considerable, ranging from about $25 to $227 per pupil; see Baily and Mosher, *ESEA: The Office of Education Administers a Law* (Syracuse, NY: Syracuse University Press, 1968), 164–165 (estimates based on the *First Annual Report, Title I, Elementary and Secondary Education Act of 1965* [USOE, 90th Cong., 1st sess., Senate, Subcommittee on Education, Notes and working papers, T1 of P.L. 89-10, 915]).

13. Berke and Kirst, *Federal Aid to Education*, 44. The significance of Title I aid is disputed. Bailey and Mosher argued that "For many states, [Title I] represented a substantial increase over average current per pupil expenditures, the national average being about $532 for 1965–66" (Bailey and Mosher, *ESEA: The Office of Education Administers a Law,* 164). Yet Feldstein argued that in the early years, for every dollar of federal aid they received, districts reduced the amount they spent on education by $0.28; M. Feldstein, "The Effect of Differential Add-on Grant: Title I and Local Education Spending," *Journal of Human Resources* 13 (1978): 450, cited in Peterson, Rabe, and Wong, *When Federalism Works,* 134.

14. John F. Jennings, "The Elementary and Secondary Education Act: The 1960s and 1970s," in *A Compilation of Papers on the Twentieth Anniversary of the Elementary and Secondary Education Act of 1965,* Subcommittee on Elementary and Secondary and Vocational Education, House of Representatives (Washington, DC: Government Printing Office, 1985), 55–60.

15. John F. Jennings, interview conducted by David K. Cohen and Susan L. Moffitt, November 1994. Rep. John Brademas, a Democrat from Indiana, played a major role in developing the child benefit concept (Christopher Cross, Personal Communication, March 2009).

16. Though private school students would receive services, public schools would typically continue to manage the funds that supported the services that private students received (Christopher Cross, Personal Communication, March 2009).

17. One Democratic House member said that "The bill itself was really categorical aid with categories so broad that the aid splattered over the face of the entire school system and could be called general aid in principle while politically remaining categorical aid"; quoted in Eidenberg and Morey, *An Act of Congress,* 90–91.

18. John F. Jennings, interview conducted by David K. Cohen and Susan L. Moffitt, November 1994. Paul Hill, interview conducted by Susan L. Moffitt, October 1994.

19. New Deal social policies also could be "dramatic" and yet quite limited: see Margaret Weir, Ann Shola Orloff, and Theda Skocpol, *The Politics of Social Policy in the United States* (Princeton, NJ: Princeton University Press, 1988), 17–18.

20. Weir, Orloff, and Skocpol (*The Politics of Social Policy in the United States,* 432) tell a similar story for Social Security—i.e., it created new benefits and bureaucratic procedures but no substantial redesign of government.

21. See Rep. Howard Smith's comments in *Congressional Record,* March 24, 1965, 5553, cited in Meranto, *The Politics of Federal Aid to Education in 1965,* 92–93. See also Eidenberg and Morey, *An Act of Congress,* 224.

22. Thomas argues that categorical aid was a compromise that allowed conservatives to support ESEA and still oppose general federal aid and that appealed to liberals who preferred some federal aid to none. Norman C. Thomas, *Education in National Politics* (New York: David McKay, 1975), 38.

23. Meranto (*The Politics of Federal Aid to Education in 1965,* 40–41) argues that the categorical nature of Title I funds and connections to fighting poverty helped quiet opponents of federal aid.

24. John Hughes, *Equal Education: A New National Strategy* (Bloomington: Indiana University Press, 1972), 22.

25. Ibid., 22–23.

26. Bailey and Mosher, *ESEA: The Office of Education Administers a Law,* 100.

27. Jerome Murphy, "Title I of ESEA: The Politics of Implementing Federal Education Reform," *Harvard Educational Review* 41, no. 1 (February 1971): 35–64. State monitoring often was informal.

28. Hughes, *Equal Education,* 45–46. This controversy stemmed from the USOE's draft guidelines, which aimed to concentrate funds on a limited number of students. Concerned about the program's impact, the USOE tried to require

that the number of children a district served could not be more than the number of eligible children under the formula. That provoked opposition from Congress and professional interest groups, which argued that the standard was not consistent with congressional intent. In November 1965, the provision was removed. See Murphy, "Title I of ESEA," 48.

29. Peterson et al. (*When Federalism Works*, 134) argue that USOE administrators viewed themselves as professional educators who were averse to federal control in education, not as program administrators.

30. Hughes, *Equal Education*, 45.

31. Bailey and Mosher, *ESEA: The Office of Education Administers a Law*, 100.

32. Murphy, "Title I of ESEA," 40.

33. See Bailey and Mosher, *ESEA: The Office of Education Administers a Law*, 89–93.

34. Michael Kirst, interview conducted by David K. Cohen and Susan L. Moffitt, September 1995.

35. Evidence for the report came from HEW's own audits and from local project applications (Phyllis McClure, Personal Communication, June 2008). Martin and McClure chose districts in which to conduct informal visits based on complaints to the NAACP about misuse of Title I funds. They noted that they tried to select representative districts, based on region, enrollment size, and racial composition (Martin and McClure, *Title I of ESEA*, xiii).

36. In addition to illustrations of misused funds and thin services, the report also called attention to districts' use of Title I to perpetuate segregation, to excessive allocations for nonacademic programs (including expenditures for equipment, nutrition, and health) at the expense of academic ones, and to a lack of community participation in district Title I decision-making (Martin and McClure, *Title I of ESEA*).

37. Ibid., iv.

38. Hearings before the U.S. House General Subcommittee on Education of the Committee on Education and Labor of the House of Representatives, *Elementary and Secondary Education Amendments of 1973, Part 1* (Washington, DC: Government Printing Office, January 31, 1973), 123.

39. Yet, Nixon selected James Allen, a Title I supporter, as Commissioner of Education.

40. Some argued that Nixon sought to tighten the administration of social programs more than to eliminate or reduce them. See Margaret Weir, ed., *The Social Divide: Political Parties and the Future of Activist Government* (Washington, DC: Brookings & Sage, 1998), 19. Political challenges to Title I did not begin with the Nixon administration. See Eidenberg and Morey, *An Act of Congress*, 183–184, and Thomas, *Education in National Politics*, 74–76, 79–83.

41. Julie Roy Jeffrey, *Education for Children of the Poor—A Study of the Origins and Implementation of the Elementary and Secondary Education Act of 1965* (Columbus: Ohio State University Press, 1978), 208. See H.R. 5823, the Better Schools Act of 1973.

42. Nixon used dismal evaluation data from the TEMPO study to justify the creation of the National Institute of Education (NIE) and no increase in Title I funds; see Milbrey W. McLaughlin, *Evaluation and Reform: Title I of the Elementary and Secondary Education Act of 1965* (Cambridge, MA: Ballanger, 1975), 64–65. USOE Commissioner Allen also wrote that the NAACP report was one reason the House held back on additional funding for Title I. See Phi Delta Kappan, "Administration Announces Major Review of Title I," *Phi Delta Kappan* 51 (January 1970): 288.

43. In stark contrast, 1990s policies that offered states more flexibility in exchange for lower funding had more enthusiastic support, particularly from Republican governors. See Weir, *The Social Divide*, 33.

44. John F. Jennings remarks to the Commission on Chapter 1, Notes from the February 11–12, 1991, Commission meeting, p. 15, unpublished, authors' personal archives. Nixon's general revenue-sharing plan was more successful in Congress and passed in 1972. Chester E. Finn, Jr., *Education and the Presidency* (Lexington, MA: Lexington Books, 1977), 83.

45. Cynthia G. Brown, interview conducted by Susan L. Moffitt, September 1995.

46. The power of exposure to school had been an article of American faith since the late eighteenth century, when social environments were seen as a powerful influence on the development of mind, and better environments were seen as a cure for all manner of mental and moral problems. Schools, asylums, prisons, libraries, and other institutions could undo the damage done by poor families, slums, papist doctrine, and other social evils. See D. Rothman, *The Discovery of the Asylum: Social Order and Disorder in the New Republic* (Boston: Little, Brown, 1971); M. Katz, "The Origins of Public Education: A Reassessment," *History of Education Quarterly* 16, no. 4 (Winter 1976): 381–407; D. Ravitch, *The Great School Wars, New York City, 1805–1973: A History of the Public Schools as Battlefield of Social Change* (New York: Basic Books, 1974); C. Kaestle, *Pillars of the Republic: Common Schools and American Society, 1780–1860* (New York: Hill and Wang, 1983).

47. Cynthia G. Brown, interview conducted by Susan L. Moffitt, September 1995.

48. The political pressures for federal aid were related to the civil rights movement; the legislation was in certain respects an effort to "do something" about

the problems the movement highlighted. Though many movement activists were skeptical about the program because it would operate in and thus seem to legitimate segregated schools, they were a primary force behind its inception and early history.

49. U.S. House General Subcommittee on Education of the Committee on Education and Labor of the House of Representatives, *Elementary and Secondary Education Amendments of 1973, Part 1* (Washington, DC: Government Printing Office, February 6, 1973), 400.

50. John F. Jennings, interview conducted by David K. Cohen and Susan L. Moffitt, November 1994.

51. Michael Kirst, interview conducted by David K. Cohen and Susan L. Moffitt, September 1995. Murphy, "Title I of ESEA."

52. U.S. Department of Health, Education and Welfare, *History of Title I ESEA*, DHEW Publication No (OE) 72-75 (Washington, DC: U.S. Department of Education, June 1969), 12.

53. Comparability provisions were included in the 1969 Elementary and Secondary Amendments, P.L. 91-230 (1970). 1969 Title I program guidelines required states to receive assurance from districts that they allocated state and local money to "project areas" at levels comparable to "non-project areas." See Timothy Wirth, *Incrementalism in Education Policy Making: A Case Study of Title I, ESEA* (PhD diss., Harvard Graduate School of Education, 1973), 44. Yet one review of state and local compliance found that comparability requirements were not met. A special task force, charged with proposing comparability standards, found that 55.8 percent of schools in eighty districts in thirty-one states were not comparable (Wirth, *Incrementalism in Education*, 49).

54. Kirst and Jung, "The Utility of a Longitudinal Approach in Assessing Implementation," 30.

55. Phyllis McClure, interview conducted by Susan L. Moffitt, December 1994. See Wirth, *Incrementalism in Education*, concerning comparability. Teacher salaries were difficult: they were about 80 percent of per pupil expenditures, and higher salaried teachers had greater mobility and would "promote themselves out of poorer schools" into wealthier schools. This would fill middle-class schools with higher-cost teachers and thereby complicate per pupil expenditures. Teacher contracts often included teachers' rights to assign themselves based on seniority. In addition, given the higher teacher costs of middle-class schools, districts would have to move teachers around to equalize expenditures and meet the comparability standard. Yet many teacher contracts prevented "arbitrary" transferring of teachers between schools, so meeting the comparability standard would create problems with unions. Wirth, *Incrementalism in Education*, 50–51.

56. Kirst and Jung, "The Utility of a Longitudinal Approach in Assessing Implementation," 30–31. These criteria included pupil-teacher ratios, pupil-nonteaching professional staff ratios, pupil-instructional nonprofessional staff ratios, and either per pupil instructional expenditures or total instructional personnel expenditures per pupil. See Phi Delta Kappan, "Clarify Use of Title I Funds," *Phi Delta Kappan* 51 (April 1970): 450.

57. The authors of one NIE study argued that these fiscal and programmatic requirements still provided districts with considerable flexibility in using federal funds. National Institute of Education, *Administration of Compensatory Education* (Washington, DC: USOE, 1977), 19. The new instruments did not, for example, deal with the general practice of allowing senior teachers to choose their assignments, which tended to leave high-poverty schools with inexperienced teachers and aides. As long as total staff salaries were comparable between these schools and others in the district, the gross lack of comparability in teacher quality met the standard.

58. Berke and Kirst, *Federal Aid to Education,* 378.

59. Ibid.

60. Phi Delta Kappan, "USOE Orders States to Repay Title I Funds Improperly Spent," *Phi Delta Kappan* 53 (November 1971): 199.

61. Phyllis McClure, interview conducted by Susan L. Moffitt, December 1994. The HEW Audit Agency, however, was separate from the USOE. Some charged that having a number of offices participate in Title I monitoring complicated the enforcement of compliance. NIE, *Administration of Compensatory Education,* 28.

62. In 1968, USOE officials did program reviews for selected states at unspecified intervals (Bailey and Mosher, *ESEA: The Office of Education Administers a Law,* 108). The USOE conducted program reviews annually for each state beginning in 1970, but they were considered "less rigorous" than audits. See Kirst and Jung, "The Utility of a Longitudinal Approach in Assessing Implementation," 30.

63. B. F. Birman, M. Orland, R. Jung, R. Anson, and G. Garcia, *The Current Operation of the Chapter 1 Program—Final Report from the National Assessment of Chapter 1* (Washington, DC: OERI, U.S. Department of Education, 1987), 143. Fact-finding program reviews included "ad hoc technical assistance" on how to implement regulations (NIE, *Administration of Compensatory Education,* 27).

64. Murphy, "Title I of ESEA," 41.

65. Michael Kirst, interview conducted by David K. Cohen and Susan L. Moffitt, September 1995.

66. See Kirst and Jung, "The Utility of a Longitudinal Approach in Assessing Implementation," 22–26.

67. It is unclear how much of a problem there was; no systematic evidence seemed to be collected, either on how much local behavior had to change or on how much it did. The new measures probably built on a large foundation of spontaneous compliance, for if many localities had not taken responsibility for legally targeting and spending federal funds when they accepted them, there would have been an impossibly huge enforcement problem, or rebellion, or both. The lack of such reactions incline us to presume that most LEAs had done the right thing and required no greater oversight and enforcement and no expanded federal effort. If so, spontaneous compliance and existing know-how meant that in most cases the dilemma of implementation had been managed with no extraordinary action by anyone.

68. See NIE, *Administration of Compensatory Education,* 35–37. The Division for Education of the Disadvantaged (DED) argued with the Office of the Associate Commissioner for Compensatory Education Programs over appropriate indicators of compliance and the burden of proof. An NIE report gave instances in which audits found the same violations but officials set different penalties as well as instances in which different program review teams issued different guidance.

69. J. Kimbrough and P. Hill pointed out that rather than allow districts to tailor programs to suit their needs, the requirements produced excessive paperwork and perverse results, such as computers sitting idly all day; see *The Aggregate Effects of Federal Education Programs* (Santa Monica, CA: RAND, 1981).

70. There is disagreement about the cause. The NIE found a significant decrease nationwide in reported instances of supplanting; some argued this stemmed from advances in fiscal accountability, but others saw it as lax monitoring and enforcement. NIE, *Administration of Compensatory Education,* 23–44.

71. Phyllis McClure, interview conducted by Susan L. Moffitt, December 1994. Peterson et al. report that "Federal audits conducted in the late 1970s also found a steady decline in the misuse of Federal funds." P. Peterson, B. Rabe, and K. Wong, "The Evolution of Compensatory Education Program," in *Federal Aid to the Disadvantaged,* ed. D. Doyle and B. Cooper (New York: Falmer Press, 1988), 44.

72. Comparability was kept from influencing local fund allocation for teachers' salaries, for instance.

73. For an extended account of these developments, see Peterson, Rabe, and Wong, *When Federalism Works* and "The Evolution of Compensatory Education Program."

4. Could Federal Policy Change Classroom Practice?

1. The best account of these developments is Milbrey Wallin McLaughlin, *Evaluation and Reform: Title I of the Elementary and Secondary Education Act of 1965* (Cambridge, MA: Ballainger, 1975).

2. See Joseph S. Wholey, Bayla White, Leona Vogt, and Richard Zamoff, *Title I Evaluation and Technical Assistance: Assessment and Prospects* (Washington, DC: USOE, 1971).

3. Systematic inquiry into the effects of schooling began after World War II, as survey research, mathematical modeling of social processes, and computers enabled large-scale data collection and analysis in which the attributes of many schools and evidence on many educational resources could be related to the performance of many students. Despite its much greater scientific quality, Coleman's study stirred up the same sort of controversy that had greeted earlier investigations, including one in Boston in the 1840s by colleagues of Horace Mann and another by Joseph Mayer Rice at the end of the nineteenth century.

4. See McLaughlin, *Evaluation and Reform*; Gerald Grant, *The Politics of the Coleman Report* (PhD diss., Harvard University, 1972); and Julie Jeffrey, *Education for Children of the Poor* (Columbus: Ohio State University Press, 1978), 143–152, for discussion of reactions to the Coleman Report. Harvey A. Averch et al., *How Effective Is Schooling? A Critical Review and Synthesis of Research Findings* (Santa Monica, CA: RAND, 1972).

5. M. J. Dunkin and B. J. Biddle, *The Study of Teaching* (New York: Holt, Rinehart and Winston, 1974).

6. This was a longitudinal survey of secondary schools that enabled researchers to weigh the effects of school resources on students' achievement near the end of high school, given knowledge of their achievement near the beginning. The analyses were published in inconspicuous mimeographed reports. In most important respects, the EEOS confirmed this large but largely unknown study.

7. Horace Mann's fourth and seventh reports to the Massachusetts Board set out his views on this point. Horace Mann, Annual Reports of the Secretary of the Massachusetts Board of Education for the years 1839–1844, *Life and Works of Horace Mann*, vol. 3 (Boston: Lee and Shepard Publishers, 1891), 53–92, 230–345.

8. For sources, see Chapter 3, note 46.

9. U.S. House Committee on Education and Labor, *Aid to Elementary and Secondary Education*, 89th Cong., 1st sess., 1965, 65–66, cited in P. Meranto, *The Politics of Federal Aid to Education in 1965: A Study in Political Innovation* (Syracuse, NY: Syracuse University Press, 1967), 36.

10. Advocates of categorical aid believed that without restrictions, states and localities would not use funds to address problems of poverty, and money would be poured "down a rat hole"; see Norman C. Thomas, *Education in National Politics* (New York: David McKay, 1975), 116.

11. Kenneth B. Clark, *Dark Ghetto: Dilemmas of Social Power* (Middletown, CT: Wesleyan University Press, 1989).

12. McLaughlin, *Evaluation and Reform,* discusses the idea. It is not far from recent efforts to use tests to create incentives for schools to improve. See Diane Ravitch's op-ed essay, "The History Lesson in Bush's School Plan," *New York Times,* January 27, 2001.

13. The amendment provided the authority for Gorham and Rivlin to undertake the G. E. TEMPO study.

14. For further discussion of how the Coleman report and other Title I evaluations challenged the idea of equal education as an antipoverty strategy, see McLaughlin, *Evaluation and Reform,* 34, 46, 63.

15. Grady McGonagill, *The Compensatory Education Study: A Case Study of Client-Centered Federal Evaluation* (PhD diss., Harvard University, 1983), 93.

16. Hearings before the U.S. House General Subcommittee on Education of the Committee on Education and Labor of the House of Representatives, *Elementary and Secondary Education Amendments of 1973, Part 1* (Washington, DC: Government Printing Office, January 31, 1973), 159.

17. Hearings before the U.S. House General Subcommittee on Education of the Committee on Education and Labor of the House of Representatives *Elementary and Secondary Education Amendments of 1973, Part 1* (Washington, DC: Government Printing Office, January 31, 1973), 130–131.

18. Cynthia G. Brown, interview conducted by Susan L. Moffitt, September 1995.

19. Christopher T. Cross, "Title I Evaluation: A Case Study in Frustration," *Educational Evaluation and Policy Analysis* 1, no. 2 (March–April 1979): 16.

20. McGonagill, *The Compensatory Education Study,* 93.

21. B. F. Birman, M. Orland, R. Jung, R. Anson, and G. Garcia, *The Current Operation of the Chapter 1 Program—Final Report from the National Assessment of Chapter 1* (Washington, DC: OERI, U.S. Department of Education, 1987), 59–64. Pullouts, however, were not required in law or regulation.

22. Paul Peterson, Barry Rabe, and Kenneth Wong, *When Federalism Works* (Washington, DC: Brookings Institution, 1986). For other arguments on the link between the supplement-not-supplant principle and pullouts, see Michael Gaffney and Daniel Schember, *The Effects of the Title I Supplement-Not-Supplant and Excess Costs and Provisions on Program Design Decisions* (Washington, DC:

Advanced Technology/Planning and Evaluation Service, U.S. Department of Education, 1982); Francis X. Archambault, Jr., "Instructional Setting: Key Issue or Bogus Concern," in *Designs for Compensatory Education: Conference Proceedings and Papers* (Washington, DC: Department of Education, June 17–18, 1986), III-68.

23. National Institute of Education, *Evaluating Compensatory Education—An Interim Report on the NIE Compensatory Education Study* (Washington, DC: U.S. Department of Health, Education, and Welfare, 1976), IV-7.

24. Ibid.

25. Several authors argue that schools and districts opted for pullouts over supportive services, such as nutrition, and innovative instruction because these were a "safe" way to protect against receiving audit exceptions. See Thomas C. Rosica, "Program and Staffing Structures: Reactions," in *Designs for Compensatory Education: Conference Proceedings and Papers* (Washington, DC: Department of Education, June 17–18, 1986), III-121; Jackie Kimbrough and Paul Hill, *The Aggregate Effects of Federal Education Programs* (Santa Monica, CA: RAND, 1981), 6.

26. One study reported that administrators were most likely to cite "a belief in the educational superiority" of pullouts as the reason they used them; see Michael J. Gaffney and Daniel M. Schember, *The Effects of the Title I Supplement-Not-Supplant and Excess Costs Provisions on Program Design Decisions. A Special Report from the Title I Practices Study* (Washington, DC: U.S. Department of Education, 1982), p. xi. Compliance with Title I accountability was the second most frequent reason.

27. Peterson et al. (*When Federalism Works*, 140) write that pullouts helped legitimize subprofessions of reading, justified the recruitment of teacher aides from low-income areas, and reflected a "widely held view that socially disadvantaged students required special instructional techniques."

28. Brenda Turnbull, Personal Communication, May 2009.

29. Support for pullouts was mixed. Worries surfaced early on about stigma and discrimination against children who were given remedial assistance. See Carter administration HEW and USOE internal memos, authors' personal archives.

30. Mary Berry testimony before the U.S. Senate Subcommittee on Education, Arts, and Humanities, Committee on Human Resources, *Education Amendments of 1977. Part 1* (Washington, DC: Government Printing Office, October 4, 1977), 17.

31. Marshall S. Smith and Brenda Turnbull, memorandum, 1977, authors' personal archives.

32. Ibid., 4.

33. Memo by Mike O'Keefe, assistant secretary of HEW, November 1977, 1, authors' personal archives.

34. Brenda Turnbull, Personal Communication, May 2009.

35. Marshall S. Smith and Brenda Turnbull, memorandum, 1977, 4, 9, 13.

36. Memo by Richard Fairley to Marshall Smith, authors' personal archives. Smith and Turnbull's concern about pullouts stemmed partly from problems associated with appropriately identifying students for Title I pullouts. They worried that errors in testing or "a fleeting problem with schoolwork could doom a student to being shunted out of the regular program and drilled on basic skills for the rest of the year, with limited hope of ever catching up." Fairley expressed greater confidence that the program appropriately identified students to receive Title I services. (Brenda Turnbull, Personal Communication, May 2009).

37. Peter Dow, *Schoolhouse Politics: Lessons from the Sputnik Era* (Cambridge, MA: Harvard University Press, 1993).

38. Chris Cross, interview conducted by David K. Cohen and Susan L. Moffitt, October 1995.

39. National Institute of Education, *The Compensatory Education Study: Executive Summary* (Washington, DC: U.S. Department of Health, Education, and Welfare, 1978), 2. One researcher, quoting unpublished sources, wrote that House Democrats supported this study "because it afforded them an opportunity to deflect attempts to change the basic purposes of Title I . . . [and] alter Title I funding criteria"; McGonagill, *The Compensatory Education Study*, 92–93.

40. M. M. Kennedy, B. F. Birman, and R. E. Demaline, *The Effectiveness of Chapter 1 Services: Second Interim Report from the National Assessment of Chapter 1* (Washington, DC: OERI, 1986); G. Kasten Tallmadge and Christine T. Wood, *ESEA Title I Evaluation and Reporting System User's Guide*, rev. ed. (Washington, DC: U.S. Department of Health, Education, and Welfare, 1976); and W. Rutherford and J. Hoffman, "Toward Implementation of the ESEA Title I Evaluation and Reporting System: A Concerns Analysis," *Educational Evaluation and Policy Analysis* 3 (1981): 5–16.

41. The most commonly used model was norm-referenced, which assumed that without Title I services, kids would have maintained, on the average, a constant positive relation to the norm. Changes in achievement were reported using the Normal Equivalency Curve.

42. Jane David, *Local Uses of Title I Evaluations* (Menlo Park, CA: SRI, 1978), 30.

43. Jane David, "Local Uses of Title I Evaluations," *Educational Evaluation and Policy Analysis* 3, no. 1 (1981): 38.

44. Richard F. Elmore and Milbrey W. McLaughlin, "Strategic Choice in Federal Education Policy: The Compliance-Assistance Trade-off," in *Policy Making*

in Education, ed. Ann Lieberman and Milbrey McLaughlin (Chicago: University of Chicago Press, 1982), 159–194.

45. Ibid., 159–194.

46. Brenda Turnbull, interview conducted by Susan L. Moffitt, June 1995.

47. Ibid.; David, "Local Uses of Title I Evaluations," 28, 31. Even if solutions to all of these problems had been found and solid evidence on how to improve projects produced, it would have remained for educators to use the knowledge. Yet changing professionals' practice is not easy, for experience, education, and beliefs inform practice. Jane David noted that when test results conflicted with professionals' views of programs, professionals relied on their views much more than on the evaluation data. Discounting the TIERS evaluations might have been wise, since they were notoriously unreliable. David noted that professional mistrust of evaluations was a central reason for not using them.

48. See D. Lortie, *Schoolteacher* (Chicago: University of Chicago, 1974).

49. General Accounting Office, *Greater Use of Exemplary Programs Could Improve Education for Disadvantaged Children* (Washington, DC: General Accounting Office, 1981).

50. Ibid., 17.

51. Ibid., 20.

52. L. Carter, "The Sustaining Effects Study of Compensatory and Elementary Education," *Educational Researcher,* August–September 1984, 6.

53. The study also included analysis of students in a sample of high-poverty schools; of economic status, socioeconomic characteristics, and attitudes of parents; of the cost and educational effectiveness of different educational activities; and of the effects of summer programs.

54. For discussion of such problems, see David K. Cohen, Steven Raudenbush, and Deborah L. Ball, "Resources, Instruction, and Research," *Educational Evaluation and Policy Analysis* 25, no. 2 (Summer 2003): 119–142.

55. Brenda Turnbull, Personal Communication, May 2009.

56. See M. Kennedy, B. Birman, and R. Demaline, *The Effectiveness of Chapter 1 Services: Second Interim Report from the National Assessment of Chapter 1,* 4–5.

57. Only Donald Trismen, Michael I. Waller, and Gita Wilder, in the related *Compensatory Reading Study* (Princeton, NJ: Educational Testing Service, 1976), 120–122, made such proposals.

58. The study, however, took many years to complete and was not able to inform the 1978 reauthorization of Title I.

59. Carter, "The Sustaining Effects Study of Compensatory and Elementary Education," 6–7; L. Carter, *A Study of Compensatory and Elementary Education:*

The Sustaining Effects Study. Final Report (Santa Monica, CA: Systems Development Corporation, 1983), 30.

60. John F. Jennings, *Why National Standards and Tests?* (Thousand Oaks, CA: Sage, 1998), 112. Students from schools that received federal Title I funds made significantly greater gains between 1970 and 1980 than did pupils from non-Title I eligible schools in all three grades tested by the NAEP. However, the NAEP does not have data that would allow direct comparisons between test scores of Title I students and those of nonparticipants. G. D. Borman, S. C. Stringfield, and R. E. Slavin eds., *Title I: Compensatory Education at the Crossroads* (Mahwah, NJ: Lawrence Erlbaum, 2001), 31.

61. Carter, "The Sustaining Effects Study of Compensatory and Elementary Education," 7.

62. Carter, *A Study of Compensatory and Elementary Education*, V-26.

63. Ibid.

64. The national assessment of Title I reanalyzed SES data in the 1980s, using improved techniques to refine comparisons between needy and Title I students. The earlier findings held up. Kennedy et al., *The Effectiveness of Chapter 1 Services: Second Interim Report from the National Assessment of Chapter 1*, 27, 35–36.

65. L. Carter, *A Study of Compensatory and Elementary Education: The Sustaining Effects Study. Interim Report* (Santa Monica, CA: Systems Development Corporation, 1980), 171–172.

66. Carter, *A Study of Compensatory and Elementary Education*, V-15, V-16.

67. Carter, *The Sustaining Effects Study: An Interim Report*, 171.

68. Patricia Sexton, *Education and Income* (New York: Viking Press, 1961); John D. Owen, *School Inequality and the Welfare State* (Baltimore: Johns Hopkins University Press, 1974); Marshall Smith, "Equality of Educational Opportunity: The Basic Findings Reconsidered," in *On Equality of Educational Opportunity; Papers Deriving from the Harvard University Faculty Seminar on the Coleman Report*, ed. Daniel P. Moynihan and Frederick Mosteller (New York: Random House, 1972); Kenneth Clark, *Dark Ghetto: Dilemmas of Social Power* (New York: Harper & Row, 1965).

69. Carter, "The Sustaining Effects Study of Compensatory and Elementary Education," 11.

70. Ibid.

71. Carter, *A Study of Compensatory and Elementary Education: The Sustaining Effects Study. Final Report*, III-6, III-7.

72. Yet, CES had conducted some studies of local programs. Though politically difficult, such studies were possible. Brenda Turnbull, Personal Communication, May 2009.

73. Jay Chambers et al., *Translating Dollars into Services: Chapter 1 Resources in the Context of State and Local Resources for Education. Final Report* (Washington, DC: U.S. Department of Education, 1993), Table 2, xi.

74. Ibid., Table 4, xvi.

75. Ibid., Table III-12, 50, 52.

76. Ibid., Table III-13, 54.

77. Ibid., Table III-14, 55.

78. Ibid., 134.

79. In addition to the problems discussed here, many needy and eligible students were not served, owing both to the program's appropriation and to differences in poverty levels among states and districts.

80. This did not violate law or regulations on the supplement-not-supplant principle, for these concerned only money.

81. Ralph Hoepfner, *Sub-studies on Allocation and Targeting of Funds and Services, Assessment of Student Growth, and Effects of Attrition, Sustaining Effects Technical Report #13* (Santa Monica, CA: Systems Development Corporation, 1981), 31–48.

82. William Cooley and Gaea Leinhardt, *Instructional Dimensions Study: The Search for Effective Classroom Processes* (Pittsburgh: Learning Research and Development Center, 1978), 32, 34–36, 39, 41–44.

83. Jere Brophy, "Research Linking Teacher Behavior to Student Achievement: Potential Implications for Instruction of Chapter 1 Students," in *Designs for Compensatory Education: Conference Proceedings and Papers* (Washington, DC: Department of Education, June 17–18, 1986), IV-121–179; Jere Brophy and Thomas Good, "Teacher Behavior and Student Achievement," in *Handbook of Research and Teaching*, 3rd ed., ed. M. C. Wittrock (New York: Macmillan, 1986), 328–377; Jere Brophy, "Teacher Influences on Student Achievement," *American Psychologist* 41, no. 10 (October 1986): 1069–1077.

84. R. Edmonds and J. R. Frederiksen, *Search for Effective Schools: The Identification and Analysis of City Schools That Are Instructionally Effective for Poor Children* (Cambridge, MA: Harvard Center for Urban Studies, 1978).

85. Brian Rowan, "Research on Effective Schools: A Cautionary Note," *Educational Researcher* 12, no. 4 (April 1983): 24–31.

86. Stewart C. Purkey and Marshall S. Smith, "Effective Schools: A Review," *Elementary School Journal* 83, no. 4 (March 1983): 427–452.

87. Ibid., 439–440.

88. Later studies supported these ideas: see Susan Rosenholtz, *Teachers' Workplace* (New York: Longmans, 1987); Anthony Bryk, Valerie Lee, and Peter Holland, *Catholic Schools and the Common Good* (Cambridge, MA: Harvard

University Press, 1993); Fred M. Newmann and Gary G. Wehlage, *Successful School Restructuring: A Report to the Public and Educators* (Madison: Wisconsin Center for Education Research, 1995).

5. Mission Revised

1. National Institute of Education, *Compensatory Education Services* (Washington, DC: U.S. Department of Health, Education, and Welfare, 1977), vii.

2. Ann Lin and Joe Soss, "Policy Discourse and Public Management: How Therapeutic Frames Organize the Politics of Administration," paper prepared for the Research Workshop on the Empirical Study of Governance, Texas A&M University, College Station, February 21–23, 2002.

3. Brenda Turnbull, Personal Communication, May 2009.

4. B. B. Kymlicka and Jean V. Matthews, *The Reagan Revolution?* (Chicago: Dorsey Press, 1988).

5. Thomas Good and Jennifer Braden, *The Great School Debate—Choice, Vouchers, and Charter Schools* (Mahwah, NJ: Lawrence Erlbaum, 2000); Ronald Reagan, "Interview with Reporters on Federalism on November 19, 1981," in *The Public Papers of President Ronald W. Reagan,* The Ronald Reagan Library, http://www.reagan.utexas.edu/resource/speeches/1981/111981b.htm.

6. The U.S. Supreme Court held that a pilot voucher program that offered tuition vouchers for poor parents to send their children to non-public schools "does not offend the Establishment clause." *Zelman, Superintendent of Public Instruction of Ohio, et al. v. Simmons-Harris et al.* No. 00-1751, argued February 20, 2002, decided June 27, 2002.

7. Good and Braden, *The Great School Debate;* H. Morken and J. R. Formicola, *The Politics of School Choice* (Lanham, MD: Rowman & Littlefield, 1999).

8. J. Murphy and P. G. Weise, *Pathways to Privatization in Education* (Greenwich, CT: Ablex Corp., 1998).

9. Maris A. Vinovskis' book—*From A Nation at Risk to No Child Left Behind: National Education Goals and the Creation of Federal Education Policy* (New York: Teachers College Press, 2009)—offers a thorough and very informative account of the developments that we discuss in this chapter, in his chapters 1 and 2.

10. National Commission on Excellence in Education, *A Nation at Risk: The Imperative for Educational Reform* (Washington, DC: United States Government Printing Office, 1983), 13.

11. Christopher T. Cross, *Political Education: National Policy Comes of Age* (New York: Teachers College Press, 2006). Cross argues, however, that Reagan went on to "embrace" the report (p. 79).

12. R. L. Thorndike, *Reading Comprehension in Fifteen Countries: An Empirical Study* (New York: Wiley, 1973), 129.

13. E. F. Vogel, *Japan as Number One* (Cambridge, MA: Harvard University Press, 1979).

14. J. Murphy, Scott W. Gilmer, Richard Weise, and Ann Page, *Pathways to Privatization in Education* (Santa Barbara, CA: Greenwood, 1998), 8.

15. D. A. Verstegen and P. Anthony, "Is There a Federal Role in Education Reform?" *Journal of Education Finance* 14, no. 2 (1988): 30–56.

16. David C. Berliner and Bruce J. Biddle, *The Manufactured Crisis: Myths, Fraud, and the Attack on America's Public Schools* (Reading, MA: Addison-Wesley, 1995).

17. For a later account, see Richard Murnane and Frank Levy, *Teaching the New Basic Skills: Principles for Educating Children to Thrive in a Changing Economy* (New York: Free Press, 1996).

18. Lauren B. Resnick, *Education and Learning to Think,* Committee on Mathematics, Science, and Technology Education, Commission on Behavioral and Social Sciences and Education, National Research Council (Washington, DC: National Academy Press, 1987), 36.

19. Bayla White, interview conducted by Susan L. Moffitt, March 1995.

20. Vinovskis, *From A Nation at Risk to No Child Left Behind,* 19.

21. Marshall S. Smith and Jennifer A. O'Day, "Systemic Reform and Educational Opportunity," in *Designing Coherent Education Policy: Improving the System,* ed. Susan H. Fuhrman (San Francisco: Jossey-Bass, 1993), 247.

22. Ibid., 267.

23. For details, see L. Carter, *A Study of Compensatory and Elementary Education: The Sustaining Effects Study: Final Report* (Santa Monica, CA: Systems Development Corporation, 1983). Readers can consult a brief summary published as L. Carter, "The Sustaining Effects Study of Compensatory and Elementary Education," *Educational Researcher,* August–September 1984, 4–13.

24. NIE, *Compensatory Education Study: Final Report* (Washington, DC: U.S. Department of Health, Education, and Welfare, 1978), 168–170.

25. Brenda Turnbull, interview conducted by Susan L. Moffitt, October 1994.

26. A. McGill-Frantzen and R. L. Allington, "The Gridlock of Low Reading Achievement: Perspectives on Practice and Policy," *Remedial and Special Education* (RASE) 12, no. 3 (May–June 1991): 20–30.

27. J. Kimbrough and P. Hill, *The Aggregate Effects of Federal Education Programs* (Santa Monica, CA: RAND, 1981), vi–vii.

28. Ibid., p. 42.

29. One federal official argued that Title I was changed not because of negative effects of regulation but because of the administration view that "prescription was bad." Bayla White, interview conducted by Susan L. Moffitt, March 1995.

30. The administration proposed the repeal of Title I, combining it with federal aid for the disabled and other federal K–12 programs in block grants and reducing Title I by 30 percent. Eileen White, "Education Programs Slashed Again," *Education Week*, October 5, 1981, http://www.edweek.org/ew/1981/ 01050089.h01. Reagan argued "that Federal aid to education amounts to only 8 percent of the total educational funding, and for this 8 percent, the Federal Government has insisted on tremendously disproportionate share of control over our schools. Whatever reductions we've proposed in that 8 percent will amount to very little in the total cost of education. They will, however, restore more authority to States and local school districts." See Address before a Joint Session of the Congress on the Program for Economic Recovery, February 18, 1981, http://www .reagan.utexas.edu/resource/speeches/1981/21881a.htm.

31. John Ashbrook, then ranking Republican member of the House Committee on Education and Labor refused to introduce the bill. The second-ranking Republican, John Erlenborn (IL) introduced it but had trouble finding cosponsors. C. W. Radcliffe, "Remarks of C. W. Radcliffe, Former Minority Counsel and Staff Director, Committee on Education and Labor," in *A Compilation of Papers on the Twentieth Anniversary of the Elementary and Secondary Education Act of 1965* (Washington, DC: United States Government Printing Office, August 1985), 61–69.

32. Mary Jean LeTendre (interview conducted by Susan L. Moffitt, May 1995) said that Bell tried to keep Title I out of a block grant: "[He] went to David Stockman personally" to request exclusion from the block grant for "Bilingual, and . . . Chapter 1. . . . Bell felt that there were appropriate Federal roles."

33. Radcliffe, "Remarks," 65.

34. Kenneth K. Wong and Anna Nicotera, "*Brown v. Board of Education* and the Coleman Report: Social Science Research and the Debate on Educational Equality," *Peabody Journal of Education* 79, no. 2 (2004): 122–135. See also Susan G. Foster, "Proposed Title I Regulations," *Education Week*, February 17, 1982, http://www.edweek.org/ew/1982/01210015.h01.

35. U.S. Department of Education, *Targeting, Formula, and Resource Allocation Issues: Focusing Federal Funds Where the Needs Are Greatest, a Supplemental*

Volume to the National Assessment of the Chapter 1 Program (Washington, DC: GPO, 1993), Exhibit I, p. 9. Appropriations began to grow in the late 1980s, from $3.7 million in 1986–1987 to $4.3 million in 1989–1990 (constant dollars). Concentration grants, begun in the Carter administration, also ceased in Fiscal Year 1981–1982 and were funded only after 1988. James Marshall, Charles Edwards, and Alvin Lin, *Title I Handbook* (Arlington, VA: Education Funding Research Council [EFRC], 1995), B-10.

36. The ECIA changed this to allow a 10 percent yearly reduction in districts' allocation to schools. If it fell below 90 percent of the previous year, the district's Chapter 1 grant could be reduced "by an amount equal to the percentage drop below 90%." Previously, districts could lose much or all of a grant if they did not meet this requirement. A later study reported that meeting the maintenance of effort requirements both before and after the ECIA changes had not been a major problem for most school districts. Beatrice F. Birman et al., *The Current Operation of the Chapter 1 Program—Final Report from the National Assessment of Chapter 1* (Washington, DC: OERI, 1987), 119–120.

37. Under Chapter 1, many states and districts allowed up to a 10 percent discrepancy between Chapter 1 and non-Chapter 1 schools before designating them as noncomparable. Title I had allowed a 5 percent discrepancy. Districts had been required to provide evidence, such as comparability reports and salary schedules, that they complied, but the ECIA required only a state's assurance that it would try to offer comparable salaries, materials, and supplies. Chapter 1 guidance urged districts to document comparability with per-pupil expenditures or pupil-staff ratios, encouraging continuing past practice, but a later analysis noted that if districts did exercise their expanded discretion and elect not to "perform comparability calculations, officials [had] no way of knowing whether their Chapter 1 schools actually receive[d] comparable state and local resources." Birman et al., *Current Operation*, 120–124.

38. The ECIA weakened the supplement-not-supplant principle by removing the requirement that districts distribute state and local compensatory education funds "proportionally" between Title I and other schools. Title I had sought to prevent districts from withdrawing state and local compensatory funds from Title I schools for use elsewhere. Removing this provision gave districts more discretion in determining the allocation of nonfederal funds and moved away from Title I's supplementary focus. Ibid., 124–125.

39. ECIA required local evaluations every three years to check on achievement, but TIERS models were not required. Many states continued to use them, but use decayed. Ibid., 130.

40. There were large staff reductions in the Department of Education from 6,849 in 1981 to 4,526 in 1986. Although the level of staffing in state departments of education did not drop overall, there was a 31 percent reduction in the number of full-time employees working in the administration of Title I/Chapter 1. Ibid., 135–139. See also J. E. Funkhouser, J. S. Michie, and M. T. Moore, *Federal Administration of Chapter 1, ECIA Staffing and Financial Support Substudy* (Washington, DC: Decision Resources Corporation, 1987).

41. Chapter 1 eliminated requirements "for State monitoring or technical assistance," which included submitting "monitoring and enforcement plans at least once every three years" and "technical assistance to districts in such areas as application preparation, program planning, evaluation, and program implementation." Birman et al., *Current Operation*, 144–145.

42. Mary Jean LeTendre, interview conducted by Susan L. Moffitt, May 1995. After the 1983 amendments, some states resumed monitoring.

43. Bayla White, interview conducted by Susan L. Moffitt, March 1995.

44. Ibid.

45. General changes in federal audit requirements made Chapter 1 audits more frequent and thorough, requiring state and district audits according to a "single audit" procedure at least once every two years, up from once every three years. Locals welcomed state oversight, for it increased certainty that they were following program guidelines. Birman et al., *Current Operation*, 146–149.

46. Ibid., 120–125. Others found changes in state and local evaluation once the requirements were modified; since 1980, there was increasing "incompleteness" in the achievement data that states reported once TIERS was no longer required. E. R. Reisner and E. L. Marks, *The Federal Administration of Evaluation, Program Improvement, and Technical Assistance under ECIA Chapter 1* (Washington, DC: Policy Studies Associates, 1987), 17–18, fn. 8.

47. Birman et al., *Current Operation*, 125.

48. Paul Pierson aptly observes that policies can change politics by changing what political actors perceive as "desirable"; Paul Pierson, "Public Policies as Institutions," in *Rethinking Political Institutions: The Art of the State,* ed. Ian Shapiro, Stephen Skowronek, and Daniel Galvin (New York: New York University Press, 2006), 118.

49. The 1980s National Assessment reported that at the time of the evaluation, state Chapter 1 directors had an average tenure of thirteen years. Birman et al., *Current Operation*, 159–160.

50. Ibid., 159.

51. Ibid., 159–160.

52. Jerome Murphy, "Progress and Problems: The Paradox of State Reform," in *Policy Making in Education,* ed. Ann Lieberman and Milbrey W. McLaughlin (Chicago: University of Chicago Press, 1982), 197.

53. Turnbull et al., "State Administration of the Amended Chapter 1 Program" (Washington, DC: U.S. Department of Education, 1990), 60, write "there is no real reason for them to see themselves in a position to launch major initiatives. Their overall staff size and composition is little changed over the past five years. If the coordinators wanted to take program administration in new directions, many of the generalists who dominate their staffs would be ill-equipped to follow. . . . Traditionally, most of the staff effort in SEA Chapter 1 offices goes into application review and monitoring." See also Virginia Plunkett, "The States' Role in Improving Compensatory Education: Analysis of Current Trends and Suggestions for the Future," *Educational Evaluation and Policy Analysis* 13, no. 4 (1991): 341.

54. Ibid.

55. Bayla White, interview conducted by Susan L. Moffitt, March 1995.

56. Birman et al., *Current Operation,* 159–160.

57. The Lawyers' Committee for Civil Rights Under Law (LCCR) in "The First Year of Chapter 1" (1984) argued that the Department of Education had not adequately informed LEAs of what was allowable under ECIA. The National Assessment of Chapter 1 reported that some districts were unaware of supplement-not-supplant exemptions; Birman et al. *Current Operation,* 125.

58. Christopher T. Cross, interview conducted by David K. Cohen and Susan L. Moffitt, October 1995.

59. P.L. 100–297, Hawkins-Stafford amendments (sec. 1012(b)).

60. Bayla White, interview conducted by Susan L. Moffitt, March 1995.

61. P.L. 100–297, Hawkins-Stafford amendments (sec. 1021 (b)(A)(i)(ii).

62. Ibid.

63. John F. Jennings, "Title I: Its Legislative History and Its Promise," in *Title I: Compensatory Education at the Crossroads,* ed. G. D. Borman, S. C. Stringfield, and R. E. Slavin (Mahwah, NJ: Lawrence Erlbaum, 2001), 15.

64. Douglas Downey, Paul von Hippel, and Beckett Broh, "Are Schools the Great Equalizer? Cognitive Inequality during the Summer Months and the School Year," *American Sociological Review* 79, no. 5 (October 2004): 613–635.

65. Vinovskis, *From A Nation at Risk to No Child Left Behind,* 42–55.

66. Christopher Cross noted, "there was an attempt by OE in the late 60s to create an 'Anchor Test' so that it would be possible to equate various tests. It was a dismal failure." (Personal Communication, March 2009).

67. See General Accounting Office, *Chapter 1 Accountability: Greater Focus on Program Goals Needed,* Report to the Chairman, Subcommittee on Elementary, Secondary, and Vocational Education, Committee on Education and Labor, House of Representatives, GAO/HRD-93-69, March 1993, 15–16.

68. Most districts evaluated Title I schools' performance on the basis of pre-post changes in school average test scores from various standardized achievement tests administered on either a fall-to-spring or annual testing cycle. If the mean change score of participating students in a school was greater than zero NCEs, which are normalized percentile scores with a mean of 50 and a standard deviation of 21.06, the program is said to be effective. A mean gain greater than zero NCEs has been interpreted as evidence of programmatic impact, on the assumption that in the absence of Title I intervention, students tended to remain at the same national rank over time; see chapter 2 in Borman et al., *Title I: Compensatory Education at the Crossroads,* 27. The validity of this approach was questioned by a number of researchers (Linn, 1979). States and districts could set higher standards if they chose. General Accounting Office, *Chapter 1 Accountability,* 16.

69. Resnick, *Education and Learning to Think.*

70. P.L. 100–297, Hawkins-Stafford amendments (sec. 1021 (a)(1)(2)(3)).

71. Brenda Turnbull, interview conducted by Susan L. Moffitt, October 1994.

72. Moreover, states typically tested for "minimum competency," which mattered more to districts and schools (Brenda Turnbull, Personal Communication, May 2009).

73. General Accounting Office, *Chapter 1 Accountability,* 16.

74. Marshall, et al., *Title I Handbook,* B-15 and 16; see also James Marshall, Charles Edwards, and Michael Brustein, *Chapter 1 Handbook* (Arlington, VA: Education Funding Research Council, 1992), A38–40.

75. P.L. 100–297, Hawkins-Stafford amendments (sec. 1015 (a)).

76. P.L. 100–297, Hawkins-Stafford amendments (sec. 1015 (c)(2)(B)), (sec. 1015 (c)(2)(C)), *Federal Register* 54, no. 90 (May 19, 1989): 21792. The regulations noted that indeed schoolwides are allowed to commingle Chapter 1 funds with other funds, but that this "does not . . . excuse an LEA from documenting separately that Chapter funds have . . . been spent in a schoolwide project."

77. P.L. 100–297 (sec. 1015 (c)(2)(A)). Schools with approved schoolwide plans would "be relieved of any requirements under this part with respect to the commingling of funds provided under this chapter with funds available for regular programs" (sec. 1015 (c)(2)(A)), but they should "supplement, and to the extent practicable, increase the level of funds that would, in the absence of such Federal funds, be made available" (sec. 1015 (c)(2)(B)). They were to comply with comparability regulations (sec. 1015 (c)(2)(C)).

78. Bayla White, interview conducted by Susan L. Moffitt, March 1995.

79. Stephanie Stullich, Brenda Donly, and Simeon Stolzberg, *Targeting Schools: Study of Title I Allocations within School Districts* (Washington, DC: Department of Education, 1999), p. vi. There were 1,626 schoolwide programs operating in 1990–1991, amounting to about 3 percent of Title I schools.

80. Mary Ann Millsap, Marc Moss, and Beth Garnse, *The Chapter 1 Implementation Study Final Report: Chapter 1 in Public Schools* (Washington, DC: Department of Education, 1993).

81. Brenda Turnbull, interview conducted by Susan L. Moffitt, October 1994.

82. Kenneth Wong and Stephen Meyer, "Title I Schoolwide Programs as an Alternative to Categorical Practices: An Organizational Analysis of Surveys from the Prospects Study," in Borman, Stringfield, and Slavin, *Title I: Compensatory Education at the Crossroads,* 222.

83. U.S. Department of Education, *Targeting, Formula, and Resource Allocation Issues,* Exhibit 3, p. 22, 12–21.

84. M. M Kennedy, R. K. Jung, and M. E. Orland, *Poverty, Achievement, and the Distribution of Compensatory Education Services* (Washington, DC: U.S. Department of Education, 1986).

85. Phyllis McClure, interview conducted by Susan L. Moffitt, December 1994; Brenda Turnbull, interview conducted by Susan L. Moffitt, October 1994.

86. John F. Jennings, comments to the National Commission on Title I, February 11–12, 1991, p. 16 of minutes. Unpublished minutes obtained from the Council of Chief State School Officers.

87. Programs like Social Security or Medicare that distribute benefits to universal populations rather than to means-tested populations are generally associated with greater political support and sustained program survival. For a review of that argument, see Andrea Louise Campbell, "Universalism, Targeting, and Participation," in *Remaking America: Democracy and Public Policy in an Age of Inequality,* ed. Joe Soss, Jacob S. Hacker, and Suzanne Mettler (New York: Russell Sage Foundation, 2007), 121–140. Title I exposes the fragility of broadly distributed benefits: its nearly universal distribution of funds produced local programs that were too weak to leverage the program's increasingly ambitious aims.

88. Bayla White, interview conducted by Susan L. Moffitt, March 1995.

89. National Education Goals Panel, *The National Goals Report: Building a Nation of Learners* (Washington, DC: National Education Goals Panel, 1999).

90. Vinovskis, *From A Nation at Risk to No Child Left Behind,* 51–63.

91. Robert Lynd and Helen Lynd, *Middletown* (New York: Harcourt Brace, 1937), chapters 13, 14, and 16; August Hollingshead, *Elmtown's Youth* (New York: Wiley, 1949), chapters 7 and 8; Arthur Powell, Eleanor Farrar, and David K. Cohen,

The Shopping Mall High School: Winners and Losers in the Marketplace (Boston: Houghton-Mifflin, 1986), chapter 5.

92. Edward McDill and Gary Natriello, "The Effectiveness of the Title I Compensatory Education Program: 1965–1997," *Journal of Education for Students Placed at Risk* 3, no. 4 (1998): 317–335.

6. A Growing Gap between Policy and Practice

1. Christopher Cross, Personal Communication, March 2009.

2. The panel included Phyllis McClure, Robert Slavin, Marshall Smith, Joe Nathan, David Hornbeck, and others. Julie A. Miller, "Chapter 1 Panel Calls for Radical Set of Revisions," *Education Week,* September 16, 1992.

3. Ibid. Joe Nathan also was reported to have objected to the proposals for testing. Rosenberg said that "the plan 'enshrines in federal policy' an unproven assessment-and-sanction system drafted by Mr. Hornbeck as part of the reform plan adopted in 1990 by the State of Kentucky."

4. Ibid. Madaus then was director of the Center for the Study of Testing at Boston College.

5. Julie A. Miller, "E.S.E.A. Plan Would Retool Chapter 1, Eliminate Block Grant," *Education Week,* August 4, 1993.

6. Michael J. Petrilli, "Leaving My Lapel Pin Behind: Is No Child Left Behind's Birthday Worth Celebrating?" *National Review Online,* January 8, 2007, http://www.publiceducation.org/nclb_articles/archive/20070108_Leaving.asp.

7. *Goals 2000: Educate America Act,* 103d Cong., 2d sess., HR 1806, 1, 6–7.

8. 103d Congress, 2d sess. HR 6, Section 1001 (d).

9. Ibid., Section 1111 (a).

10. Marshall S. Smith and Jennifer O'Day, "Systemic School Reform," in *Politics of Education Association Yearbook 1990,* ed. Susan H. Fuhrman and Betty Malen (London: Taylor and Francis, 1990), 233–267. This seems to be the first published version, but the authors note that "A brief form of some of the ideas in this paper were shared with the Advisory Council for the Science and Engineering Education Directorate of the National Science Foundation over two years ago."

11. Maris A. Vinovskis, *From A Nation at Risk to No Child Left Behind: National Education Goals and the Creation of Federal Education Policy* (New York: Teachers College Press, 2009), 97–98.

12. Vinovskis, *From A Nation at Risk to No Child Left Behind,* offers a helpful account of these events, especially pp. 97–102.

13. R. E. Floden, A. C. Porter, W. H. Schmidt, D. J. Freeman, and J. R. Schwille, "Responses to Curriculum Pressures: A Policy-Capturing Study of Teacher Decisions about Content," *Journal of Educational Psychology* 73 (1981): 129–141.

14. These attributes were evident in a stream of studies dating from the early twentieth century; see Arthur Powell, Eleanor Farrar, and David K. Cohen, *The Shopping Mall High School* (Boston: Houghton-Mifflin, 1985), chapter 5.

15. For more on salience, see Chapter 2.

16. Chester Finn and Michael Petrilli, eds., *The State of State Standards* (Washington, DC: Thomas B. Fordham Foundation, 2000), vii.

17. American Federation of Teachers, *Making Standards Matter 2001* (Washington, DC: American Federation of Teachers, 2001), 5.

18. Ibid., 6.

19. Jean Johnson, Ana Maria Arumi, and Amber Ott, *Is Support for Standards Fading?* (New York: Public Agenda, 2006).

20. In his analyses, McGuinn explains Title I's transformation in terms that are somewhat similar and somewhat different. He points to changing public perceptions of schools' performance, from the belief that American schools generally provided decent education to concerns that they did not. He argues that these ideas coincided with growing beliefs that access to material resources was insufficient for improving performance. These ideas found expression in federal policies promoting greater accountability. He suggests that changes in Title I's political environment account for why more aggressive federal accountability policies emerged when they did. He argues, "The new federal focus on accountability . . . was only possible because of important shifts in the political alignment and policymaking arrangements. The development of a more competitive national electoral environment and the rise of education to the top of the public agenda in the 1990s eventually led both parties to embrace a more proactive and reform-oriented federal role in improving schools." Patrick J. McGuinn, *No Child Left Behind*, 193–194.

21. Elizabeth Debray, *Politics, Ideology, and Education*, 130.

22. Christopher Cross, Personal Communication, March 2009.

23. National Center for Education Statistics (NCES), *Digest of Education Statistics: 2007* (Washington, DC: NCES, 2007), table 362.

24. These are the targeted and education finance incentive grants.

25. The NCES reported that federal spending on the education of disadvantaged students grew from $8.5 billion in 2000 to $14.8 billion in 2007 and that most of that increase was in Title I. NCES, *Digest of Education Statistics: 2007,* table 162.

26. Jay G. Chambers, Irene Lam, Kanya Mahitivanichcha, Phil Esra, Larisa Shambaugh, and Stephanie Stullich, *State and Local Implementation of the*

No Child Left Behind Act: Volume VI—Targeting and Uses of Federal Education Funds (Washington, DC: U.S. Department of Education, 2009), Exhibit 12, p. 26.

27. The evidence for our discussion of this matter derives from Wayne Riddle, *Education for the Disadvantaged: Overview of ESEA Title I-A. Amendments under the No Child Left Behind Act* (Washington, DC: Congressional Research Service, 2001), esp. table 1.

28. For more details, see the discussion in Chambers et al., *State and Local Implementation of the No Child Left Behind Act.*

29. Riddle, quoted in Center on Education Policy, *Implementing the No Child Left Behind Teacher Requirements* (Washington, DC: Center on Education Policy, 2007), 21.

30. B. Birman, K. LeFloch, A. Klokota, M. Ludwig, J. Taylor, K. Walters, A. Wayne, and K. Yoon, *State and Local Implementation of the No Child Left Behind Act, Volume II—Teacher Quality under NCLB: Interim Report* (Washington, DC: U.S. Department of Education, Office of Planning, Evaluation, and Policy Development, 2007), 39.

31. Ibid.

32. R. C. Pianta, J. Belsky, R. Houts, F. Morrison, and NICHD Early Child Care Research Network, "Teaching Opportunities to Learn in America's Elementary Classrooms," *Science* 315 (2007): 1795–1796.

33. Birman et al., *State and Local Implementation of the No Child Left Behind Act Volume II*, 76.

34. Ibid., 84.

35. Dan Goldhaber, *Exploring the Use and Efficacy of Incentives to Reward Teachers for Tough Assignments* (Seattle: Center on Reinventing Public Education, University of Washington, 2008).

36. Lynn Olson, "Analysts Worry NCLB Won't Solve Teacher Issue," *Education Week,* November 24, 2004.

37. Earlier initiatives had moved in this direction. The first national efforts to develop techniques to improve failing schools—President George H. W. Bush's New American School Development Corporation and the Clinton-era Comprehensive School Reform Design program—responded to the rising interest in reform. Both sponsored "whole school" reforms, like Success for All and the School Development Program, which sought to develop and implement methods for improving high-poverty schools.

38. American Federation of Teachers, *Sizing up State Standards, 2008* (Washington, DC: American Federation of Teachers, 2008), 4–5.

39. Chester E. Finn, Jr., Liam Julian, and Michael J. Petrilli, *The State of State Standards* (Washington, DC: Thomas B. Fordham Foundation, 2006), 9.

40. Ibid., 9.

41. Ibid., 18–19.

42. See, for example, the work of social scientists at RAND: Laura S. Hamilton, Brian M. Stecher, Julie A. Marsh, Jennifer Sloan McCombs, Abby Robyn, Jennifer Lin Russell, Scott Naftel, and Heather Barney, *Standards-Based Accountability under No Child Left Behind Experiences of Teachers and Administrators in Three States* (Santa Monica, CA: RAND, 2007), 99–101.

43. P. Barton, "Staying on Course in Education Reform," Educational Testing Service, April 2002, 10.

44. For a discussion of the limits on using such tests to measure growth, see A. Bryk, Y. Thum, J. Easton, and S. Luppescu, "Academic Productivity of Chicago Public Elementary Schools," Consortium on Chicago School Research, March 1998.

45. D. Ballou, "Sizing up Test Scores," *Education Next,* Summer 2002, 10.

46. Marshall Smith, the leading theorist of these reforms, opposed the use of tests for "high-stakes" purposes. Vinovskis, *From A Nation at Risk to No Child Left Behind,* 54.

47. There also is an experimental effort to distinguish schools that are making substantial progress from those that are not and to calibrate penalties and assistance accordingly. This response is reasonable and overdue, but it does not deal with the underlying sources of schools' weak capability; less crude measures could make the regulatory regime less heavy-handed, but it will not address schools' capability to improve teaching and learning.

48. See our discussion of this point in Chapter 2.

49. Hamilton et al., *Standards-Based Accountability under No Child Left Behind,* 106.

50. For example, see Diane Ravitch, "Every State Left Behind," *New York Times,* November 7, 2005.

51. Phyllis McClure, *School Improvement under No Child Left Behind* (Washington, DC: Center for American Progress, 2005), 23.

52. Title I, Section 1003 (a) and (b).

53. McClure, *School Improvement under No Child Left Behind,* 12.

54. Ibid., 12–13.

55. Ibid., 23.

56. Ibid., 28.

57. Ibid., 27.

58. Center on Education Policy, *Moving beyond Notification: Assisting Schools in Improvement* (Washington, DC: Center on Education Policy, 2007), 8.

59. Ibid., 11.

60. Ibid., 17–18.

61. Ibid., 16–17.

62. Hamilton et al., *Standards-Based Accountability under No Child Left Behind,* 103–104; table 6.5, 108.

63. David J. Hoff, "Schools Struggling to Meet Key Goal on Accountability: Number Failing to Make AYP Rises 28 Percent," *Education Week,* updated January 7, 2009 (Table: Schools and Districts—Stages of Improvement under NCLB), http://www.edweek.org/ew/articles/2008/12/18.

64. Institute of Education Sciences, *Mapping 2005 State Proficiency Standards onto the NAEP Scales* (Washington, DC: Institute of Education Sciences, 2007), 16.

65. Ibid., 12.

66. Robert Linn, *Accountability: Responsibility and Reasonable Expectations,* CSE Report 601 (Boulder: CRESST/University of Colorado, 2003).

67. "Each state study statistically linked the minimum scores required for basic, proficient, and advanced levels of performance on each states' tests with the minimum scores associated with that performance level on a Northwest Evaluation Association exam that was aligned to the state's curriculum standards. All scores for the NWEA tests in a subject area reference a single, cross-grade, equal-interval scale developed using Item Response Theory methodology." From G. Gage Kingsbury, Allan Olson, John Cronin, Carl Hauser, and Ron Houser, *The State of State Standards: Research Investigating Proficiency Levels in Fourteen States* (Portland, OR: Northwest Evaluation Association, 2003), 4, http://www.nwea.org/support/reportsLogin.aspx.

68. Ibid., 11.

69. Ibid., 12; for sample question 1, see p. 13, Figure 1.

70. Ibid., 16–18.

71. Ibid., 21 and 27.

72. P. L. Donahue, *NAEP 2008 Trends in Academic Progress* (NCES 2009–479) (Washington, DC: National Center for Education Statistics, Institute of Education Sciences, U.S. Department of Education, 2009), 9, 14, 29.

73. This was not the first time that change in practice occurred in this way. The classroom effects of the "back-to-basics" movement in the 1970s seemed to be the joint result of state policies, extensive public concern about weak student performance, media attention, and educators' attention to these developments. The changes discussed in Chapter 5, which led to the reforms, were much broader than policy, and found many avenues into education.

74. For several perspectives on the CSRDs designs, see Christopher Cross, ed., *Putting the Pieces Together: Lessons from Comprehensive School Reform Research* (Washington, DC: National Clearinghouse for Comprehensive School Reform, 2004).

75. Brian Rowan, Richard Correnti, Robert J. Miller, and Eric M. Camburn, "School Improvement by Design: Lessons from a Study of Comprehensive School Reform Programs," in *Handbook of Education Policy Research,* ed. Gary Sykes, Barbara Schneider, and David N. Plank (New York: Routledge, 2009), 637–651.

76. Ibid.

77. Core Knowledge (CK) is another CSR design that requires common curriculum, among other elements of infrastructure, and evaluations report significant achievement gains for students in CK schools, though the research is not as rigorous as that of Rowan et al. See *Core Knowledge Overview of Research 2004,* http://www.coreknowledge.org/CK/about/research/eval12_2002 .htm.

78. ScimathMN, Minnesota TIMSS Report, December 2008, pp. 1–7. www. scimathmn.org. Sandra Gaumond Rummel, *Changing Math Changing Minds,* 2001, www.scimathmn.org.

79. Institute of Education Sciences, The Nation's Report Card: Mathematics 2007, State Snapshot Report, Minnesota Grade 4, http://nces.ed.gov/nationsreport card/states/.

80. Ibid.

81. Institute of Education Sciences, The Nation's Report Card: Mathematics 2007, State Snapshot Report, Minnesota Grade 8, http://nces.ed.gov/nationsreportcard/ states/.

82. Emily Johns, "Minnesota's Must-Pass Math Test Goes by Wayside," *Minneapolis Star-Tribune,* May 30, 2009, http://www.startribune.com/local/46508322 .html?page=1&c=y.

83. Marc Moss, Alyssa Rulf Fountain, Beth Boulay, Megan Horst, Chris Rodger, and Melanie Brown-Lyons, *Reading First Implementation Evaluation Final Report* (Washington, DC: U.S. Department of Education, 2008), chapters 3–7. The program was plagued with problems: it gave unbalanced emphasis to one particular view of reading and was badly mismanaged in the Department of Education. Yet it was the first time that the federal government tried to prescribe curriculum content and teaching. The Democratic Congress cut it very far back after the 2006 midterm elections gave them a majority in the U.S. House.

84. Ibid., chapter 8.

85. Marguerite Roza, *Allocation Anatomy: How District Policies That Deploy Resources Can Support (or Undermine) District Reform Strategies* (Seattle: Center on Reinventing Public Education, University of Washington, 2008).

86. Goldhaber, *Exploring the Use and Efficacy of Incentives.*

7. Title I

1. Patrick J. McGuinn, *No Child Left Behind and the Transformation of Federal Education Policy, 1965–2005* (Lawrence: University of Kansas Press, 2006); Elizabeth Debray, *Politics, Ideology, and Education: Federal Policy during the Clinton and Bush Administrations* (New York: Columbia University Teachers College Press, 2006).

2. Margaret Weir offers a useful distinction between these types of ideas, distinguishing between "public philosophies" and "a more pragmatic set of statements about cause and effect relationships attached to a method for influencing those relationships"; Margaret Weir, "Ideas and the Politics of Bounded Innovation," in *Structuring Politics: Historical Institutionalism in Comparative Analysis,* ed. Sven Steinmo, Kathleen Thelen, and Frank Longstreth (New York: Cambridge University Press, 1992), 207–208.

3. On this point, McGuinn (*No Child Left Behind,* 201) observes, "although the existence of new ideas is a necessary condition for major policy change, ideas alone are not sufficient to create a new policy regime. Ideas must be paired with political will and institutional capacity to be effectively implemented."

4. Our view of this matter is similar to Robert Lieberman's account of the shift from color-blind civil rights. He wrote "that neither ideas nor institutions can rightly claim priority in an account that purports to explain significant political change. . . . Rather, what has changed is the very relationships among factors that and processes by which a set of underlying conditions generates outcomes. . . . An idea's time arrives not simply because the idea is compelling on its own terms, but because opportune political circumstances favor it." Robert C. Lieberman, "Ideas, Institutions, and Political Order: Explaining Political Change," *American Political Science Review* 96, no. 4 (2002): 709–710.

5. Margaret Weir ("Ideas and the Politics of Bounded Innovation," 208) tells a similar story for the development of American employment policy, particularly in the 1970s: "In the absence of sufficient applicable research, purely political criteria held sway."

6. On this point, see Debray, *Politics, Ideology, and Education,* 130.

7. Edward McDill and Gary Natriello, "The Effectiveness of the Title I Compensatory Education Program: 1965–1997," *Journal of Education for Students Placed at Risk* 3, no. 4 (1998): 317–335.

8. Epilogue

1. Alyson Klein, "Dual Aims in Stimulus Stir Tension," *Education Week*, June 9, 2009, http://www.edweek.org/ew/articles/2009/06/10/33stimreform.h28.html ?tkn=UQBFOcWKvVyDGEbz9Q0qS611IC4kl9NqvUXB.

2. U.S. Department of Education, "The American Recovery and Reinvestment Act of 2009: Saving and Creating Jobs and Reforming Education" (Washington, DC: U.S. Department of Education, March 7, 2009), 3, http://www.ed .gov/policy/gen/leg/recovery/implementation.html.

3. Klein, "Dual Aims in Stimulus Stir Tension."

4. Ibid.

5. U.S. Department of Education, "The American Recovery and Reinvestment Act of 2009," 2.

6. Klein, "Dual Aims in Stimulus Stir Tension."

7. Michele McNeil, "Stimulus Aid's Pace Still Slow: States Aim to Plug Holes, Application Review Shows," *Education Week*, June 17, 2009.

8. Klein, "Dual Aims in Stimulus Stir Tension."

9. Alyson Klein, "Key Democrats Question Parts of Obama Budget," *Education Week*, June 10, 2009.

10. Marguerite Roza, "Ranking the States: Federal Education Stimulus Money and the Prospects for Reform" (Seattle: Center on Reinventing Public Education, University of Washington, 2009), http://www. crpe.org.

11. Ibid.

12. Javier C. Hernandez, "For Many Teachers, a Famously Fertile Market Dries Up Overnight," *New York Times*, May 11, 2009. See also Jennifer Medina, "Finding Jobs for Teachers Already on City's Payroll," *New York Times*, November 18, 2008.

13. The New Teacher Project, "Overview," http://www.tntp.org/ourimpact/ overview.html.

14. Teach for America, "Teach for America Adds Largest Number of New Teachers and Regions in 20-Year History," May 28, 2009, http://www.teachfor america.org/newsroom/documents/20090528_Teach_For_America_Adds_ Largest_Number_of_Teachers_in_History.htm.

15. The elementary school study is Paul T. Decker, Daniel P. Mayer, and Steven Glazerman, *The Effects of Teach for America on Students. Findings from a National Evaluation* (Princeton, NJ: Mathematica Policy Research, 2004). The high school study is Zeyu Xu, Jane Hannaway, and Colin Taylor, *Making a Difference?: The Effects of Teach for America in High School* (Washington, DC: National Center for Analysis of Longitudinal Data in Educational Research [CALDER], 2007), http://www.urban.org, or www.CALDERcenter.org.

16. R. Pianta, L. Belsky, N. Vandergrift, R. Houts, and F. Morrison, "Classroom Effects on Children's Achievement Trajectories in Elementary School," *American Educational Research Journal* 45, no. 2 (2008): 388.

17. Heather C. Hill, "Evaluating Value-Added Models: A Validity Argument Approach," *Journal of Policy Analysis and Management,* forthcoming. Several other studies are summarized there as well.

18. The first study compared scores on two math sub-scales from the Stanford 9, and found correlations of value-added gains of between .01 and .46, depending on model specification. This means that there is "a strong sensitivity of value-added estimate to the domain of mathematics sampled," which varies among tests. The other study used scores on three reading tests, and correlations among the value-added scores among the tests ranged between .17 and .51. Hill, "Evaluating Value-Added Models."

19. Ibid.

20. Several papers from the National Bureau of Economic Research discuss these issues: Jesse Rothstein, "Teacher Quality in Educational Production: Tracking, Decay, and Student Achievement," National Bureau of Economic Research Working Paper No. 14442, March 2009; Cory Koedel and Julian R. Betts, "Value-Added to What? How a Ceiling in the Testing Instrument Influences Value-Added Estimation," National Bureau of Economic Research Working Paper No. 14778, March 2009. See also Daniel McCaffrey, J. R. Lockwood, Tim R. Sass, and Kata Mihaly, "The Inter-Temporal Variability of Teacher Effect Estimates," unpublished paper.

21. Hill, "Evaluating Value-Added Models."

22. Laura S. Hamilton, Brian M. Stecher, Julie A. Marsh, Jennifer Sloan McCombs, Abby Robyn, Jennifer Lin Russell, Scott Naftel, and Heather Barney, *Standards-Based Accountability under No Child Left Behind: Experiences of Teachers and Administrators in Three States* (Santa Monica, CA: RAND, 2007), 106.

23. Tammi Chun, Gail Zellman, Brian Stecher, and Elizabeth Giddens, *An Evaluation Strategy Developed by RAND for the Broad Foundation* (Santa Monica, CA: RAND, 2001), iii.

24. Broad Center, "The Broad Superintendents Academy: Results," May 18, 2009, http://www.broadacademy.org/fellows/results.html.

25. Broad Center, "The Broad Center for the Management of School Systems Announces 2008 Broad Residency Class" (Los Angeles, CA: Broad Center, September 16, 2008).

26. Broad Center, "The Broad Superintendents Academy."

27. Kathy Emery and Susan Ohanian, *Why Is Corporate America Bashing Our Schools?* (Portsmouth, NH: Heinemann, 2004), 77–99.

28. Chancellor Rhee's proposal to eliminate tenure and create a two-track teaching force is stalled, in part because she failed to even talk with teachers about her ideas. The City Council stalled appropriations for the schools in part because she ignored the Council. In a recent detailed analysis, the *Washington Post* found both "pockets of promise" and "painful lessons." Chancellor Rhee herself said, "The reality in Washington, D.C., is that we continue to fail the majority of kids who are put in our care every day." For a discussion of these points, see Bill Turque, "Two Years of Hard Lessons for D.C. Schools' Agent of Change," *Washington Post*, June 14, 2009, http://www.washingtonpost.com/wp-dyn/content/article/2009/06/13/AR2009061302073_5.html?hpid=topnews&sid=ST2009061302085.

29. Between 2003 and 2007, the fraction of Chicago's fourth grade students whose math scores on the Urban NAEP were "below basic" fell from 50 percent to 42 percent, but the fraction who were "basic" was essentially unchanged, at 40 percent and 41 percent; the percentage of students whose scores were "proficient" rose from 9 percent to 15 percent. The latter is a large percentage increase, but, viewed against the other scores, it means that only a very small fraction of the city's fourth graders could do math relatively well. In math in grade eight, the Chicago picture was more discouraging: the fraction below basic fell from 58 percent to 51 percent between 2003 and 2007, while the fraction of students at basic rose slightly from 33 percent to 36 percent; the fraction of students whose scores were proficient went from 8 percent to 11 percent. Thus the percentage of Chicago eighth graders who could only do math at a level that failed or barely passed fell from 91 percent to 87 percent; although it is a gain, it is a tiny gain in a very discouraging larger landscape. See A. Lutkus, W. Grigg, and G. Dion, *The Nation's Report Card: Trial Urban District Assessment Mathematics 2007 (NCES 2008–452)* (Washington, DC: National Center for Education Statistics, Institute of Education Sciences, U.S. Department of Education, 2007), 40–41. Reading scores were similar. In fourth grade, 66 percent of students were below basic in 2002, and 23 percent were at basic, while in 2007 56 percent were below basic and 28 percent were at basic; the fraction of students who were proficient rose from 9 percent to 13 percent. Again, this was a slight improvement in a generally discouraging situation. The eighth grade results were worse: 38 percent were below basic and 47 percent were basic in 2002, and 39 percent were below basic and 44 percent were at basic in 2007. See A. Lutkus, W. Grigg, and P. Donahue, *The Nation's Report Card: Trial Urban District Assessment Reading 2007 (NCES 2008–455)* (Washington, DC: National Center for Education Statistics, Institute of Education Sciences, U.S. Department of Education, 2007), 40–41.

30. Michael Jonas, "Held Back," *Commonwealth Magazine* 13 no. 3 (2008). Also available at http://www.massinc.org. See also Thomas Downes, Jeffrey

Zabel, and Dana Ansel, *Incomplete Grades: Massachusetts Education Reform at 15* (Boston, MA: MassInc, 2009).

31. Jonas, "Held Back."

32. David J. Hoff, "Schools Struggling to Meet Key Goal on Accountability," *Education Week,* January 7, 2009, 1, 14–15.

33. For example, see the work of MassInsight, an advocacy group that vigorously supports the Massachusetts state education reform: http://www.massinsight.org/

34. Libby Quaid writes, "The plan is to beef up funding for the federal school turnaround program, created by the No Child Left Behind law, which gets about $500 million a year. The stimulus legislation boosted funding to $3.5 billion. Obama's budget would add another $1.5 billion by shifting dollars away from traditional formula programs." Libby Quaid, "Obama Wants to See 5,000 Failing Schools Close," *Seattle Times,* May 11, 2009, http://seattletimes.nwsource.com/html/politics/2009206020_apusobamafailingschools.html.

35. Ibid.

36. Ibid. Secretary Duncan offers a more hopeful interpretation in a recent op-ed: Arne Duncan, "Turnarounds Should Be the First Option for Low-Performing Schools," *Education Week,* June 17, 2009.

37. The studies include Public Impact, *School Turnarounds: A Review of the Cross-Sector Evidence on Dramatic Organizational Improvement* (Chapel Hill, NC: Public Impact, Academic Development Institute, 2007); Ronald C. Brady, *Can Failing Schools Be Fixed?* (Washington, DC: The Thomas B. Fordham Foundation, 2003); Emily Ayscue Hassell and Bryan C. Hassel, "The Big U-Turn," *Education Next,* Winter 2009, http://www.hoover.org/publications/ednext/34686334.html; Center on Education Policy, *Managing More Than a Thousand Remodeling Projects: School Restructuring In California* (Washington, DC: Center on Education Policy, 2008).

38. See, for example, Fred Hess, "Back To School," *The American: The Journal of the American Enterprise Institute,* April 24, 2008, http://www.american.com/archive/2008/april-04-08/back-to-school.

39. Center on Education Policy, *Managing More Than A Thousand Remodeling Projects,* 21.

40. Ibid.

41. Public Impact, *School Turnarounds.*

42. Ron Zimmer, Brian Gill, Kevin Booker, Stephane Lavertu, Tim R. Sass, and John Witte, *Charter Schools in Eight States: Effects on Achievement, Attainment, Integration, and Competition* (Santa Monica, CA: RAND, 2009), 19.

43. Zimmer et al. write, "The analysis suggests that nonprimary charter schools are producing achievement gains that are approximately equivalent to those of

TPSs in most locations, with moderately negative effects in math and reading in Texas middle schools and in reading in Chicago middle schools. While our results for Ohio's virtual charter schools should be viewed with a level of caution because of the uniqueness of the students who attend these schools and because much of the analysis relies on charter schools with primary grades, they suggest that these schools should be examined more carefully because of the poor achievement results." Zimmer et al., *Charter Schools in Eight States*, 50–51. In another large study, the Center for Research on Education Outcomes offered a similar conclusion: "Our national pooled analysis reveals, on the whole, a slightly negative picture of average charter school performance nationwide. On average, charter school students can expect to see their academic growth be somewhat lower than their traditional public school peers, though the absolute differences are small. Charter students trail the academic growth of TPS students by .01 standard deviations in reading, and by .03 standard deviations in math. Though small, these effects are statistically significant. These findings hold for students across the board of initial starting scores, except for students in the lowest and highest starting deciles in reading. There is some good news as well. Nationally, elementary and middle school charter students exhibited higher learning gains than equivalent students in the traditional public school system. In addition, some subgroups demonstrated greater academic growth than their TPS twins. Specifically, students in poverty and ELL students experience larger learning gains in charter schools. Other subgroups, however, including Black and Hispanic students as a whole, have learning gains that are significantly smaller than those of their TPS twins." Center for Research on Education Outcomes, *Multiple Choice: Charter School Performance in 16 States* (Stanford, CA: Stanford University, 2009), 45.

44. Steven F. Wilson, "Success at Scale in Charter Schooling," Working Paper 2008-02 (Washington, DC: American Enterprise Institute, 2008), 4, www.aei .org/futureofeducation.

45. Ibid.

46. Ibid., cites Samuel Casey Carter, *No Excuses: Lessons from 21 High-Performing, High-Poverty Schools* (Washington, DC: Heritage Foundation, 2001).

47. Wilson, "Success at Scale in Charter Schooling," 23. Wilson continues: "Unsurprisingly, Achievement First [a charter network] places a candidate's attendance at a 'top notch university' at the top of its list of 23 attributes in its summary of 'teacher quality.'" Second is a "high GPA" and "legitimate major." Achievement First prefers "two to five years teaching experience." Candidates are sought who have a "history of getting high student achievement, tight discipline and culture," believe that "measurable student achievement is the number one goal," and "[like] standards, statewide testing, and accountability." "Student achievement is a part of a teacher's evaluation."

48. Ibid., 26.

49. Ibid., 27.

50. Ibid., 28.

51. Ibid.

52. Anthony Bryk discusses instructional systems in "Support a Science of Instructional Improvement," *Phi Delta Kappan,* April 2009, 597–600.

53. "The SABIS® Educational System consists of a demanding curriculum, an intense, disciplined, and interactive approach to deliver the intellectual material, and rigorous homework requirements. In SABIS schools, all students, regardless of their ability levels, can learn and achieve very high academic standards provided they want to learn. For this purpose, students undergo continuous monitoring to prevent the development of knowledge gaps during their learning process. By motivating students, fostering a desire to learn, and providing an efficient and high-quality educational experience, the SABIS® Educational System helps each student achieve his/her full potential." In the United States, SABIS Educational Systems, Inc. currently operates eight charter schools (Arizona, Louisiana, Massachusetts, Michigan, Ohio) and one private school (Minnesota). http://www.sabis.net/educational-systems/Default.aspx.

54. Wilson, "Success at Scale in Charter Schooling," 31.

55. National Governors Association, Council of Chief State School Officers, and Achieve, *Benchmarking for Success: Ensuring U.S. Students Receive a World-Class Education* (Washington, DC: National Governors Association, Council of Chief State School Officers, and Achieve, 2008), 1.

56. Ibid., 6.

57. Ibid., 7.

58. Council of Chief State School Officers, "Common Core State Standards Initiative" (Washington, DC: Council of Chief State School Officers, 2009).

59. U.S. House of Representatives Committee on Education and Labor, "Congress Must Support State Efforts for Rigorous Common Standards," April 29, 2009, http://edlabor.house.gov/newsroom/2009/04.

60. See our discussion in Chapter 6.

61. Council of Chief State School Officers, "Common Core State Standards Initiative."

62. Michelle McNeil, "NGA, CCSSO Launch Common Standards Drive," *Education Week,* June 1, 2009.

63. The Center on Education Policy (CEP) addressed part of this issue. See Angela Minnici and Deanna D. Hill, *Educational Architects: Do State Education Agencies Have the Tools Necessary to Implement NCLB?* (Washington, DC: Center on Education Policy, 2007). CEP (pp. 2–3) reported, "Our surveys and interviews

identified four major challenges to the capacity of SEAs to implement the requirements of NCLB: (1) limitations in staffing and infrastructure; (2) inadequate federal funding; (3) lack of guidance and technical support from the U.S. Department of Education; and (4) barriers in NCLB and within state education agencies." It continued: "Providing technical assistance to school districts with schools in improvement continues to be very challenging for most states, and many are worried about the future. Only 11 states reported they were able to provide technical assistance to districts with schools in improvement, corrective action, or restructuring 'to a great extent.' Survey data reveal that insufficient numbers of staff, lack of in-house expertise, and inadequate federal and state funding were the major impediments to implementing this requirement."

64. Maria Glod, "46 States, D.C. Plan to Draft Common Education Standards," *Washington Post,* June 1, 2009.

65. Ibid.

66. Alyson Klein, "Duncan Unveils Details on Race to the Top Aid," *Education Week,* June 15, 2009, http://www.edweek.org/ew/articles/2009/06/15/36duncan .h28.html?r=475744911.

67. National Governors Association et al., *Benchmarking for Success,* 30.

68. The demand for these services was initially prompted by state and federal standards-based reform in the 1980s and 1990s, but NCLB's very tight, test-driven accountability requirements had appreciable negative effects on demand.

69. These CSRDs are much more vulnerable to the environment than the local districts that adopt their designs. As the economic crash has squeezed state and local governments, there are reports that school systems are cutting their work with the CSRDs to save money, and that threatens to put some of the parent organizations out of business. If that happens, one of the most promising efforts to develop organizations that can build the capability to improve schools could be eliminated. That would be serious a loss, for we know of no other organizations that have their capability to stimulate and support school improvement.

70. See, for example, Richard Correnti, "Examining CSR Program Effects on Student Achievement: Causal Explanation through Examination of Implementation Rates and Student Mobility," paper presented at 2nd annual conference of the Society for Research on Educational Effectiveness, Washington, DC, March 2009.

Bibliography

American Federation of Teachers. *Making Standards Matter 2001.* Washington, DC: American Federation of Teachers, 2001.

———. *Sizing up State Standards, 2008.* Washington, DC: American Federation of Teachers, 2008.

Archambault, Francis X., Jr. "Instructional Setting: Key Issue or Bogus Concern." In *Designs for Compensatory Education: Conference Proceedings and Papers,* edited by B. I. Williams, P. A. Richmond, and B. J. Mason. Washington, DC: Department of Education, June 17–18, 1986, III-59–93.

Averch, Harvey A., Stephen J. Carroll, Theodore S. Donaldson, Herbert J. Kiesling, and John A. Pincus. *How Effective Is Schooling? A Critical Review and Synthesis of Research Findings.* Santa Monica, CA: RAND, 1972.

Bailey, Stephen, and Edith Mosher. *ESEA: The Office of Education Administers a Law.* Syracuse, NY: Syracuse University Press, 1968.

Ballou, D. "Sizing up Test Scores." *Education Next,* Summer 2002, 10–15.

Bardach, Eugene. *The Implementation Game.* Cambridge, MA: MIT Press, 1977.

Barton, P. "Staying on Course in Education Reform." Princeton, NJ: Educational Testing Service, April 2002.

Berke, J., and Michael Kirst. *Federal Aid to Education—Who Benefits? Who Governs?* New Britain, CT: Lexington Books, 1972.

Berliner, David C., and Bruce J. Biddle. *The Manufactured Crisis: Myths, Fraud, and the Attack on America's Public Schools.* Reading, MA: Addison-Wesley, 1995.

Berman, Paul, and Milbrey W. McLaughlin. *Federal Programs Supporting Educational Change.* Vol. 8. Santa Monica, CA: RAND, 1979.

Birman, B., K. LeFloch, A. Klokota, M. Ludwig, J. Taylor, K. Walters, A. Wayne, and K. Yoon. *State and Local Implementation of the No Child Left Behind Act,* Vol. 2, *Teacher Quality under NCLB: Interim Report.* Washington, DC: U.S. Department of Education, Office of Planning, Evaluation, and Policy Development, 2007.

Birman, B. F., M. Orland, R. Jung, R. Anson, and G. Garcia. *The Current Operation of the Chapter 1 Program—Final Report from the National Assessment of Chapter 1.* Washington, DC: OERI, U.S. Department of Education, 1987.

Borman, G. D., S. C. Stringfield, and R. E. Slavin, eds. *Title I: Compensatory Education at the Crossroads.* Mahwah, NJ: Lawrence Erlbaum, 2001.

Brady, Ronald C. *Can Failing Schools Be Fixed?* Washington, DC: Thomas B. Fordham Foundation, 2003.

Brehm, John, and Scott Gates. *Working, Shirking, and Sabotage: Bureaucratic Response to a Democratic Public.* Ann Arbor: University of Michigan Press, 1997.

Broad Center. "The Broad Superintendents Academy: Results." May 18, 2009. http://www.broadacademy.org/fellows/results.html.

———. "The Broad Center for the Management of School Systems Announces 2008 Broad Residency Class." Los Angeles, CA: Broad Center, September 16, 2008.

Brodkin, Evelyn Z. "Implementation as Policy Politics." In *Implementation and the Policy Process: Opening up the Black Box,* edited by Dennis J. Palumbo and Donald J. Calista. New York: Greenwood, 1990, 107–118.

Brophy, Jere. "Research Linking Teacher Behavior to Student Achievement: Potential Implications for Instruction of Chapter 1 Students." In *Designs for Compensatory Education: Conference Proceedings and Papers,* edited by B. I. Williams, P. A. Richmond, and B. J. Mason. Washington, DC: Department of Education, June 17–18, 1986, IV 121–179.

———. "Teacher Influences on Student Achievement." *American Psychologist* 41, no. 10 (October 1986): 1069–1077.

Brophy, Jere, and Thomas Good. "Teacher Behavior and Student Achievement." In *Handbook of Research and Teaching,* 3rd ed., edited by M. C. Wittrock. New York: Macmillan, 1986, 328–377.

Bryk, A., Y. Thum, J. Easton, and S. Luppescu. "Academic Productivity of Chicago Public Elementary Schools." Chicago: Consortium on Chicago School Research, March 1998.

Bryk, Anthony, Valerie Lee, and Peter Holland. *Catholic Schools and the Common Good.* Cambridge, MA: Harvard University Press, 1993.

Bryk, Anthony S., and Barbara Schneider. *Trust in Schools: A Core Resource for Improvement.* New York: Russell Sage, 2002.

Campbell, Andrea Louise. *How Policies Make Citizens: Senior Political Activism and the American Welfare State.* Princeton, NJ: Princeton University Press, 2003.

———. "Universalism, Targeting and Participation." In *Remaking America: Democracy and Public Policy in an Age of Inequality,* edited by Joe Soss, Jacob S. Hacker, and Suzanne Mettler. New York: Russell Sage Foundation, 2007, 121–140.

Carter, L. *A Study of Compensatory and Elementary Education: The Sustaining Effects Study. Final Report.* Santa Monica, CA: Systems Development Corporation, 1983.

———. *A Study of Compensatory and Elementary Education: The Sustaining Effects Study. Interim Report.* Santa Monica, CA: Systems Development Corporation, 1980.

———. "The Sustaining Effects Study of Compensatory and Elementary Education." *Educational Researcher,* August–September 1984, 4–13.

Carter, Samuel Casey. *No Excuses: Lessons from 21 High-Performing, High-Poverty Schools.* Washington, DC: Heritage Foundation, 2001.

Center for Research on Education Outcomes. *Multiple Choice: Charter School Performance in 16 States.* Stanford, CA: Stanford University, 2009.

Center on Education Policy. *Implementing the No Child Left Behind Teacher Requirements.* Washington, DC: Center on Education Policy, 2007.

———. *Managing More Than a Thousand Remodeling Projects: School Restructuring in California.* Washington, DC: Center on Education Policy, 2008.

———. *Moving beyond Notification: Assisting Schools in Improvement.* Washington, DC: Center on Education Policy, 2007.

Chambers, Jay G., Irene Lam, Kanya Mahitivanichcha, Phil Esra, Larisa Shambaugh, and Stephanie Stullich. *State and Local Implementation of the No Child Left Behind Act: Volume VI—Targeting and Uses of Federal Education Funds.* Washington, DC: United States Department of Education, Office of Planning, Evaluation and Policy Development, 2009.

Chambers, Jay, Thomas Parrish, Margaret Goertz, Camille Marder, and Christine Padilla. *Translating Dollars into Services: Chapter 1 Resources in the Context of State and Local Resources for Education. Final Report.* Washington, DC: United States Department of Education, Office of Policy and Planning, 1993.

Chun, Tammi, Gail Zellman, Brian Stecher, and Elizabeth Giddens. *An Evaluation Strategy Developed by RAND for the Broad Foundation.* Santa Monica, CA: RAND, 2001.

Clark, Kenneth. *Dark Ghetto Dilemmas of Social Power.* New York: Harper & Row, 1965.

——. "Education of Minority Poor: The Key to the War on Poverty." In *Disadvantaged Poor: Education and Employment, Third Report of the Task Force on Economic Growth Opportunity.* Washington, DC: Chamber of Commerce of the United States, 1966.

Coburn, Cynthia E., and Mary Kay Stein. "Communities of Practice Theory and the Role of Teacher Professional Community in Policy Implementation." In *New Directions in Education Policy Implementation: Confronting Complexity,* edited by Meredith I. Honig. Albany: State University of New York Press, 2006, 25–46.

Cohen, David K. "Revolution in One Classroom." *Educational Evaluation and Policy Analysis* 12, no. 3 (1990): 311–329.

Cohen, David K., and Carol A. Barnes. "A New Pedagogy for Policy?" In *Teaching for Understanding: Challenges for Policy and Practice,* edited by David K. Cohen, Milbrey W. McLaughlin, and Joan E. Talbert. San Francisco: Jossey-Bass, 1993, 240–275.

——. "Pedagogy and Policy." In *Teaching for Understanding: Challenges for Policy and Practice,* edited by David K. Cohen, Milbrey W. McLaughlin, and Joan E. Talbert. San Francisco: Jossey-Bass, 1993, 207–239.

Cohen, David K., and Heather C. Hill. *Learning Policy: When State Education Reform Works.* New Haven, CT: Yale University Press, 2001.

Cohen, David K., Susan L. Moffitt, and Simona Goldin. "Policy and Practice: The Dilemma." *American Journal of Education* 134, no. 4 (September 2007): 515–548.

Cohen, David K., Steven Raudenbush, and Deborah L. Ball. "Resources, Instruction and Research." *Educational Evaluation and Policy Analysis* 25, no. 2 (2003): 119–142.

Cohen, David K., and James P. Spillane. "Policy and Practice: The Relations between Governance and Instruction." In *Review of Research in Education,* edited by Gerald Grant. Washington, DC: American Educational Research Association, 1992, 3–49.

Cooley, William, and Gaea Leinhardt. *Instructional Dimensions Study: The Search for Effective Classroom Processes.* Pittsburgh: Learning Research and Development Center, 1978.

Correnti, Richard. "Examining CSR Program Effects on Student Achievement: Causal Explanation through Examination of Implementation Rates and Student Mobility." Paper presented at 2nd annual conference of the Society for Research on Educational Effectiveness, Washington, DC, March 2009.

Council of Chief State School Officers. "Common Core State Standards Initiative." Washington, DC: Council of Chief State School Officers, 2009.

Cross, Christopher T. *Political Education: National Policy Comes of Age.* New York: Teachers College Press, 2006.

——. *Putting the Pieces Together: Lessons from Comprehensive School Reform Research.* Washington, DC: National Clearinghouse for Comprehensive School Reform, 2004.

——. "Title I Evaluation: A Case Study in Frustration." *Educational Evaluation and Policy Analysis* 1, no. 2 (March–April 1979): 15–21.

David, Jane. *Local Uses of Title I Evaluations.* Menlo Park, CA: SRI, 1978.

——. "Local Uses of Title I Evaluations," *Educational Evaluation and Policy Analysis* 3, no. 1 (1981): 27–39.

Debray, Elizabeth. *Politics, Ideology, and Education.* New York: Teachers College Press, 2006.

Decker, Paul T., Daniel P. Mayer, and Steven Glazerman. *The Effects of Teach for America on Students. Findings from a National Evaluation.* Princeton, NJ: Mathematica Policy Research, 2004.

Donahue, P. L., *NAEP 2008 Trends in Academic Progress.* Washington, DC: National Center for Education Statistics, Institute of Education Sciences, U.S. Department of Education, 2009.

Dow, Peter. *Schoolhouse Politics: Lessons from the Sputnik Era.* Cambridge, MA: Harvard University Press, 1993.

Downes, Thomas, Jeffrey Zabel, and Dana Ansel. *Incomplete Grades: Massachusetts Education Reform at 15.* Boston, MA: MassInc, 2009.

Downey, Douglas B., Paul T. von Hippel, and Beckett A. Broh. "Are Schools the Great Equalizer? Cognitive Inequality during the Summer Months and the School Year." *American Sociological Review* 79, no. 5 (October 2004): 613–635.

Duncan, Arne. "Turnarounds Should Be the First Option for Low-Performing Schools." *Education Week*, June 17, 2009.

Dunkin, M. J., and B. J. Biddle. *The Study of Teaching*. New York: Holt, Rinehart and Winston, 1974.

Edmonds, R., and J. R. Frederiksen. *Search for Effective Schools: The Identification and Analysis of City Schools That Are Instructionally Effective for Poor Children*. Cambridge, MA: Harvard Center for Urban Studies, 1978.

Eidenberg, Eugene, and Roy Morey. *An Act of Congress: The Legislative Process and the Making of Education Policy*. New York: W. W. Norton, 1969.

Ellis, Joseph J. *Founding Brothers: The Revolutionary Generation*. New York: Vintage, 2000.

Elmore, Richard F. "Agency, Reciprocity, and Accountability in Democratic Education." In *The Public Schools,* edited by Susan Fuhrman and Marvin Lazerson. Oxford: Oxford University Press, 2005, 277–301.

———. "Backward Mapping: Implementation Research and Policy Decisions." *Political Science Quarterly* 94, no. 4 (1979–1980): 601–616.

———. "Organizational Models of Social Program Implementation." *Public Policy* 23, no. 2 (1978): 185–228.

Elmore, Richard F., and Milbrey W. McLaughlin. *Steady Work: Policy, Practice, and the Reform of American Education*. Santa Monica, CA: RAND, 1988.

———. "Strategic Choice in Federal Education Policy: The Compliance-Assistance Trade-off." In *Policy Making in Education,* edited by Ann Lieberman and Milbrey W. McLaughlin. Chicago: University of Chicago Press, 1982, 159–194.

Emery, Kathy, and Susan Ohanian. *Why Is Corporate America Bashing Our Schools?* Portsmouth, NH: Heinemann, 2004.

Feldstein, M. "The Effect of Differential Add-on Grant: Title I and Local Education Spending." *Journal of Human Resources* 13 (1978): 443–458.

Finn, Chester E., Jr. *Education and the Presidency*. Lexington, MA: Lexington Books, 1977.

Finn, Chester E., Jr., Liam Julian, and Michael J. Petrilli. *The State of State Standards*. Washington, DC: Thomas B. Fordham Foundation, 2006.

Finn, Chester, and Michael Petrilli, *The State of State Standards*. Washington, DC: Thomas B. Fordham Foundation, 2000.

Floden, R. E., A. C. Porter, W. H. Schmidt, D. J. Freeman, and J. R. Schwille. "Responses to Curriculum Pressures: A Policy-Capturing Study of Teacher Decisions about Content." *Journal of Educational Psychology* 73 (1981): 129–141.

Foster, Susan G. "Proposed Title I Regulations." *Education Week,* February 17, 1982. http://www.edweek.org/ew/1982/01210015.h01.

Fuhrman, Susan H., and Richard F. Elmore. "Ruling Out Rules: The Evolution of Deregulation in State Education Policy." *Teachers College Record* 97, no. 2 (1995): 279–309.

———. "Takeover and Deregulation: Working Models of New State and Local Regulatory Relationships." CPRE Research Report no. RR-24. New Brunswick, NJ: Consortium for Policy Research in Education, Rutgers University, 1992.

Fuller, B., K. Gesicki, E. Kang, and J. Wright. *Is the No Child Left Behind Act Working? The Reliability of How States Track Achievement.* Berkeley, CA: PACE, 2006.

Funkhouser, J. E., J. S. Michie, and M. T. Moore. *Federal Administration of Chapter 1, ECIA Staffing and Financial Support Substudy.* Washington, DC: Decision Resources Corporation, 1987.

Gaffney, Michael, and Daniel Schember. *The Effects of the Title I Supplement-Not-Supplant and Excess Costs and Provisions on Program Design Decisions.* Washington, DC: Advanced Technology/Planning and Evaluation Service, U.S. Department of Education, 1982.

Glod, Maria. "46 States, D.C. Plan to Draft Common Education Standards." *Washington Post,* June 1, 2009.

Goals 2000: Educate America Act, 103d Cong., 2d sess., HR 1806.

Goldhaber, Dan. *Exploring the Use and Efficacy of Incentives to Reward Teachers for Tough Assignments.* Seattle: Center on Reinventing Public Education, University of Washington, 2008.

Good, Thomas, and Jennifer Braden. *The Great School Debate—Choice, Vouchers, and Charter Schools.* Mahwah, NJ: Lawrence Erlbaum, 2000.

Graham, Hugh Davis. *The Uncertain Triumph: Federal Education Policy in the Kennedy and Johnson Years.* Chapel Hill: University of North Carolina Press, 1984.

Grant, Gerald. *The Politics of the Coleman Report.* PhD diss., Harvard University, 1972.

Grant, W. Vance. "Statistics in the U.S. Department of Education: Highlights from the Past 120 Years." In *120 Years of American Education: A Statistical Portrait,* edited by Thomas D. Snyder. Washington, DC: National Center for Education Statistics, 1993, 1–4.

Hamilton, Laura S., Brian M. Stecher, Julie A. Marsh, Jennifer Sloan McCombs, Abby Robyn, Jennifer Lin Russell, Scott Naftel, and Heather Barney. *Standards-Based Accountability under No Child Left Behind: Experiences of Teachers and Administrators in Three States.* Santa Monica, CA: RAND, 2007.

Hanushek, Eric. "School Resources and Student Performance." In *Does Money Matter? The Effect of School Resources on Student Achievement and Adult Success,* edited by Gary Burtless. Washington, DC: Brookings Institution, 1996, 43–73.

Hassell, Emily Ayscue, and Bryan C. Hassel. "The Big U-Turn." *Education Next,* Winter 2009. http://www.hoover.org/publications/ednext/34686334.html.

Hernandez, Javier C. "For Many Teachers, a Famously Fertile Market Dries Up Overnight." *New York Times,* May 11, 2009.

Hess, Fred. "Back To School." *The American: The Journal of the American Enterprise Institute,* April 24, 2008. http://www.american.com/archive/2008/april-04-08/back-to-school.

Hill, Heather C. "Evaluating Value-Added Models: A Validity Argument Approach." Forthcoming in *Journal of Policy Analysis and Management.*

——. "Language Matters: How Characteristics of Language Complicate Policy Implementation." In *New Directions in Education Policy Implementation: Confronting Complexity,* edited by Meredith I. Honig. Albany: State University of New York Press, 2006, 65–82.

Hoepfner, Ralph. *Sub-studies on Allocation and Targeting of Funds and Services, Assessment of Student Growth, and Effects of Attrition, Sustaining Effects Technical Report #13.* Santa Monica, CA: Systems Development Corporation, 1981.

Hoff, David J. "Schools Struggling to Meet Key Goal on Accountability: Number Failing to Make AYP Rises 28 Percent." *Education Week.* http://www.edweek.org/ew/articles/2008/12/18 (updated January 7, 2009).

Hoff, David J. "Schools Struggling to Meet Key Goal on Accountability." *Education Week*, January 7, 2009.

Hollingshead, August. *Elmtown's Youth*. New York: Wiley, 1949.

Honig, Meredith I. *New Directions in Education Policy Implementation*. Albany: State University of New York Press, 2006.

Hughes, John. *Equal Education: A New National Strategy*. Bloomington: Indiana University Press, 1972.

Institute of Education Sciences. *Mapping 2005 State Proficiency Standards onto the NAEP Scales*. Washington, DC: Institute of Education Sciences, 2007.

Jeffrey, Julie Roy. *Education for Children of the Poor: A Study of the Origins and Implementation of the Elementary and Secondary Education Act of 1965*. Columbus: Ohio State University Press, 1978.

Jennings, John F. "The Elementary and Secondary Education Act: The 1960s and 1970s." In *A Compilation of Papers on the Twentieth Anniversary of the Elementary and Secondary Education Act of 1965*, Subcommittee on Elementary and Secondary and Vocational Education, House of Representatives. Washington, DC: Government Printing Office, 1985, 55–60.

———. "Title I: Its Legislative History and Its Promise." In *Title I: Compensatory Education at the Crossroads*, edited by G. D. Borman, S. C. Stringfield, and R. E. Slavin. Mahwah, NJ: Lawrence Erlbaum, 2001, 1–25.

———. *Why National Standards and Tests?* Thousand Oaks, CA: Sage, 1998.

Johns, Emily. "Minnesota's Must-pass Math Test Goes By Wayside." *Minneapolis Star-Tribune*, May 30, 2009.

Johnson, Jean, Ana Maria Arumi, and Amber Ott. *Is Support for Standards Fading?* New York: Public Agenda, 2006.

Jonas, Michael. "Held Back." *Commonwealth Magazine* 13, no. 3 (2008). Also available at http://www.massinc.org.

Kaestle, Carl. *Pillars of the Republic: Common Schools and American Society, 1780–1860*. New York: Hill and Wang, 1983.

Katz, M. "The Origins of Public Education: A Reassessment." *History of Education Quarterly* 16, no. 4 (Winter 1976): 381–407.

Katznelson, Ira, and Margaret Weir. *Schooling for All: Class, Race, and the Decline of the Democratic Ideal*. New York: Basic Books, 1985.

Kennedy, M., B. Birman, and R. Demaline. *The Effectiveness of Chapter I Services.* Washington, DC: U.S. Department of Education (OERI), 1987.

———. *The Effectiveness of Chapter 1 Services: Second Interim Report from the National Assessment of Chapter 1.* Washington, DC: OERI, 1986.

Kennedy, M. M., R. K. Jung, and M. E. Orland. *Poverty, Achievement, and the Distribution of Compensatory Education Services.* Washington, DC: U.S. Department of Education, 1986.

Kimbrough, Jackie, and Paul Hill. *The Aggregate Effects of Federal Education Programs.* Santa Monica, CA: RAND, 1981.

Kingsbury, G. Gage, Allan Olson, John Cronin, Carl Hauser, and Ron Houser. *The State of State Standards: Research Investigating Proficiency Levels in Fourteen States.* Portland, OR: Northwest Evaluation Association, 2003. http://www.nwea.org/support/reportsLogin.aspx.

———. *The State of State Standards: Research Investigating Proficiency Levels in Fourteen States.* Portland, OR: Northwest Evaluation Association, 2004.

Kirst, Michael, and R. Jung. "The Utility of a Longitudinal Approach in Assessing Implementation: A Thirteen-Year View of Title I, ESEA." *Educational Evaluation and Policy Analysis* 2, no. 5 (1980): 17–34.

Klein, Alyson. "Dual Aims in Stimulus Stir Tension." *Education Week,* June 9, 2009. http://www.edweek.org/ew/articles/2009/06/10/33stimreform.h28.html?tkn=UQBFOcWKvVyDGEbz9Q0qS611IC4kl9NqvUXB.

———. "Duncan Unveils Details on Race to the Top Aid." *Education Week,* June 15, 2009. http://www.edweek.org/ew/articles/2009/06/15/36duncan.h28.html?r=475744911.

———. "Key Democrats Question Parts of Obama Budget." *Education Week,* June 10, 2009.

Koedel, Cory, and Julian R. Betts. "Value-Added to What? How a Ceiling in the Testing Instrument Influences Value-Added Estimation." National Bureau of Economic Research Working Paper No. 14778, March 2009.

Koretz, Dan. *Measuring Up.* Cambridge, MA: Harvard University Press, 2008.

Kymlicka, B. B., and Jean V. Matthews. *The Reagan Revolution?* Chicago: Dorsey Press, 1988.

Lieberman, Robert C. "Ideas, Institutions, and Political Order: Explaining Political Change." *American Political Science Review* 96, no. 4 (2002): 697–712.

Lin, Ann Chih. *Reform in the Making: The Implementation of Social Policy in Prison.* Princeton, NJ: Princeton University Press, 2000.

Lin, Ann, and Joe Soss. "Policy Discourse and Public Management: How Therapeutic Frames Organize the Politics of Administration." Paper prepared for the Research Workshop on the Empirical Study of Governance, Texas A&M University, College Station, February 21–23, 2002.

Lindblom, Charles. "The Science of 'Muddling Through.'" *Public Administration Review* 19, no. 2 (Spring 1959): 79–88.

Linn, R. L. "The Validity of Inferences Based On the Proposed Title I Evaluation Models." *Educational Evaluation and Policy Analysis* 1 (1979): 23–32.

Linn, Robert. *Accountability: Responsibility and Reasonable Expectations.* CSE Report 601. Boulder: CRESST/University of Colorado, 2003.

Lipsky, Michael. *Street-Level Bureaucracy: Dilemmas of the Individual in Public Service.* New York: Russell Sage, 1980.

Lortie, D. *Schoolteacher.* Chicago: University of Chicago, 1974.

Lutkus, A., W. Grigg, and G. Dion. *The Nation's Report Card: Trial Urban District Assessment Mathematics 2007 (NCES 2008–452).* Washington, DC: National Center for Education Statistics, Institute of Education Sciences, U.S. Department of Education, 2007.

Lutkus, A., W. Grigg, and P. Donahue. *The Nation's Report Card: Trial Urban District Assessment Reading 2007 (NCES 2008–455).* Washington, DC: National Center for Education Statistics, Institute of Education Sciences, U.S. Department of Education, 2007.

Lynd, Robert, and Helen Lynd. *Middletown.* New York: Harcourt Brace, 1937.

Mann, Horace. *Life and Works of Horace Mann,* Vols. 3–4. Boston, MA: Lee and Shepard Publishers, 1891.

Martin, Ruby, and Phyllis McClure. *Title I of ESEA: Is It Helping Poor Children?* Washington, DC: Washington Research Project of the Southern Center for Studies in Public Policy and the NAACP Legal Defense and Education Fund, 1969.

Marshall, James, Charles Edwards, and Michael Brustein. *Chapter 1 Handbook.* Arlington, VA: Education Funding Research Council, 1992.

Marshall, James, Charles Edwards, and Alvin Lin. *Title I Handbook.* Arlington, VA: Education Funding Research Council, 1995.

Mazmanian, Daniel A., and Paul A. Sabatier. *Implementation and Public Policy.* Lanham, MD: University Press of America, 1989.

McCaffrey, Daniel, J. R. Lockwood, Tim R. Sass, and Kata Mihaly. "The Inter-Temporal Variability of Teacher Effect Estimates." Unpublished paper.

McClure, Phyllis. *School Improvement under No Child Left Behind.* Washington, DC: Center for American Progress, 2005.

McDill, Edward, and Gary Natriello. "The Effectiveness of the Title I Compensatory Education Program: 1965–1997." *Journal of Education for Students Placed at Risk* 3, no. 4 (1998): 317–335.

McDonnell, Lorraine M., and Richard F. Elmore. "Getting the Job Done: Alternative Policy Instruments." *Educational Evaluation and Policy Analysis* 9, no. 2 (1987): 133–152.

McGill-Frantzen, A., and R. L. Allington. "The Gridlock of Low Reading Achievement: Perspectives on Practice and Policy." *Remedial and Special Education (RASE)* 12, no. 3 (May–June 1991): 20–30.

McGonagill, Grady. *The Compensatory Education Study: A Case Study of Client-Centered Federal Evaluation.* PhD diss., Harvard University, 1983.

McGuinn, Patrick J. *No Child Left Behind and the Transformation of Federal Education Policy, 1965–2005.* Lawrence: University of Kansas Press, 2006.

McLaughlin, Milbrey W. *Evaluation and Reform: Title I of the Elementary and Secondary Education Act of 1965.* Cambridge, MA: Ballanger, 1975.

———. "Learning from Experience: Lessons from Policy Implementation." In *Education Policy Implementation,* edited by Allan R. Odden. Albany: State University of New York Press, 1991, 185–196.

———. "The RAND Change Agent Study: Ten Years Later." In *Education Policy Implementation,* edited by Allan R. Odden. Albany: State University of New York Press, 1991, 143–156.

McNeil, Michelle. "Stimulus Aid's Pace Still Slow: States Aim to Plug Holes, Application Review Shows." *Education Week,* June 17, 2009.

Medina, Jennifer. "Finding Jobs for Teachers Already on City's Payroll." *New York Times,* November 18, 2008.

Meranto, P. *The Politics of Federal Aid to Education in 1965: A Study in Political Innovation.* Syracuse, NY: Syracuse University Press, 1967.

Mettler, Suzanne. *Soldiers to Citizens: The G.I. Bill and the Making of the Greatest Generation.* New York: Oxford University Press, 2005.

Miller, Julie A. "Chapter 1 Panel Calls for Radical Set of Revisions." *Education Week,* September 16, 1992.

———. "E.S.E.A. Plan Would Retool Chapter 1, Eliminate Block Grant." *Education Week,* August 4, 1993.

Millsap, Mary Ann, Marc Moss, and Beth Garnse. *The Chapter 1 Implementation Study Final Report: Chapter 1 in Public Schools.* Washington, DC: U.S. Department of Education, 1993.

Minnici, Angela, and Deanna D. Hill. *Educational Architects: Do State Education Agencies Have the Tools Necessary to Implement NCLB?* Washington, DC: Center on Education Policy, 2007.

Morken, H., and J. R. Formicola. *The Politics of School Choice.* Lanham, MD: Rowman & Littlefield, 1999.

Mosbaek, E. J., F. R. Frola, K. F. Gordon, and J. W. Harrison. *Analysis of Compensatory Education in Five School Districts.* Washington, DC: TEMPO, 1969.

Moss, Marc, Alyssa Rulf Fountain, Beth Boulay, Megan Horst, Chris Rodger, and Melanie Brown-Lyons. *Reading First Implementation Evaluation Final Report.* Washington, DC: U.S. Department of Education, 2008.

Munger, F. J., and R. F. Fenno. *National Politics and Federal Aid to Education.* Syracuse, NY: Syracuse University Press, 1962.

Murnane, Richard, and Frank Levy. *Teaching the New Basic Skills: Principles for Educating Children to Thrive in a Changing Economy.* New York: Free Press, 1996.

Murphy, J. *Grease the Squeaky Wheel.* Lexington, MA: Lexington Books, 1974.

Murphy, Jerome. "Progress and Problems: The Paradox of State Reform." In *Policy Making in Education,* edited by Ann Lieberman and Milbrey W. McLaughlin. Chicago: University of Chicago Press, 1982, 195–214.

———. "Title I: Bureaucratic Politics and Poverty Politics." *Inequality in Education* 6 (November 1970): 9–15.

——. "Title I of ESEA: The Politics of Implementing Federal Education Reform." *Harvard Educational Review* 41, no. 1 (February 1971): 35–64.

Murphy, J., Scott W. Gilmer, P. G. Weise, and Ann Page. *Pathways to Privatization in Education.* Greenwich, CT: Ablex Corp., 1998.

National Center for Education Statistics. *Digest of Education Statistics: 2007.* Washington, DC: National Center for Education Statistics, 2007.

——. *Revenues and Expenditures for Public Elementary and Secondary Education: School Year 2005–06.* http://nces.ed.gov/pubs2008/2008328.

National Commission on Excellence in Education. *A Nation at Risk: The Imperative for Educational Reform.* Washington, DC: National Commission on Excellence in Education, 1983.

National Education Goals Panel. *The National Goals Report: Building a Nation of Learners.* Washington, DC: National Education Goals Panel, 1999.

National Governors Association, Council of Chief State School Officers, and Achieve. *Benchmarking for Success: Ensuring U.S. Standards Receive a World Class Education.* Washington, DC: National Governors Association, Council of Chief State School Officers, and Achieve, 2008.

National Institute of Education. *Administration of Compensatory Education.* Washington, DC: U.S. Office of Education, 1977.

——. *Compensatory Education Services.* Washington, DC: U.S. Department of Health, Education, and Welfare, 1977.

——. *The Compensatory Education Study: Executive Summary.* Washington, DC: U.S. Department of Health, Education, and Welfare, 1978.

——. *Compensatory Education Study: Final Report.* Washington, DC: U.S. Department of Health, Education, and Welfare, 1978.

——. *Evaluating Compensatory Education—An Interim Report on the NIE Compensatory Education Study.* Washington, DC: U.S. Department of Health, Education, and Welfare, 1976.

Newmann, Fred M., and Gary G. Wehlage. *Successful School Restructuring: A Report to the Public and Educators.* Madison: Wisconsin Center for Education Research, 1995.

The New Teacher Project. "Overview." http://www.tntp.org/ourimpact/overview.html.

Nussbaum, Martha C., and Amartya K. Sen, eds. *The Quality of Life*. Oxford: Oxford University Press, 1993.

O'Day, Jennifer A., and Marshall S. Smith. "Systemic Reform and Educational Opportunity." In *Designing Coherent Education Policy: Improving the System*, edited by Susan H. Fuhrman. San Francisco: Jossey-Bass, 1993, 250–312.

Olson, Lynn. "Analysts Worry NCLB Won't Solve Teaching Issue." *Education Week*, November 24, 2004.

———. "A 'Proficient' Score Depends on Geography." *Education Week*, February 20, 2002.

———. "States Weigh 'Value Added' Models." *Education Week*, November 24, 2004.

Owen, John D. *School Inequality and the Welfare State*. Baltimore: Johns Hopkins University Press, 1974.

Patashnik, Eric M. *Reforms at Risk: What Happens after Major Policy Changes Are Enacted*. Princeton, NJ: Princeton University Press, 2008.

Peterson, Paul, Barry Rabe, and Kenneth Wong. "The Evolution of Compensatory Education Program." In *Federal Aid to the Disadvantaged*, edited by D. Doyle and B. Cooper. New York: Falmer Press, 1988, 33–60.

———. *When Federalism Works*. Washington, DC: Brookings Institution, 1986.

Petrilli, Michael J. "Leaving My Lapel Pin Behind: Is No Child Left Behind's Birthday Worth Celebrating?" *National Review Online*, January 8, 2007. http://www .publiceducation.org/nclb_articles/archive/20070108_Leaving.asp.

Phi Delta Kappan. "Administration Announces Major Review of Title I." *Phi Delta Kappan* 51 (January 1970): 288.

———. "Clarify Use of Title I Funds." *Phi Delta Kappan* 51 (April 1970): 450.

———. "Support a Science of Instructional Improvement." *Phi Delta Kappan* (April 2009): 597–600.

———. "USOE Orders States to Repay Title I Funds Improperly Spent." *Phi Delta Kappan* 53 (November 1971): 199.

Pianta, R., L. Belsky, N. Vandergrift, R. Houts, and F. Morrison. "Classroom Effects on Children's Achievement Trajectories in Elementary School." *American Educational Research Journal* 45, no. 2 (2008): 365–397.

Pianta, R. C., J. Belsky, R. Houts, F. Morrison, and NICHD Early Child Care Research Network. "Teaching Opportunities to Learn in America's Elementary Classrooms." *Science* 315 (2007): 1795–1796.

Pierson, Paul. "Public Policies as Institutions." In *Rethinking Political Institutions: The Art of the State,* edited by Ian Shapiro, Stephen Skowronek, and Daniel Galvin. New York: New York University Press, 2006, 114–134.

———. "When Effect Becomes Cause: Policy Feedback and Political Change." *World Politics* 45 (July 1993): 595–628.

P.L. 100–297, Hawkins-Stafford amendments.

Plunkett, Virginia. "The States' Role in Improving Compensatory Education: Analysis of Current Trends and Suggestions for the Future." *Educational Evaluation and Policy Analysis* 13, no. 4 (1991): 339–344.

Powell, Arthur, Eleanor Farrar, and David K. Cohen. *The Shopping Mall High School: Winners and Losers in the Marketplace.* Boston: Houghton-Mifflin, 1986.

Pressman, Jeffrey L., and Aaron B. Wildavsky. *Implementation,* 3rd ed. Berkeley: University of California Press, 1984.

Public Impact. *School Turnarounds: A Review of the Cross-Sector Evidence on Dramatic Organizational Improvement.* Chapel Hill, NC: Public Impact, Academic Development Institute, 2007.

Purkey, Stewart C., and Marshall S. Smith. "Effective Schools: A Review." *Elementary School Journal* 83, no. 4 (March 1983): 427–452.

Quaid, Libby. "Obama Wants to See 5,000 Failing Schools Close." *Seattle Times,* May 11, 2009. http://seattletimes.nwsource.com/html/politics/2009206020_apusobamafailingschools.html.

Radcliffe, C. W. "Remarks of C. W. Radcliffe, Former Minority Counsel and Staff Director, Committee on Education and Labor." *A Compilation of Papers on the Twentieth Anniversary of the Elementary and Secondary Education Act of 1965, Print of the Subcommittee on Elementary, Secondary and Vocational Education.* Washington, DC: United States Government Printing Office, August 1985, 61–69.

Ravitch, Diane. "Every State Left Behind." *New York Times,* November 7, 2005.

———. *The Great School Wars, New York City, 1805–1973: A History of the Public Schools as Battlefield of Social Change.* New York: Basic Books, 1974.

———. "The History Lesson in Bush's School Plan." *New York Times*, January 27, 2001.

Reagan, Ronald. "Interview with Reporters on Federalism on November 19, 1981." In *The Public Papers of President Ronald W. Reagan*. The Ronald Reagan Library. http://www.reagan.utexas.edu/resource/speeches/1981/111981b.htm.

Reese, William J. *America's Public Schools*. Baltimore: Johns Hopkins University Press, 2005.

Reisner, E. R., and E. L. Marks. *The Federal Administration of Evaluation, Program Improvement, and Technical Assistance under ECIA Chapter 1*. Washington, DC: Policy Studies Associates, 1987.

Resnick, Lauren B. *Education and Learning to Think*. National Research Council Committee on Mathematics, Science, and Technology Education, Commission on Behavioral and Social Sciences and Education. Washington, DC: National Academy Press, 1987.

Riddle, Wayne. *Education for the Disadvantaged: Overview of ESEA Title I-A. Amendments under the No Child Left Behind Act*. Washington, DC: Congressional Research Service, 2001.

Rosenholtz, Susan. *Teachers' Workplace*. New York: Longmans, 1987.

Rosenstone, Steven, and John Mark Hansen. *Mobilization, Participation, and Democracy in America*. New York: Macmillan, 1993.

Rosica, T. "Program and Staffing Structures: Reactions." In *Designs for Compensatory Education: Conference Proceedings and Papers*, edited by B. I. Williams, P. A. Richmond, and B. J. Mason. Washington, DC: Department of Education, June 17–18, 1986, III-117–130.

Rothman, D. *The Discovery of the Asylum: Social Order and Disorder in the New Republic*. Boston: Little, Brown, 1971.

Rothstein, Jesse. "Teacher Quality in Educational Production: Tracking, Decay, and Student Achievement." National Bureau of Economic Research Working Paper No. 14442, March 2009.

Rothstein, Richard. *Class and Schools: Using Social, Economic, and Educational Reform to Close the Black-White Achievement Gap*. Washington, DC: Economic Policy Institute, 2004.

Rowan, Brian. "Research on Effective Schools: A Cautionary Note." *Educational Researcher* 12, no. 4 (April 1983): 24–31.

Rowan, Brian, Richard Correnti, Robert J. Miller, and Eric M. Camburn. "School Improvement by Design: Lessons from a Study of Comprehensive School Reform Programs." In *Handbook of Education Policy Research*, edited by Gary Sykes, Barbara Schneider, and David N. Plank. New York: Routledge, 2009, 637–651.

Roza, Marguerite. *Allocation Anatomy: How District Policies That Deploy Resources Can Support (or Undermine) District Reform Strategies*. Seattle: Center on Reinventing Public Education, University of Washington, 2008.

———. "Ranking the States: Federal Education Stimulus Money and the Prospects for Reform." Seattle: Center on Reinventing Public Education, University of Washington, 2009.

Roza, Marguerite, and Paul Hill. "How Within-District Inequalities Help Some Schools to Fail." In *Brookings Papers on Education, 2004*, edited by Diane Ravitch. Washington, DC: Brookings Institution Press, 2004, 201–218.

Rutherford, W., and J. Hoffman. "Toward Implementation of the ESEA Title I Evaluation and Reporting System: A Concerns Analysis." *Educational Evaluation and Policy Analysis* 3 (1981): 5–16.

Sarason, Seymour. *The Culture of the School and the Problem of Change*. New York: Wiley, 1973.

Saulny, Susan. "State to State: Varied Ideas of Proficient." *New York Times*, January 19, 2005.

Schattschneider, E. E. *Politics, Pressures, and the Tariff*. New York: Prentice-Hall, 1935.

Sexton, Patricia. *Education and Income*. New York: Viking Press, 1961.

Sharp, James Roger. *American Politics in the Early Republic*. New Haven, CT: Yale University Press, 1993.

Simon, Herbert A., Donald W. Smithburg, and Victor A. Thompson. *Public Administration*. New York: Knopf, 1950.

Skocpol, Theda. *Social Policy in the United States: Future Possibilities in Historical Perspective*. Princeton, NJ: Princeton University Press, 1997.

Skowronek, Stephen. *Building a New American State: The Expansion of National Administrative Capacities, 1877–1920*. New York: Cambridge University Press, 1982.

Smith, Marshall. "Equality of Educational Opportunity: The Basic Findings Reconsidered." In *On Equality of Educational Opportunity; Papers Deriving from the Harvard University Faculty Seminar on the Coleman Report,* edited by Daniel P. Moynihan and Frederick Mosteller. New York: Random House, 1972, 230–342.

Smith, Marshall S., and Jennifer O'Day. "Systemic School Reform." In *Politics of Education Association Yearbook 1990,* edited by Susan H. Fuhrman and Betty Malen. London: Taylor and Francis, 1990, 233–267.

Soss, Joe. "Lessons from Welfare: Policy Design, Political Learning, and Political Action." *American Political Science Review* 93, no. 2 (1999): 363–380.

Spillane, James P. "Cognition and Policy Implementation: District Policy-Makers and the Reform of Mathematics Education." *Cognition and Instruction* 18, no. 2 (2000): 141–170.

Spillane, James P., Brian J. Reiser, and Louis M. Gomez. "Policy Implementation and Cognition: The Role of Human, Social, and Distributed Cognition in Framing Policy Implementation." In *New Directions in Education Policy Implementation: Confronting Complexity,* edited by Meredith I. Honig. Albany: State University of New York Press, 2006, 47–64.

Spillane, James P., and Charles L. Thompson, "Reconstructing Conceptions of Local Capacity: The Local Education Agency's Capacity for Ambitious Instructional Reform." *Educational Evaluation and Policy Analysis* 19, no. 2 (1997): 195–203.

Spillane, James P., and John S. Zeuli. "Reform and Mathematics Teaching: Exploring Patterns of Practice in the Context of National State Reforms." *Educational Evaluation and Policy Analysis* 21, no. 1 (1999): 1–27.

Stullich, Stephanie, Brenda Donly, and Simeon Stolzberg. *Targeting Schools: Study of Title I Allocations within School Districts.* Washington, DC: Department of Education, 1999.

Tallmadge, G. Kasten, and Christine T. Wood. *ESEA Title I Evaluation and Reporting System User's Guide,* rev. ed. Washington, DC: U.S. Department of Health, Education, and Welfare, 1976.

Teach for America. "Teach for America Adds Largest Number of New Teachers and Regions in 20-Year History." May 28, 2009. http://www.teachforamerica.org/newsroom/documents/20090528_Teach_For_America_Adds_Largest_Number_of_Teachers_in_History.htm.

Thomas, Norman C. *Education in National Politics.* New York: David McKay, 1975.

Thorndike, R. L. *Reading Comprehension in Fifteen Countries: An Empirical Study.* New York: Wiley, 1973.

Trismen, Donald, Michael I. Waller, and Gita Wilder. *Compensatory Reading Study.* Princeton, NJ: Educational Testing Service, 1976.

Turnbull, B. J., S. Zeldin, and T. Cain. "State Administration of the Amended Chapter 1 Program." Washington, DC: U.S. Department of Education, August 1990.

Turque, Bill. "Two Years of Hard Lessons for D.C. Schools' Agent of Change." *Washington Post,* June 14, 2009. http://www.washingtonpost.com/wp-dyn/content/article/2009/06/13/AR2009061302073_5.html?hpid=topnews&sid=ST2009061302085.

U.S. Department of Education. "The American Recovery and Reinvestment Act of 2009: Saving and Creating Jobs and Reforming Education." Washington, DC: Department of Education, 2009. http://www.ed.gov/policy/gen/leg/recovery/implementation.html.

——. *Targeting, Formula, and Resource Allocation Issues: Focusing Federal Funds Where the Needs Are Greatest, a Supplemental Volume to the National Assessment of the Chapter 1 Program.* Washington, DC: GPO, 1993.

U.S. Department of Health, Education, and Welfare. *History of Title I ESEA,* DHEW Publication No. (OE) 72-75. Washington, DC: U.S. Department of Education, 1969.

U.S. GAO. *Chapter 1 Accountability: Greater Focus on Program Goals Needed.* Report to the Chairman, Subcommittee on Elementary, Secondary, and Vocational Education, Committee on Education and Labor, House of Representatives. GAO/HRD-93-69, March 1993.

——. *Greater Use of Exemplary Programs Could Improve Education for Disadvantaged Children.* Washington, DC: U.S. GAO, 1981.

U.S. House Committee on Education and Labor. *Aid to Elementary and Secondary Education.* 89th Cong., 1st sess., 1965.

U.S. House General Subcommittee on Education of the Committee on Education and Labor of the House of Representatives. *Elementary and Secondary Education Amendments of 1973, Part 1, Jan. 31, Feb. 1, 5-8, 20-22, 1973.* Washington, DC: Government Printing Office, 1973.

U.S. House of Representatives Committee on Education and Labor. "Congress Must Support State Efforts for Rigorous Common Standards." April 29, 2009. http://edlabor.house.gov/newsroom/2009/04.

U.S. Senate. Committee on Labor and Public Welfare. *Elementary and Secondary Education Act of 1965: Background Material with Related Presidential Recommendations,* 89th Cong., 1st sess., Washington, DC: Government Printing Office, 1965.

U.S. Senate Subcommittee on Education, Arts, and Humanities, Committee on Human Resources. *Education Amendments of 1977, Part 1.* Washington, DC: Government Printing Office, 1977.

Van Meter, Donald S., and Carl E. Van Horn. "The Policy Implementation Process: A Conceptual Framework." *Administration and Society* 6, no. 4 (1975): 445–488.

Verba, Sidney, Kay Lehman Schlozman, and Henry E. Brady. *Voice and Equality: Civic Voluntarism and American Politics.* Cambridge, MA: Harvard University Press, 1995.

Verstegen, D. A., and P. Anthony. "Is There a Federal Role in Education Reform?" *Journal of Education Finance* 14, no. 2 (1988): 30–56.

Vinovskis, Maris A. *From A Nation at Risk to No Child Left Behind: National Education Goals and the Creation of Federal Education Policy.* New York: Teachers College Press, 2009.

Vogel, E. F. *Japan as Number One.* Cambridge, MA: Harvard University Press, 1979.

Weir, Margaret. "Ideas and the Politics of Bounded Innovation." In *Structuring Politics: Historical Institutionalism in Comparative Analysis,* edited by Sven Steinmo, Kathleen Thelen, and Frank Longstreth. New York: Cambridge University Press, 1992, 188–216.

———. *The Social Divide: Political Parties and the Future of Activist Government.* Washington, DC: Brookings & Sage, 1998.

Weir, Margaret, Ann Shola Orloff, and Theda Skocpol. *The Politics of Social Policy in the United States.* Princeton, NJ: Princeton University Press, 1988.

Weiss, Janet A. "Ideas and Inducements in Mental Health Policy." *Journal of Policy Analysis and Management* 9, no. 2 (1990): 178–200.

Weiss, Janet A., and Judith E. Gruber. "Using Knowledge for Control in Fragmented Policy Arenas." *Journal of Policy Analysis and Management* 3, no. 2 (1984): 225–247.

Weiss, Janet A., and Mary Tschirhart. "Public Information Campaigns as Policy Instruments." *Journal of Policy Analysis and Management* 13, no. 1 (1994): 82–119.

White, Eileen. "Education Programs Slashed Again." *Education Week,* October 5, 1981. http://www.edweek.org/ew/1981/01050089.h01.

Wholey, Joseph S., Bayla White, Leona Vogt, and Richard Zamoff. *Title I Evaluation and Technical Assistance: Assessment and Prospects.* Washington, DC: USOE, 1971.

Wilson, Steven F. "Success at Scale in Charter Schooling." Working Paper 2008-02. Washington, DC: American Enterprise Institute, 2008. http://www.aei.org/futureofeducation.

Wirth, Timothy. *Incrementalism in Education Policy Making: A Case Study of Title I, ESEA.* PhD diss., Harvard Graduate School of Education, 1973.

Wolfinger, Raymond, and Steven Rosenstone. *Who Votes?* New Haven, CT: Yale University Press, 1980.

Wong, Kenneth, and Stephen Meyer. "Title I Schoolwide Programs as an Alternative to Categorical Practices: An Organizational Analysis of Surveys from the Prospects Study." In *Title I: Compensatory Education at the Crossroads,* edited by Geoffrey Borman, Samuel Stringfield, and Robert Slavin. Mahwah, NJ: Lawrence Erlbaum, 2001, 195–234.

Wong, Kenneth K., and Anna Nicotera. "*Brown v. Board of Education* and the Coleman Report: Social Science Research and the Debate on Educational Equality." *Peabody Journal of Education* 79, no. 2 (2004): 122–135.

Xu, Zeyu, Jane Hannaway, and Colin Taylor. *Making a Difference?: The Effects of Teach for America in High School.* Washington, DC: National Center for Analysis of Longitudinal Data in Educational Research (CALDER), 2007.

Yanow, Dvora. *How Does a Policy Mean?* Washington, DC: Georgetown University Press, 1996.

Young, Alexander, Aurelius D. Parker, Winslow Lewis, Samuel G. Howe, and Ezra Palmer. *Reports of the Annual Visiting Committees of the Public Schools of the City of Boston.* Boston: J. H. Eastburn, City Printer, 1845.

Zelman, Superintendent of Public Instruction of Ohio, et al. v. Simmons-Harris et al. No. 00-1751.

Zimmer, Ron, Brian Gill, Kevin Booker, Stephane Lavertu, Tim R. Sass, and John Witte. *Charter Schools in Eight States: Effects on Achievement, Attainment, Integration, and Competition.* Santa Monica, CA: RAND, 2009.

Index